W9-ABO-045

The Orchestral Composer's Point of View

UNIVERSITY OF OKLAHOMA PRESS : NORMAN

Essays on Twentieth-Century Music by Those Who Wrote It

EDITED BY ROBERT STEPHAN HINES

With an Introduction by William Schuman

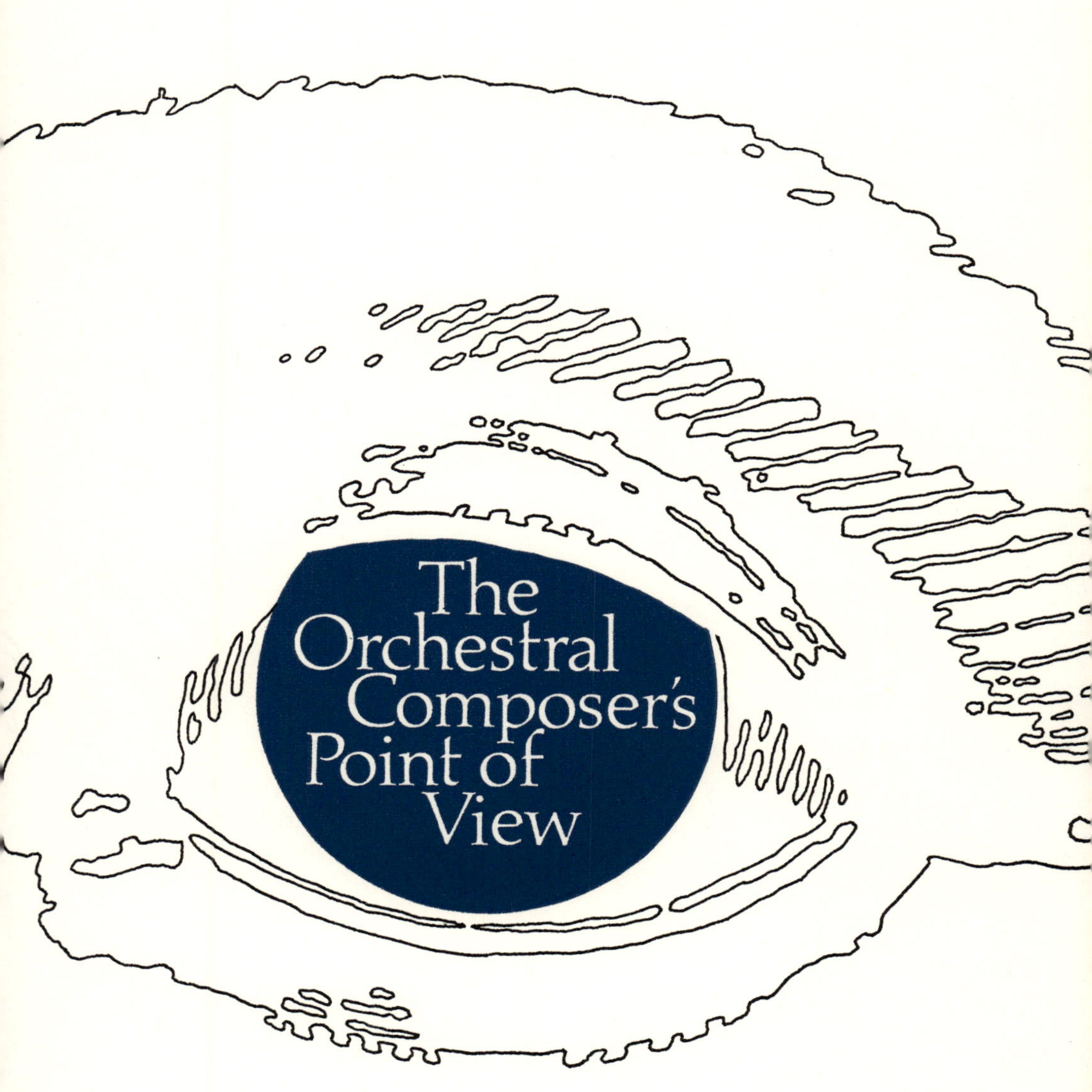

Edited by Robert Stephan Hines

The Composer's Point of View: Essays on Twentieth-Century Choral Music by Those Who Wrote It (Norman, 1963)
The Orchestral Composer's Point of View: Essays on Twentieth-Century Music by Those Who Wrote It (Norman, 1970)

International Standard Book Number: 0–8061–0862–2

Library of Congress Catalog Card Number: 69–16733

 Composed and printed at Norman, Oklahoma, U.S.A., by the University of Oklahoma Press. First edition.

TO MY WIFE Germaine
Lahiff
Hines

ROBERT STEPHAN HINES: Foreword

THIS COLLECTION of essays by twentieth-century composers on their orchestral music is actually a companion volume to an earlier book which I edited, *The Composer's Point of View: Essays on Twentieth-Century Choral Music by Those Who Wrote It*, published by the University of Oklahoma Press in December, 1963.

Even though this book and its predecessor were initiated and published within a decade, the second collection of essays comes at a time when society in general is, belatedly, taking a rather self-conscious look at itself—taking stock of itself in all areas of human endeavor. The phenomenal evolution of the sciences has startled other facets of life and art into questioning whether they too should be moving at the same rapid pace. Perhaps they should and perhaps they could if a similar amount of fiscal resources and manpower had been placed at their disposal. Even without huge sums of money, it is clearly evident that the velocity of scientific advances has quickened the pulse of the arts. The effect is that ours is an era of music in which there has been tremendous innovation and change. Unless we accept this truth, we are ignoring the quintessence of our times. We must not be blind to the fact that fundamental concepts of musical composition, music form, and musical ensembles, large and small, have changed dramatically; therefore, audiences and, above all, performers must be intellectually viable, willing to explore and understand these challenging, often delightful, transformations in the evolution of music in history.

A part of the current phase of questioning or "stock-taking" is the debate concerning the role of the symphony orchestra as we know it. There are musicologists, composers, performers, and informed laymen who contend that the symphony orchestra, functioning as it does in our society, is dedicated mainly to the preservation of symphonic works of the eighteenth, nineteenth, and early twentieth centuries. These people also allege that the small amount of contemporary literature that does reach the public is generally conservative, works which will not offend or stimulate too many patrons or board members. On the opposite side of the argument stand those who maintain that the orchestra is still capable of new musical expression in the skillful hands of composers who comprehend and have an affection for large musical forces. Both groups agree on one central point: there is not enough twentieth-century music on orchestral programs, and there is too little rehearsal time when it is programmed.

Perhaps the public—laymen, symphony board members, conductors, and instrumentalists—will be stimulated by something they read here to take a fresh approach to the problems of rehearsing and performing twentieth-century symphonic works. I would urge a flexible yet fair rehearsal schedule: one which would permit fewer hours on standard repertoire well known to instrumentalists and audiences alike and more hours on contemporary scores. This approach must become a reality if our composers are to evolve artistically as have other generations of composers.

Although articles and interviewed opinions have appeared in various newspapers and journals, there is no single place where this problem has been discussed in detail by composers. It seemed logical that this new collection of essays would be an obvious place to explore this question; therefore, the contributors were asked to comment and offer observations concerning where the symphony orchestra and symphonic forms seem to be going. Some spoke to the question directly, while others answered within the contexts of their essays.

With the exception of one minor change in format which I will point out shortly, this new collection parallels the 1963 publication's objectives in every respect. Outstanding composers from all nations were invited to contribute essays—men who represented diverse styles of musical composition being practiced in the final third of the twentieth century and men who have established themselves as composers beyond the scope of one or two experimental works which might have brought brief recognition.[1] Those composers who accepted were urged to write introspective, reflective essays recording musical as well as nonmusical factors that shaped their music. I reasoned that their insights into the creative act would be invaluable to the historian seeking knowledge of this period of the twentieth century, to the performer occupied with re-creating works by the composers, to the young musician learning and trying to understand the magnitude of the disciplines encompassing music, and to the layman seeking a broader knowledge of contemporary orchestral music. The composers were given freedom to express themselves openly in their discussions of their works. In correspondence with them, I did recommend general points of information which readers would expect, but there was no effort on my part to enforce a rigid outline on the contributors.

Some of the essays are technical, some autobiographical, some philosophical, and some are the composers' rethinking and wrestling with orchestral forces and forms. Despite this contrast in content and emphasis, readers will be able to draw valid conclusions from the common threads of thought here. Now and in the future, the essays will be useful primary sources for musicians and musicologists in search of an understanding of these composers and of our age.

This book, any book, cannot be all things to all people. This collection is not and should not be considered complete or definitive. If it were, there would be essays by Bartók, Berg, Hindemith, Honegger, Schönberg, Vaughan Williams, Webern, and many other deceased composers. If a favorite living composer is missing,

[1] Electronic music was consciously avoided, not because of any personal prejudice on my part, but because it was felt that electronic music was a subject which deserved individual attention in a separate collection.—R.S.H.

understand that there are composers who cannot and will not write about their music, composers who have binding literary contracts with other publishers, and composers who favored the premise of the book but had compositional commitments which prevented them from meeting the deadline.

I have arranged the present composers alphabetically rather than grouping them as composers of the United States, England, and Europe. The latter format, which I chose for the 1963 collection and which seemed logical at that time, is obviously outdated. It implied nationalism when, in reality, the second half of the twentieth century is definitely international in the free exchange of compositional methods and styles.

A primary objective of this book must be to stimulate more interest in live and recorded performances of the works discussed within the various chapters. One of the rewarding results of the first book was the number of performances which were a direct outcome of the essays. The catalogues of composers' choral works printed at the end of the book led to a remarkable number of performances of choral compositions not touched upon in the essays. Another surprising consequence was the quantity of performances of pieces in completely different mediums which resulted from reader interest in the composers. Accordingly, lists of orchestral works and publishers are included in this collection as a supplement to the essays in the hope that their printing will stimulate the same kind of general interest in the composers' music.

If I possessed the craftsmanship of a professional author, I could form phrases which would adequately express the depth of my gratitude to the composers who set aside valuable time to write for this book. The collection exists because of their unselfish dedication to contemporary music—a cause where the aesthetic and financial rewards rarely approximate the effort expended. My personal associations with them and our correspondence will be counted among my life's most treasured experiences.

There are many other people who faithfully gave support to this project over the years that it took to prepare the manuscript for publication. From the beginning Walter J. Duerksen, dean of the College of Fine Arts in Wichita State University, and Howard E. Ellis, assistant dean of the School of Music, loyally defended my requests for research funds at times when these monies were at a premium. My thanks are also extended to the Wichita State University Research Committee for its faith and understanding when the collection took longer than estimated.

I shall always be thankful to the late Nathan Broder, associate editor of the *Musical Quarterly*, for recommending the gifted and devoted translator, Willis J. Wager. Mr. Wager was on leave of absence from Boston University as a Fulbright scholar to Turkey during the time we worked together. Distance alone could have complicated our collaboration, but it did not. And, when a phrase or sentence in translation presented a thorny problem, he was the first to suggest alternate versions which the composer might prefer.

Someone once commented that the ultimate test of the strength of the bands of matrimony was to write or edit a book. In most cases, and particularly my own, this statement is an exaggeration, but it does point up the fact that there are many evenings, weekends, and vacations that are spent with "the book" and not with one's wife. With this book and its predecessor, my wife, Germaine, helped greatly with all the chores that are a part of any scholarly, detail-laden manuscript. For this reason and many others beyond, I wish to dedicate this book to her.

In conclusion, I would like to extend my sincere thanks to the music publishers who permitted the reprinting of the many musical examples which appear throughout this book and which are an invaluable supplement to the essays. The publishers are Associated Music Publishers, Inc., New York (Milton Babbitt, Elliott Carter, Hans Werner Henze, Gunther Schuller); Bärenreiter-Verlag, Kassel (Ernst Krenek); Elkan-Vogel Co., Inc., Philadelphia (Ernst Krenek, Vincent Persichetti); Franco Colombo, Inc., New York, the United States representative for Edizioni G. Ricordi & Co., Milan (Wladimir Vogel); Henmar Press, Inc., New York (Ross Lee Finney); Edward B. Marks Music Corp., New York (Ernst Krenek); Theodore Presser Co., Bryn Mawr, Pa., the United States representative for Universal Edition, Vienna (Ernst

Krenek, Frank Martin); Schott and Co., Ltd., London (Peter Racine Fricker, Michael Tippett); and SESAC, Inc., New York, representative for Polskie Wydawnictwo Muzyczne, Warsaw, Cracow (Witold Lutoslawski). Special thanks are due Associated Music Publishers, Inc., New York, and B. Schott's Söhne, Mainz, for graciously allowing the translation of Hans Werner Henze's essay from the composer's collection entitled *Essays*.

ROBERT STEPHAN HINES

Wichita, Kansas
June 10, 1969

Contents

Table of Musical Examples

The Orchestral Composer's Point of View

WILLIAM SCHUMAN : Introduction

WILLIAM SCHUMAN (born in New York City on August 4, 1910) planned a career in business and entered New York University School of Commerce. However, he left college after hearing his first orchestral concert to devote his life to music. Max Persin at the Malkin Conservatory of Music was his harmony teacher, and Charles Haubiel privately guided his studies in counterpoint. Schuman returned to his education at Columbia University Teachers' College, where he received a B.S. in 1935 and a M.A. in 1937. The summer of 1935 he attended the Mozart Academy at Salzburg to study conducting. Back in the United States that fall he accepted a faculty appointment at Sarah Lawrence College, where he conducted the choir and composed many choral works. During the summer of 1936, Schuman began composition studies with Roy Harris, who was to be a dynamic influence on his output as a composer. Two orchestral pieces established Schuman as a young composer of great promise—the *Second Symphony*, first performed by Howard Barlow and the CBS Symphony and, in February, 1938, by Serge Koussevitzky and the Boston Symphony Orchestra; and the *American Festival Overture* which was premiered by Koussevitzky the same year. Two years later the *Third Symphony*, also introduced in Boston, won the New York Critics' Circle Award. In 1945, Schuman accepted two important positions: the presidency of the Juilliard School of Music, and director of publications for G. Schirmer, Inc. (1945–52). His tenure at Juilliard was marked by the gathering of a distinguished faculty of composers—Bergsma, Giannini, Goeb, Goldman, Lloyd, Mennin, Persichetti, and Ward—with whom he developed the L & M (Literature and Materials) concept of teaching music theory, history, and literature as one course. The L & M approach was to have a profound, lasting effect upon the philosophy of American music instruction on all levels of private and formal music education. Schuman left the Juilliard post in 1962 to become the president of the new arts complex, the Lincoln Center for the Performing Arts. In December, 1968, he resigned the presidency of Lincoln Center in order to have more time for composing. Throughout his life, Schuman has been extremely successful in combining two careers—one as a composer and one as an administrator. His honorary degrees, prizes, commissions, and professional affiliations are legion and testimony to the energetic, effective leadership he has maintained for over thirty years. Among them are two Guggenheim Fellowships, the first Pulitzer Prize for music, Brandeis Creative Arts Award, Columbia University Bicentennial Anniversary Medal, and the Gold Medal of Honor from the National Arts Club. Commissioning groups have included the Ford Foundation, New York Philharmonic, Dallas Symphony, and UNESCO. He holds honorary degrees from sixteen leading American universities plus an honorary membership in England's Royal Academy of Music. In addition, Schuman is active as a fellow of the National Institute of Arts and Letters, American Academy of Arts and Sciences; a director of the Koussevitzky Music Foundation, the Walter W. Naumburg Foundation, and the Composers Forum; and chairman of the board of judges for the Broadcast Music, Inc. Student Composers Award.

ACCORDING TO SOME of the Cassandra-like statements that have been appearing increasingly in late years, the orchestra is doomed. It is said by some, including leading figures of our musical life, to be simply a museum, with the conductor as custodian. It is finished. *Kaput*. Composers no longer write for it, and when they do, it is said by these prophets of doom, they give a note here and a note there to a few instruments at a time, thus not only failing to exploit the orchestra but also emasculating its capabilities.

What, then, am I doing writing an introduction to a subject that requires an epitaph? The answer is quite simple. The prophets of doom talk sheer nonsense. The orchestra is a medium for the making of music. And it will exist as long as composers desire to use large forces of instrumentalists, and as long as there are sufficient funds at hand to pay for such forces. This does not mean that the orchestra in the middle of the next century, as it will be used by composers then, will necessarily be the standard symphony orchestra of today, any more than our orchestra of today is a replica of Monteverdi's. But the big point to make is that the introduction of electronic music is not the introduction of a substitute for the symphony orchestra, but the introduction of another instrument.

There seem to me three basic issues at hand: One is the contemporary literature (say, the last fifty years) composed for symphony orchestra; the second is the present attitude toward composition for symphony orchestra; and the third is the move to eliminate or at least neutralize the performer through the introduction of direct composer-sound media—electronics.

Taking the last point first, it is interesting to examine what has actually happened so far with electronic music. My own personal view is that any development in music which can extend its means of expression is welcome. And the introduction of electronics is particularly exciting because it gives promise of new and extended means of expression. To date, however, evaluation of the evidence of the achievement of electronic music as a new means of expressive content is complicated, because of those champions of electronic causes who believe in what is described as non-music. I myself do not know how to enter into this realm of specialized appreciation, and therefore must at once be disqualified. I do not think anyone can fairly evaluate what he knows he does not understand.

The problem of non-music I find extraordinarily difficult. What happens to the listener? What special tutoring does he require in which he tells himself, "Now I am not listening to this as I would to regular music. It is not meant to engage my intellect; to arouse my emotions, or, heaven forbid, to stir my heart." It may well be —I am no prophet—that the day will come when music is listened to as a series of abstract sound and noise relationships, and that music appreciation will have nothing to do with the criteria which we normally associate with it. I do not know. I can guess, however, and my guess is that the introduction of electronics can, will, and should make a great contribution to the art of music when it is developed to the point of entering the art's main historic stream.

There is no music in history known to me that is not in the mainstream. Now, you can quickly add that while much of the main-stream music was being composed—invented, if you will—it certainly did not seem as though it were going to enter the main stream. The point is that the great composers changed the course of the stream by the genius of their creative powers. If *avant-garde* composers remain *avant-garde* after a generation or two, the chances are that they will have joined the *derrière-garde.* There is no need in an introduction to a book which will be read only by those with highly specialized interests to repeat clichés about the history of music, but let us not forget its lessons.

To me, the great promise of electronic music is the inherent capacity of this new medium to make sounds which are impossible for human beings to produce. This would include intricacies of speed, rhythm, timbre, new concepts of pitch levels, and many other aspects of making of sound which human beings cannot physically accomplish. This indeed is a new element of music. Whether this element is used separately from live music or in combination with it is not the point. The point is that it does supply a new possibility. What electronic music awaits is its exploitation by a composer of genius. I believe it is only the few extreme proponents who see in electronic music the elimination altogether of the performer.

There are those who argue, philosophically and in deep earnestness, that the machine can indeed take over the functions of man. Such arguments as applied to music actually contend that there is nothing in music produced by the human performer which cannot be duplicated or even improved upon by the machine. It is even claimed that eventually the machine can have the same improvisatory element that is basic to the human performer. I don't believe it. I do not believe that any machine can substitute for the bow drawn across the string with the instinct, insight, learning, technique, and—hear it—heartbeat of the gifted instrumentalist. Nor do I believe a machine can replace the inescapable identity which we experience in the presence of a human voice. The live performer is to music what the hearth is to the home: an endless fascination built into the whole historic psyche of our beings. The answer to electronic music: Yes and No.

The second of the points which seems to me appropriate for this introduction concerns the present attitude toward composition for symphony orchestra. I would say that this attitude is not caused so much by the lack of desire on the part of the composers to write for symphony orchestra, as the reluctance of all but a few conductors to put strange music on their programs. Historically there is, of course, nothing new in this. But that does not make it any better. There is, however, a different element.

Many of today's younger composers do indeed prefer to write for smaller instrumental combinations (even those who do not include electronic means). The symphony orchestra as such does not attract them and indeed it should not, since their thinking is not germane to the use of large forces. There is no point in having an aggregation of eighty to one hundred or more men on a stage when the melodic line shifts swiftly from a note in a trombone to an oboe, a piano, a timpani, and a solo violin. It is not that there is anything "wrong" with the attempt of such music-making (the bounding melodic line is certainly a viable aesthetic goal, and music's history is filled with a successful expansion of this approach). It is merely the same case as not putting into the form of a novel an anecdote that takes but two minutes to tell. The symphony orchestra cannot subsist on stinginess. For the composer who is intrigued by the potentialities of the orchestra—and to some of us they are never ending and endlessly wondrous—there remains a fertile field for exploration if—and here is a big "if"—the composer desires to come to grips with the problem of adjusting his aesthetic aims and technical procedures to the inherent and natural appetite of large groups of performers.

The above in no way implies conventionality. The use of the present-day orchestra is wholly different from that of a century and a half or more ago, and there is no reason why the composer of ingenuity cannot create further evolutions within its basic framework. I would say that the conductor who rejects the performance of new symphonic music because it is not truly written in a manner that exploits the nature of the orchestra has a point on his side, although of course he must be awfully sure of his judgments. And this brings me to my last and most important point: the existing contemporary literature for the symphony orchestra.

If symphony orchestras do not continually program new repertory pieces, in long time they will, in fact, become solely the custodians of the past. But, the problem is even more serious than that. Without new music the orchestra—or any other performing medium—cannot survive. The nourishment of fresh repertory is a prerequisite for musical health. For this reason, it is clear that one of the most unfortunate aspects of the current symphonic scene is its very lack of contemporaneity, not only in repertory but in general attitude. This attitude reflects a lack of conviction and leads, despite a number of happy exceptions, to the programming of safe, short, and easily accessible pieces.

If those who form the musical policies of our orchestras—the conductors and others—really believe that the orchestra is fast becoming obsolete, they could do much to reverse the trend by more enlightened programming, which would in no way belittle or de-emphasize the glorious works of the past. This is the road to a healthier situation.

There *is* a viable contemporary symphonic literature; some of it is composed by some of the men who have contributed to this book. Taken *in toto,* the symphonic literature of the twentieth century is a rich one. Yet, its exposure is anemic. The real problem comes from the lack of willingness of conductors to continue successful works in the repertory—especially, although not exclusively, the works of American composers.

There are a number of examples of contemporary symphonic compositions that have been widely acclaimed by musicians—even by some critics—and fully appreciated by audiences. Instead of so many of the unproductive musicological documents that abound in some of our learned journals and of which we have a plethora in our academic institutions, let the scholars awaken to the music of their own times. If another study must be made, let it deal with the symphonic works of, say, the last thirty years which continue to receive sporadic performances here and there around the country, often skipping years at a time, but which are always acclaimed by the audiences. Why are these works not given the status of repertory pieces? If one speaks of sickness, here is where it is.

It is true that there are a handful of living composers whose works continue to be performed. What concerns me is that there are other composers who have written worth-while compositions that are neglected and which would enliven the repertory. But, even speaking of the few of us who make no claim of being misunderstood or neglected, even here the fact remains that it is usually the shorter and more easily playable and accessible compositions that are programmed time and time again at the expense of the larger statements in the longer and more difficult compositions.

And so there existed a need for composers to speak about their own symphonic music in a day where fashion and fad move in the opposite direction (for the short time that they will have the stage). Our admiration for this book is in no way diminished when we say that we have no illusions that this volume or the thoughts here expressed in introducing it will have any effect on the present scene. They won't. But fundamentally those of us who are involved in composing for the symphony orchestra do not derive our satisfaction from performances, from recognition, from proving dire predictions wrong, or from anything except being artists. We have the deep satisfaction of having composed the music—and against this, all the small conceits pale. We can regret that the life expectancy tables indicate that, barring a yet-to-be-invented pill, we will not be around in one hundred years to witness the remarkable health of the twenty-first-century symphony orchestra. The great orchestras have somehow survived their many heralded burials. Let us be thankful to our Cassandras for leading us to challenge their defeatist views with a reassertion of the health and viability and the will to survive of the symphony orchestra as a medium, and of the old-fashioned composers who continue to believe in it.

CHAPTER ONE: Milton Babbitt

MILTON BABBITT (born in Philadelphia on May 10, 1916) was educated in Jackson, Mississippi, public schools and at New York and Princeton universities. From 1935 to 1938 he studied composition privately with Roger Sessions. Babbitt joined the faculty of Princeton's music department in 1938, and between 1943 and 1945 he was a member of the mathematics department. He has also served on the composition faculties of the Salzburg Seminar of American Studies, Berkshire Music Center (Tanglewood), Princeton Seminars in Advanced Musical Studies, and the Darmstadt Summer Course. Commissions for musical compositions have been granted from the Fromm Foundation, the Serge Koussevitzky Memorial Foundation in the Library of Congress, the New York Philharmonic, the Juilliard School of Music, the Brandeis Festival of the Creative Arts, and many other organizations. He has been honored with the Joseph Bearns Prize, a Guggenheim Fellowship, two Citations by the New York Critics' Circle, and a grant from the National Institute of Arts and Letters. In addition to his composition and teaching, Babbitt is active as a member of the Committee of Direction of the Electronic Music Center of Columbia and Princeton universities, on the editorial board of the periodical *Perspectives of New Music*, and a member of the National Institute of Arts and Letters. Although his discussion in this book is confined to non-electronic music, he has been preoccupied with the electronic medium for thirty years. In 1939 he was interested in handwritten sound track, and in 1947 he applied concepts of twelve-tone practice to non-pitch elements of sound.

The Orchestral Composer's Point of View

I HAVE HAD a number of occasions in the past—and the present article is but another such occasion—to contemplate the hazardous temptations besetting the composer seeking words to assist the understanding of his music. Therefore, it is less the lack of the customary professional immodesty that initially inhibits my discussion of my own music than the awareness that, when presented with such an opportunity, the composer is likely to point with pride to the singularities of his accomplishments, to the most immediate manifestations of his originality, to those of his music's properties which he deems historically unprecedented and chronologically unparalleled. For, however conscious one may be of history's tendency to honor—at most—an innovator's name rather than his works, one still is strongly inclined to stake a claim as a prophet in—at least—one's own time. And, since in our time such claims to innovations in musical composition more often have been founded on nationalism and journalism than on evidence or warrant, more often have been asserted in the language of polemic and propaganda than in the considered discourse of fact and reason, one's self-restraint often is severely tested. But to direct a listener's attention to the unique aspects of a work, particularly when he probably knows the work little or not at all, and is likely to hear it in the near future little if at all, is to emphasize that which will provide least aid in initial comprehension, for—to such a listener—uniqueness is far less significantly helpful than is communality, however far removed from the immediate musical foreground such shared characteristics may be. Indications of the procedural sources, the technical traditions—even though the sources and traditions may be of recent origin—provide not only a point of entry but, eventually, the bases for determining the depth, extent, and genuineness of the work's originality.

The composer is further constrained by the realization that his words, as those of the creator of the work, are expected to reflect a "privileged access" to knowledge about the work, when—in truth—the most he possesses of this sort is the memory of what he thought were the reasons, if any, for his choices and decisions at the time he made them. Even if properly identified at that time, and accurately recalled in retrospect, such reasons have privileged status only as autobiography, only to explain how the so-explained events happened to have come to be in the work, not what they are doing in the work. And so there is the compounding of the genetic error with the realization that the primary component of the intentional error is not the unverifiability of the composer's "true" intention, but simply that even if there were means of discovering and confirming the "true" intention, there would not thereby necessarily be conferred on this statement of intention any value as a statement about the work. In other words, and only too obviously, the descriptive exactness and explanatory scope of a statement about a composition depends upon the statement itself and not upon the role of the formulator of the statement. In the light of the difficulties and responsibilities so entailed, it is little wonder, then, that many composers happily assume the traditional stance, one welcomed by that sector of the public and profession which finds it comfortable and comforting to regard the composer as a kind of *idiot savant* (who actually doesn't even know much of anything), of invoking the ineffable untranslatability of inspiration and the fragility of the *objet d'art* under the weight of words. But there is still another sector of the public and the public profession today which shares a quaint notion with, apparently, certain sixteenth-century musicians, the notion that there are "secrets of composition" which have the power to endow works with desirable properties, but which are themselves not inferable from the works themselves. Now, apparently, these "secrets" are assumed to take the form of "mathematical expressions" or "cryptanalytic keys," which—when they are revealed—explain all, and leave nothing. If such simple and exhaustive explanations did indeed exist, that is, did serve musically to explain all or even a great deal, it would be natural then to characterize the works themselves as simple, even simple-minded. Of course, I (or anyone else) could produce polynomials or Goedel numbers or other mathematical expressions which, under suitable interpretations, could generate *Relata I* or any other composition ever written; I trust only that it is no longer necessary to belabor the point that such an explanation would be as trivial as it would be musically unsatisfactory. So, just as I, as a composer, compose for me, as a listener, that which I would like to hear, so I, as an analyst, shall attempt to discover and formulate that which I, as a listener, would like to know.

Relata I, which was commissioned by the Serge Koussevitzky Music Foundation in the Library of Congress, was mentally formed and preliminarily sketched beginning in late 1964; the final stage of composition occupied me from June 21 to December 6, 1965. The first performance, by The Cleveland Orchestra under the direction of Gunther Schuller, took place in Cleveland on March 3, 1966. The work is sixteen minutes four and one-half seconds long, and the orchestra employed consists of three flutes (with one doubling piccolo), two oboes and an English horn, two clarinets and a bass clarinet, three bassoons (one doubling contra bassoon), four trumpets, four horns, three tenor trombones and a tuba, xylophone, marimba, vibraphone, celesta, harp, piano, violins (usually divided into four), violas (divided into four), cellos (divided into two), and double basses (also divided into two). The disposition of the woodwinds suggests their treatment as four trios, that of the brass as three quartets, while the sextet of polylinear percussion instruments of "definite" pitch can be regarded and employed as a sextet of registrally bilinear pairs, and the division of the strings makes feasible their treatment as two sextets, one of bowed strings and the other of plucked strings. Cymbal, tam-tam, three drums, and wood block are used only, and—thus—extravagantly, in the opening eight measures, and the corresponding final seven measures. There is one tempo indicated for the entire work: quarter-note = 84; "tempo changes" are effected through changes of "speed," the number of attacks per unit time, with the unit provided by the explicit subdividing of the durational metrical unit into 3, 4, 5, 6, 7, and 8.

The opening eight measures separate themselves from the main body of the work texturally, rhythmically, and in their dynamic and repetitional character, and constitute literally and pervasively an introduction, by introducing the main features of the pitch structures of the total work (more precisely, the relations of proximity among the pitch-classes, and the transformations of these relations), of the temporal structure, the dynamic range, and the total orchestra to be used. This introduction divides into four short subsections, in each of which a different one of the four timbral "families" sustains a twelve-tone chord, stated as two temporally overlapping hexachords, while the remaining three timbral families, in rhythmic co-ordination, present the other three twelve-tone transformations of the spatially ordered, sustained twelve-tone chord, cumulatively in three short attacks, supporting the entrance of the first hexachord, the second hexachord, and the conclusion of the sustained chord. Example I, 1, shows the disposition of the sustained chords in the woodwinds at the very opening of the work, along with the accompanying chords in the other timbral groups, whose transpositional levels are so selected that the initial three tetrachords of the three different set forms constitute a twelve-tone aggregate. If one regards the set presented by the woodwinds as the referential norm, then the sustained chords of the introduction are, in order, spatio-temporal representations of its retrograde inversion in the strings, its inversion in the brass, and its retrograde in the percussion. Viewing the introduction as a whole: each timbral family presents each transformation of the (temporally) referential set exactly once in each of the four sections, just as each of the sections presents each of the four transformations exactly once, one in each timbral family, while each individual instrument presents just one pitch-class (the percussion instruments, as suggested previously, present two in each section, with a fixed registral relation), which is the pitch-class to which belongs the first pitch of its part in the main body of the movement. Already there appears to be sufficient evidence to suggest that the composition employs the common practice syntax of the twelve-tone, or twelve–pitch-class, system.

The opening of the main body of the movement has the obvious attributes of a "beginning." The aggregate is, throughout the composition, the constant unit of harmonic succession, not an irreducible element—since it is composed of simultaneities of different pitch and interval structures which vary throughout the course of the work, and serve to differentiate primary areas of the work—but the smallest invariant element, and the first aggregate is stated within the minimal registral span (an octave), in a "non-extreme" octave ranging upward from middle C. Each pitch-class, therefore, is represented by only one member, and each member

EXAMPLE I, 1

Examples I, 1–7, used by permission of Associated Music Publishers, Inc.

is represented by just one instrument. The dynamic range is limited to a mid-range *mp-mf*. Manifestly, this aggregate is virtually a minimal statement in many dimensions; however, it is presented by two different timbral families (obviously, a minimal statement in this respect would employ only a single member of a single timbral family, a condition which is more closely approached, but never reached, at the "mid-points" of the sections of the work, as discussed below); the relation between the pitch successions (which are unequivocally ordered temporally within the groups) of these two timbral groups suggests that one of the compositional realizations of the twelve-tone set of the work is as timbrally presented "lines."

The first aggregate consists, then, of what can be construed as —in the strings—the first hexachord of the set form which, with reference to the opening woodwind chord of the introduction regarded as ordered from top to bottom within the temporally ordered hexachords, would be termed the retrograde, and—in the woodwinds in this first aggregate therefore—the retrograde inversion, with the two hexachords relatively transposed to create an aggregate, revealing that this hexachord is inversionally combinatorial,[1] and, indeed, is an ordering of one of the familiar first-order, hexachordally all-combinatorial source hexachords.[2] Equivalently, of course, and perhaps more apparently to the casual "ear," the pitch succession of the strings can be regarded as a transposition (and linearization) of the first hexachordal chord of the percussion in the introduction, and that of the woodwinds a transposition of the first hexachordal chord of the strings.

The next aggregate, in the cause of continuing clarity and simplicity articulated from the first by a rest, similarly is contained within minimal registral span, is limited to a *mp-mf* dynamic range, represents each pitch-class therefore by a single member, but—while continuing the participation of the strings and woodwinds—introduces the remaining two timbral groups in associa-

[1] See my article: "Set Structure as a Compositional Determinant," *Journal of Music Theory* (April, 1961), 74–77.—M.B.

[2] See my article: "Some Aspects of Twelve-Tone Composition," *I.M.A.* and *Score* (June, 1955), 57–58.—M.B.

tion with a single pitch-class line, so that—in this aggregate—one line of pitch-class members is represented by a doubling of percussion and brass instruments, and another by a doubling of strings and woodwinds, while the latter continue their unfolding of their individual, undoubled lines. The percussion and brass line introduces a transposition of the first three pitch-classes of the initial hexachord of the woodwinds, and the doubled string and woodwind line is, in parallel with the individual string and woodwind lines, an inversion, or, equivalently, a transposition of the first three notes of the brass hexachordal chord of the introduction. As early as this stage of the work, then, the strings and woodwinds are participating in two timbrally defined lines, and the second aggregate is partitioned by all of these timbral lines into four trichords. Also, by this point, since the individual string and woodwind lines have presented nine pitches each, it is inferable that these lines are compositionally interpreted sets, which is verified by the next aggregate, in which these individual lines complete their first, inversionally related, set statements.

Example I, 2, indicates the pitch-class presentation of the first seven aggregates; it must be emphasized that the pitch notations are of pitch-classes, and therefore do not represent necessarily registral placement, and rhythmic relations are here represented not at all except to the extent that the aggregates are temporally ordered, as units. It will be observed and heard that the linear components of the aggregates (the timbrally projected lines) are initially presented in inversional pairs, excepting the last two entrances. The "reason" for this, that is, the property of these last two sets to which this deviating presentation should direct attention can be understood by again considering the first aggregate in the light of the two hexachords which constitute it, and the dyads defined by the elements of the same order number in each of these two inversionally related hexachords. In Example I, 2, these hexachords are notated in a "note-against-note" manner to make these dyads easily identifiable, but it is also characteristic of the simplicity and the presentational nature of the early part of the work that such a note-against-note presentation is maintained explicitly in the compositional realization of the pitch structure, and that these dyads are the so contextually defined pitch associations for this section of the work, and until a new, "parallel" section re-

EXAMPLE I, 2

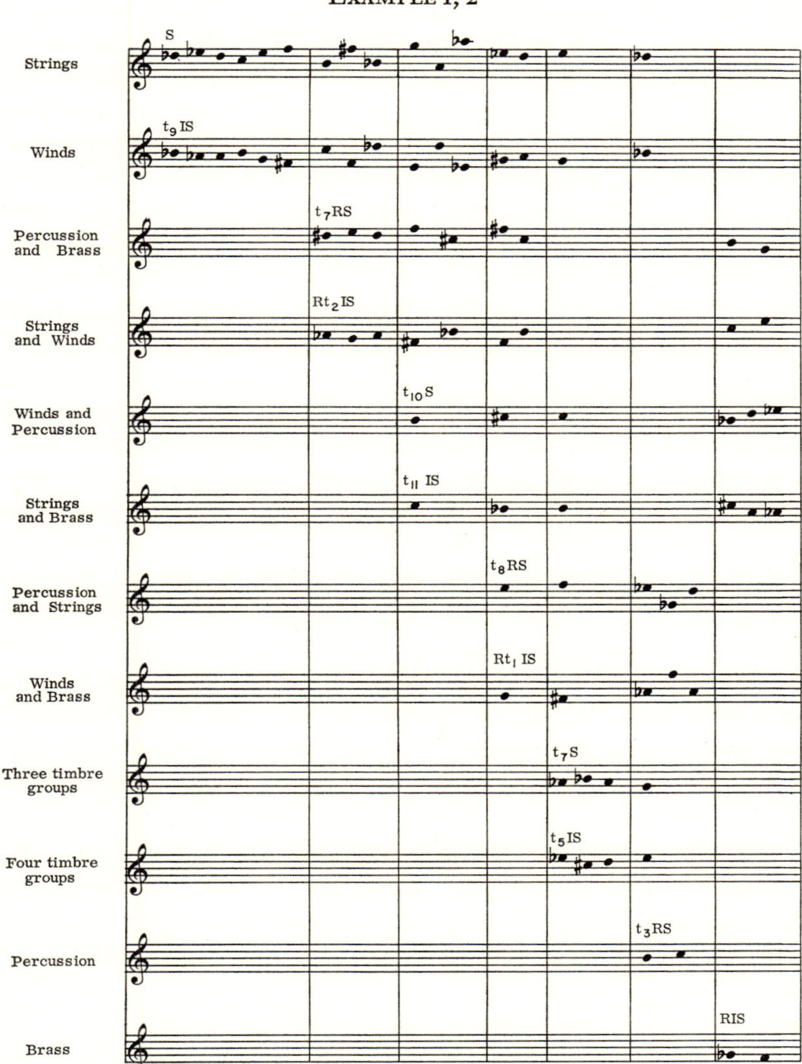

defines the pitch relations, and it is then obvious that the five inversionally related pairs of "set-lines" which enter in each of the first five aggregates not only are hexachordally combinatorial, but maintain these relations between pitch-classes of the same order number;[3] the index, the sum of the pitch-class numbers, is "three," assuming the B-flat of the woodwind to be 0. The inversionally related eleventh and twelfth lines of this underlying "polyphony" however, though still maintaining hexachordal combinatoriality, do not preserve this dyadic relationship; clearly, they could have been so chosen, since there are twelve such pairs of inversionally related sets, but this final pair was chosen to function as a linear summation of the "simultaneous" dyads. By selecting this pair so that the index number 3 occurs as the sum of successive pitch-class numbers, what had been simultaneously defined dyads between sets are now successively defined dyads within a set.[4] So, the percussion line presents B—C, B-flat—D-flat, and A—D in its first hexachord, while the brass line contains G-flat—F, G—E, and A-flat—E-flat in its first hexachord; these are the six dyads which characterize completely the note-against-note relations of the preceding five set pairs, the six dyads presented in the first aggregate.

The instrumental disposition of just the first two aggregates of this underlying what might be termed "pitch-class canon" reveals the functional flexibility to which these procedures give rise; for instance, the string and wind line in the second aggregate supplies a trichord which, in the strings, taken together with the nine pitch-classes of the string line of the first two aggregates, produces an aggregate which can be and is compositionally presented by the initial pitches of each of the twelve string instrumental lines, so that by the end of the second aggregate all of the participating string instruments have been introduced. However, the same trichord in the winds provides a repetition of three pitches already presented in the wind hexachord of the first aggregate; these pitches could have been, but are not, compositionally presented

[3] See my article: "Twelve-Tone Rhythmic Structure and the Electronic Medium," *Perspectives of New Music* (Fall, 1962), 57–58.—M.B.

[4] "Set Structure as a Compositional Determinant," *loc. cit.*, 91.—M.B.

as repetitions within the wind instrumental parts (respectively: bass clarinet, third bassoon, third flute), but are presented as the second notes of the lines of, respectively, third bassoon, third flute, and English horn, thus directing attention to the timbral reorientation of the already heard instruments in their unison doubling with the new string instruments that collaborate in the presentation of this trichord.

The structure of the individual instrumental lines is, then, a further determinant of the mode of unfolding of this twelve-part "polyphony." Example I, 3, shows these forty-eight pitch-class lines which provide the ordered pitch material of the instrumental lines for the first half of the first of the six sections of the main body of the work. These are the forty-eight different set forms which can be derived under the three operations (inversion, retrogression, and transposition) of the system. It will be observed that, within each timbral family, each pitch-class occurs exactly once at each order number position; each timbral family contains three transpositions of each of the four transformed forms (including the identity) of the set, and so on. But perhaps the extent of the multiple functionality of each instrumental pitch-class and subset of pitch-classes through association by pitch-class identity or, complementarily, aggregate formation best can be understood by considering briefly one such instrumental line, say, the first horn. (The quantitative degree of such association is, by the symmetry induced by the operations of the system, the same for all of the instrumental lines.) The first pitch-class of the first horn is identical with that of the third flute, the upper register of the celesta, and the first viola; it can occur in (4^{11}) aggregates of the (1^{12}) partitional type,[5] restricting the components of the partitions to pitch-classes standing in the same order-number position as that of the first horn pitch-class. The first dyad of the horn is pitch-class content identical with the initial dyad of the lower-register marimba, and can participate in a (2^{6}) aggregate with, for

[5] This notation is explained in "Twelve-Tone Rhythmic Structure and the Electronic Medium," *loc. cit.*, 54. For instance, (3^{4}) denotes an aggregate consisting of four parts of three pitch-classes each.—M.B.

EXAMPLE I, 3

(Percussion and strings on facing page.)

Xylophone
Marimba
Vibes
Celesta
Harp
Piano
Violins
Violas
'Celli
Basses

example, horns 2, 3, and 4, trumpet 2, and trombone 3, or trumpets 1, 2, 3, and 4, and trombone 1, or—to choose a "mixed family" instance—with oboe 1, bassoon 3, lower-register harp, upper-register piano, and violin 3, and these are only characteristic examples. So on with the trichordal, tetrachordal, pentachordal, etc. segments of the set. The hexachordal associations perhaps are the most evident, since they are the most traditionally familiar, and again the first hexachord of the first horn is content identical with that of trombone 2, violin 3, and double bass 2, and combinatorial with horn 3, trombone 1, violin 1, and double bass 1.

In explicit compositional terms, these relationships are revealed by the resources of register, simultaneity, attack mode, phrasing, etc., and the compounds of these properties. Perhaps it should be noted that instrumental doublings within, between, and among timbral families, as required to delineate the timbral lines, occur at octaves and multiple octaves as well as at the unison, for the unisons of the initial aggregates simply reflect the minimalization of register at the outset.

The work's twelve-tone set, that singular pre-compositional conjunction of the systematically generic and the compositionally unique, is explicitly interpreted and compositionally projected, then, by two independent components of the work: the twelve timbral lines, and the forty-eight instrumental lines, but its structure pervades every aspect of the composition, from the most local "harmony" to the associatively defined dependencies and contingencies of harmonic succession, through the structure of the total, ensemble aggregates, of the instrumentally formed aggregates, including the interrelation and progression of these aggregates, to the structure of the whole, its surface patterns and "form," its cumulative subsumptions. This functional ubiquity should become apparent quite early in *Relata I*, and, therefore, Example I, 4, presents the set in the form first formulated by the string line; its aggregate forming potential can now be understood in terms of the extent of its inversional combinatoriality, which in turn can be observed simply by examining the set's highly redundant internal structure: its initial and final trichords, tetra-

EXAMPLE I, 4

chords, pentachords, and hexachords are content identical under inversion and transposition, its discrete tetrachords are all-combinatorial, while only the first and final trichords are degenerate, order identical, under twelve-tone operations. The juxtaposition of the designated S with t_8IS yields aggregates of (9 3), (8 4), (7 5), (5 7), (4 8), (3 9), where the first number signifies the initial segment length of the S extracted segment, and the second that of the initial segment extracted from t_8IS; similarly, S with t_9IS yields (6 6). Correspondingly, but independently, the S produces with Rt_3IS (10 2), (8 4), (6 6), and with Rt_2IS (9 3), (7 5), (5 7), (3 9), (2 10), and with Rt_1IS (4 8). Obviously, under both transformational cases (1 11) and (11 1) can be secured trivially. The corresponding segmental content identities are correspondingly derivable. The prolific complexity of contextual hierarchizations made available by these combinational identities and complementarities of the subsets within the over-all permutational system is reflected in the explicit modes of their compositional realizations, with the superimposition of the additional levels of complexity resulting from the general characteristic that, when registrally specified, the elements of the twelve-tone set are not necessarily or even usually permuted under the systematic operations, for they are permuted only as representatives of their pitch class, and therefore compositionally combinational hierarchical criteria determine local measures of affinity. Herein probably lies the cause of much of the initial difficulty of the work's performance and understanding, just as surely as another more persistent source is the rhythmic structure, which in this work is projected at the surface by dynamics in a manner precisely analogous to that in which the pitch lines of the over-all progression are projected by timbral combinations. That is, dynamics are employed in their simplest and most readily perceived mode of manifestation, as susceptible to merely nominal scaling, in order to differentiate the linear constituents of the ensemble rhythm which together make up the rhythmic aggregates, with the measure always functioning modularly, and with all of the combinatorial aspects of the pitch sets, therefore, present accordingly in the temporal domain.

The set "table" or "matrix" of Example I, 5, consequently, provides an over-all insight into the temporal structure as well as the

EXAMPLE I, 5

S:	0	2	1	11	3	4	10	5	9	6	8	7	R
	10	0	11	9	1	2	8	3	7	4	6	5	
	11	1	0	10	2	3	9	4	8	5	7	6	
	1	3	2	0	4	5	11	6	10	7	9	8	
	9	11	10	8	0	1	7	2	6	3	5	4	
	9	10	9	7	11	0	6	1	5	2	4	3	
	2	4	3	1	5	6	0	7	11	8	10	9	
	7	9	8	6	10	11	5	0	4	1	3	2	
	3	5	4	2	6	7	1	8	0	9	11	10	
	6	8	7	5	9	10	4	11	3	0	2	1	
	4	6	5	3	7	8	2	9	1	10	0	11	
	5	7	6	4	8	9	3	10	2	11	1	0	
	RI												

pitch structure. This table is cast in the familiar form, with the first row—from left to right—representing, say, the first set form of the strings, so that the rows, from left to right, represent transpositions of this form; inversional forms correspondingly fill the columns from top to bottom, retrograde the rows from right to left, and retrograde inversions the columns from bottom to top.

To return to the general course of the composition: there is a gradual registral, dynamic, and textural expansion to the harmonic midpoint of what would later be viewed as the first section, a point of singular structural simplicity, for it is a convergence of the aggregate structure to the only point where the aggregate is a form of the set (or, strictly speaking, where the aggregate necessarily is contextually defined compositionally as a set) as a result of being a (12^1) partition; accordingly, this is also the only point of the section at which a single timbral line is associated with the total aggregate. Example I, 6a, which is measure 29 of the composition, shows that at this point the strings present the aggregate which can be identified as the first set form of the opening string line of the main body of the movement, now functioning as the sixth set

EXAMPLE I, 6a

EXAMPLE I, 6b

EXAMPLE I, 6c

statement in this line. Perhaps something of the degree of the differences and similitudes among the sections can be inferred from a comparison of the first five of the (12[1]) occurrences (Examples I, 6a–6e). These locations necessarily are the closest to total repetition, and as a result emphasize the extent to which the "sections" do not and cannot embrace conjoined repetition of all dimensions to anything approaching the degree found in the "form" defining sections of more traditional works, and yet serve the function of clearly delineating the transformational and pitch functional relations among the large sections.

The point of least timbral complexity in the first section also

EXAMPLE I, 6d

275
Piccolo
Flutes 1 2
Oboes 1 2
English Horn
1 2
Clarinets
Bass
Bassoon 1 2
Contra Bassoon
1 2
Horns
3 4
1 2
Trumpets
3 4
1 2
Trombones
3
Tuba

Example I, 6e

performs the role of transition to the second half of the section, which, while continuing the underlying aggregate progression, alters the structure of the instrumental lines. Here, rather than explicit set forms, derived sets[6] are presented by the individual instruments, and so to the end of the first large section, where the last aggregate is that which is the conjugate of the (12^1) partition: a (1^{12}) partition, the only aggregate which requires the involvement of all twelve timbral lines. This most timbrally heterogeneous of the aggregates is reduced, a pitch-class at a time, while the underlying "canon" continues, to a hexachord, that hexachord

[6] See "Some Aspects of Twelve-Tone Composition," *loc. cit.*, 59.—M.B.

which is transpositionally combinatorial at the transpositional interval which maintains combinatoriality between the first and second sections, so that, at the point of junction of these two sections, an aggregate is created. Unfortunately, the total complexity of this and the two corresponding locations precludes the presentation of a musical example, while forcefully, and yet reassuringly, reminding one that all of these words depend for their comprehension and consequence on, at least, a knowledge of the printed score, and ultimately an auditory intimacy with the performed score.

From the standpoint of aggregate structures, the second section is a pitch-class retrograde of the first, while from the standpoint of the set structures of the instrumental lines, it is a pitch-class inversion, but it must be emphasized and understood—and, perhaps, already has been from Example I, 6—that since aggregate structure does not define the orderings of its component parts, the total pitch progression of the second section is by no means a retrogression of the first section, and since the component timbral lines are timbrally reinterpreted on the basis of combinatorial connection, neither is the linear pitch progression. Again, the over-all transformational relation is revealed most explicitly at the corresponding midpoint (Example I, 6b), which in this section represents a reduction from the (1^{12}) with which it opens, and is compositionally presented totally linearly by the doubling of clarinet 2 and violin 4, and similarly opens the second part of the section, a chamber orchestra–like part, which is most obviously characterized by greater timbral and linear homogeneity than has appeared thus far in the work. The pitch-class dyadic associations, which determine harmonic contingencies in the small, are literally revealed at the end of the section with the return of the (6^2) partition (see Example I, 7).

From the standpoint of external pattern, the remainder of the main body of the composition could be viewed as two further analogous double sections, within each of which the timbral lines are timbrally reinterpreted, and within each a twelve-tone operational transformation is applied separately to the timbral lines

Example I, 7

and the instrumental lines, and within each is a hexachordal junction which heralds the transformation, defines the new hexachordal transpositional level, and thereby the pitch dependencies of the new section. By direct virtue of the structure of the set and its influence on the structure of the whole, no two of the six sections are founded on the same pitch dependencies.

As has been indicated, the work ends with a short section analogous with the introduction. The sustained chords now occur in the transformational succession (now with respect to the introduction): R, I, RI, and S, associated with the timbral succession: strings, woodwinds, percussion, and brass.

I am aware that my discussion has centered about, has been obliged to center about, "atomic" musical features: the atomic pitch-class, and the atomic collection of pitch-class relationships: the twelve-tone set, if only because these are the most incorrigibly incontrovertible auditory correlates of the acoustical event, and because the progression from these minimal units through structural strata to the totality is founded on extensive interactions of differentiation and association, inter- and intra-dimensional, which demand musical experience and developed memorative capacity for their perception, and for their explication concepts that have not yet been generally or completely or accurately formulated, and for which we do not yet have therefore reliable abbreviational verbal characterizations. For those whose music strives, successfully or unsuccessfully, to make music as much as it can possibly be, rather than as little, the sense of verbal tentativeness and inadequacy is particularly saddening.

It would appear that a few words are due regarding *Relata II*, which—like *Relata I*—is self-contained, but which—unlike *Relata I*—can be performed as a continuation of *Relata I*. *Relata II* employs the same orchestra, but the strings are not divided throughout; the set is the same, but the background structure is different in almost every detail, if not entirely in general conception. From the position of the knowing performer and listener, it is probably less intricate and less demanding than *Relata I*, but for the only slightly knowing performer and listener, I suspect that the difference in conception and realization between the two works would be insignificant unto imperceptibility.

That I have undertaken to compose three orchestral works in the past three years after not having written for orchestra for nearly a quarter of a century, not since a long-buried, never-performed symphony of 1941 (twelve-tone, to be sure, but I am less than sure about any other aspect of it), is not to be interpreted as a change of mind as to the relation—or more defensibly, the lack of relation—of the professional symphony orchestra to the world of demanding, sophisticated, genuinely "advanced" contemporary composition. But the commission from the Koussevitzky Foundation for the first of these three works, *Relata I*, did remove—if only partially, and even only slightly—one of the major, if mundane, obstacles to orchestral composition: the cost and time of the preparation of performance materials. And yet, since there was provided only relatively slight assistance for the copying of parts and none for the copying of the score, this practical inducement would have been negligible had I not believed and even hoped to demonstrate that the resources of the symphony orchestra, far from having been "exhausted" or "outdated," have been applied but little and slightly to the fulfillment of the needs and conceptions of informed contemporary music. I mean not just the superficialities of timbral and sonic resources as things in themselves—no more with respect to the orchestra than with respect to electronic media—but the employment of these resources as vehicles for the structuring of pitch, temporal, dynamic, registral, and textural relationships: the manifold extensions of those applications with which contemporary composition has transformed the use of solo and chamber media.

So, to attempt to realize some of those inviting possibilities, I accepted the opportunity to write *Relata I*. The occasion of its first performance in Cleveland reconfirmed my worst apprehensions. The guest conductor, Gunther Schuller, having been invited to present an "all contemporary" program (ranging chronologically from Prokofiev's *Scythian Suite* to my work), was obliged to prepare five works, all unfamiliar to that orchestra; for this task, he was generously allowed the rehearsal time—about ten hours—usually allotted to the permanent conductor for the preparation of his far-from-first performances of historically certified masterpieces. The orchestra was mechanically and mentally largely unprepared and massively uninterested, ranging up and down from, for example, the oboist who suggested that the highest notes of his part (in *Relata I*) be transferred summarily to the piccolo, on the assumption that such a reassignment—since the original assignment presumably had been arrived at in the first place only by oversight or ignorance—would not affect crucially and disastrously (in my music, at least, and probably in any music) the pitch, rhythmic, and contour structure of the oboe and piccolo lines, and therefore decisively, manifestly, and immediately the structure of the total work in every respect.

So, for all of the knowing concern and ability in preparation and performance of Gunther Schuller and a few of the orchestral musicians, the performance was a profoundly unsatisfactory representation of the work; in the last of the three public performances—therefore, the most "rehearsed"—only about 80 per cent of the notes of the composition were played at all, and only about 60 per cent of these were played accurately rhythmically, and only about 40 per cent of these were played with any regard for dynamic values.

Given such consequences, even the friendly are likely to inquire as to why one should write so difficult a piece for orchestra. The equivalent question can be only why one writes at all for orchestra, since one does not begin a non-pedagogical composition with an artificial preconception of its difficulty, for performance difficulty is a complex compositional supervenient, not a separable property. After all, a composer hardly revels in his composition's difficulty, for the rehearsals and performance of such a work are hardly a revel. But, let it not even be breathed that we write such difficult pieces because we cannot write easy, easily accessible—as they say—music, not because such an allegation may or may not be true, but because it is utterly irrelevant, to the issue and to our music.

In the midst of the mutual antagonisms provoked between orchestra and composer by the unrealistically anachronistic conditions of such performances, I have felt obliged to point out (for example, at the time of a comparable rehearsal problem with the Minneapolis Symphony, when, as a result, only excerpts from

Relata I could be performed) that the piece is 516 measures long, and that probably no two of these measures are identical (I say "probably" since I have never checked the work in this respect, and certainly did not compose it in such terms, but neither was it conceived in terms of dimensionally conjoined repetitions). If only five minutes were spent on each measure, in attempting to master its variety of ensemble requirements and intricacies (and I know no soloist who spends as little as five minutes per measure in the learning of a solo work with no ensemble problem), over forty hours' rehearsal time would be required. For each performance *Relata I* has thus far received, there have been less than four hours of rehearsal time.

This might suggest that the means of achieving satisfactory orchestral performance would be the subsidization, at enormous cost, of a few adequately rehearsed works. But this overlooks the further manifest fact that the competences and dispositions of the orchestral performers, conductors, and audiences simply are inappropriate to the performance of complex contemporary works. Nor would such an ingenuous and spotty solution attract to the orchestras those young performers whose individual abilities, educations, and interests have led them to spurn positions in such orchestras, and whose presence in them would ironically reduce the necessary rehearsal time. The only satisfactory solution appears to be that formulated by a number of us in collaboration with Dimitri Mitropoulos well over a decade ago: the formation of an orchestra of such young performers, with suitable young conductors, which would prepare, say, one program of contemporary works a month, a program which could be toured and recorded. Such a repertory of about fifty new works a year could be prepared for a total subsidy of a mere $1,000,000 a year (very "mere" when compared with the $80,000,000 recently provided for the artificial perpetuation of the standard and substandard repertory). Also, orchestras at conservatories and schools of music, where additional rehearsal time can compensate for immaturity and inexperience, could, under knowing conductors, prepare a few difficult works, but theirs would be a far more fundamental contribution if they were enabled to train performers for such an elite contemporary orchestra.

Until, if ever, such an orchestra is formed, few demanding contemporary works will be performed, and fewer still will be accurately performed, and the composers of such works who have access to electronic media will, with fewer and fainter pangs of renunciation, enter their electronic studios with their compositions in their heads, and leave those studios with their performances on the tapes in their hands.

CHAPTER TWO: Elliott Carter

ELLIOTT CARTER (born in New York City on December 11, 1908) took his B.A. in English from Harvard University in 1930. He stayed on for graduate work in music for two years under Walter Piston, Archibald T. Davison, and the visiting British composer Gustav Holst. Carter traveled to Paris in 1932 to study composition and counterpoint with Nadia Boulanger. When he returned to the United States, he first settled in Cambridge but, finding the depression had made financial conditions difficult for a composer, he moved to New York City. There he contributed articles to the periodical *Modern Music* and, between 1937 and 1939, acted as music director for the Ballet Caravan. Carter served as a music consultant to the Office of War Information during World War II. Since the war there have been several academic appointments: Peabody Conservatory of Music (1946–48), Columbia University (1948–50), Salzburg Seminars in Austria (1958), and Yale University (1960–62). He was composer-in-residence at the American Academy in Rome in 1963 and composer-in-residence of the City of West Berlin and the Ford Foundation the following year. Despite the demands of composition, Carter has been active in professional societies, often serving on boards or holding offices in the League of Composers, International Society of Contemporary Music, and the American Composers Alliance. Awards and honors have been frequent: National Institute of Arts and Letters (1956), Sibelius Medal for Music (1961), New York Music Critics Circle Award for the *Double Concerto* (1961), Brandeis University Creative Arts Award (1965), Premio delle Muse, "Polimnia," Florence (1969), and honorary doctorates from the New England Conservatory of Music, Swarthmore College, and Princeton University. It is in the realm of chamber music that Carter has received the greatest acclaim: his *Second String Quartet* was awarded a Pulitzer Prize (1959), New York Music Critics Circle Award (1960), and UNESCO First Prize (1961). Carter's independent spirit and philosophy toward composition are summed up in what he once said: "I just can't bring myself to do something that someone else has done before. Each piece is a kind of crisis in my life; it has to be something new, with an idea that is challenging." The *première* of a new Carter work is, consequently, always a challenge to the performers, audience, and critics for they have learned to expect excellence, originality, and no compromises.

MERELY TO CONSIDER the possibility of writing orchestral music of any quality as a field of endeavor for a composer in the United States calls up a barrage of contradictory problems, each of which would seem to militate against any kind of new, vital, or original music being produced. It would even seem impossible to work out an intelligent program that would provide a situation in which this could be accomplished by anyone but a confirmed masochist seeking a heavy burden of self-punishment. The fact that such music has been written here, though not often, amid miserable circumstances, at great human cost to its creators and in almost utter neglect—that Edgard Varèse, Charles Ives, Carl Ruggles, Stefan Wolpe, and others fought this desperate battle—means that these composers had such a strong inner vision that they were able to overlook the preposterous circumstances that surrounded them in our musical society, particularly in the orchestral field. Younger composers who write in an original way are often filled with illusions about the present situation (which, it is to be hoped, is changing), encouraged as they are by commissions, fellowships, and contests bent on stimulating what must seem like an appalling overproduction of an unwanted commodity. Such commissions, for instance, are very often given by those entirely concerned with publicity, a kind that feeds on the composer's reputation but is not interested in his actual work. This is clear from the fact that commissions are too often given by groups who have shown no previous interest in a composer's work by performing it or arranging for performances of it. Very often, a little research will reveal that the commissioners do not even know what kind of music the composer has written and hence is likely to write—with the curious result that the finished score comes as a disagreeable surprise to conductor and performers, who then churn through it desultorily or with hostility misrepresenting the score to the public and ruining the possibility of future performances for a long time. The commissioning sums, themselves, are seldom attractive, and are usually far less than a professional copyist would be paid to copy the score. The rewards, if one cares about them—artistic results, kudos, and money—are each so small that commissions rarely seem worth the trouble.

Composers with fewer illusions about the present orchestral situation in our country suffer through these nonsensical performances in the hope that they will get ones supported by educational funds, such as the Rockefeller Foundation–supported modern-music symphony concerts played in universities, or performances with some of our better conservatory orchestras (Oberlin, Iowa, Michigan, or the New England Conservatory) where student performers are eager to play new music and have plenty of time to rehearse and be taught the score by a conductor who really knows it thoroughly. A somewhat similar result can sometimes be obtained by performances with European radio orchestras, which do not play as well as American orchestras but can devote much more rehearsal time to new music. In fact, a number of American composers living abroad have been able to develop styles of orchestration by constant contact with orchestral performances that they could not have evolved in this country.

Because it is difficult to get multiple performances with American symphony orchestras, since they are interested mainly in *premières*, composers do not write for this medium unless they are commissioned or have the stimulus of a prize contest. There is little satisfaction in a poorly rehearsed *première*. And, under the present rehearsal and performance situations, there are such absurdly small performance and royalty fees that the copying of the parts is seldom repaid except by potboilers. (No performance or royalty fees would be given if a number of us had not fought a bitter battle twenty-five years ago to try and establish what one would have thought was an obvious principle.) Prize contests do not solve the problem any better since the authority of juries is infrequently respected by musicians. Even when an honorific prize like the Pulitzer Prize has been given in music, sometimes resulting in a number of performances (as with my *Second String Quartet*), this can cause a great deal of dissatisfaction on the part of those who question the jury's choice.

Here is an example of what can happen at a prize contest: My *Holiday Overture* won a prize of $500, publication, and performance by one of the major symphonies whose conductor was one of the jurors. The score and parts were taken from me, remained in the orchestra's library four years without ever being performed, and were then returned. I had no copy of the parts, and I could not get other performances during this time, for when I tried to withdraw the parts, the possibility of a performance that might take place very soon and which I might lose if the parts were not in the library was held before me. Finally, I sneaked the parts out without the librarian's knowing it, had them photostated, and returned. From these parts the work got its first performance in Frankfurt, Germany, and later in Berlin with Serge Celibidache conducting. The American orchestra never knew of this. Why it held up the *Holiday Overture* I never learned, but the experience did not add to my desire to deal with American conductors and orchestras.

Such mishaps are a constant part of the composer's routine. Conditions do not improve much even when such relationships are handled through a publisher, as has been my frequent experience since 1936 when my first orchestral work was written. The reasons for these vexations and others have been a constant source of concern for composers, yet no one has been able to find a way to solve them. Perhaps all these problems can be traced to the habit of applying traditional economic standards by a large segment of our population to all its efforts and products, which inevitably causes confusions and misapprehensions between composers and many performers, critics, publishers, and publics.

Looked at in this way, a piece of music is assimilated to a typical item of consumption in the traditional frame of a consumers' market. However, such a piece cannot be physically owned as can a painting or sculpture, cannot generally be figuratively owned by being retained in the memory as the contents of a book, movie, or play. This very fact means that its consumption value lies only in the immediate present during which it is heard and during which it must be experienced, if it is. Hence, it must cater to the listener's immediate abilities, interests, and experiences, in much the same way a performer does on a far more accessible level. Although recordings have somewhat lessened the composition's mere present existence for the public, still it is the very evanescence, which is part of its attractiveness, that makes it an anomaly as an item of consumption and alters drastically the bases on which music can be compared to any of the other arts, both in terms of historical development and economic remuneration. This accounts for the underdeveloped nature of its economic aspect; particularly in America it was (and probably still is) assumed that musical repertory is a European importation and that Europe can take care of composers' payments and exploitation while we do not have to consider these seriously. From this follows that the investment of money in publicity and salesmanship in compositions in the United States need be very little since so little return can be expected. However, with the explosion of the publicity industry, more and more emphasis has been put on the public image of the composer as the real item of consumption. His musical composition is only one of the contributing elements, others being his ability to perform, to talk, to write, to teach, and to be photographed—all of these being more salable, and hence more highly paid, than his music. The public, often, must wonder why composers persist in writing music that so few can understand. They must think—and perhaps rightly—that the musical work is intended to help his public image through reviews and reports in widely circulated periodicals, and thus lead the composer to more important positions in domains peripheral to composition, but more remunerative. Except for American opera, symphony orchestra, and community-concert subscribers where the group must be very small, there usually exists a sizable minority of musical public that understands what an important role new music could play. This special public realizes that the development of musical composition is affected by many more important factors than that of immediate popular consumption. This group has little power, even though its point of view—that contact with the new brings new attitudes toward the old, new insights into the art itself and interesting, even important new experiences—is generally accepted in the other arts and in most of American life. Contemporary music, music that is to be listened to for itself rather than for its performance, is in another class from older music, and this distinction keeps it out of competition with the "performance industry," where the stakes are high, and whose efforts assume the solid foundation of accepted "masterworks."

A solid foundation? Commercial exploitation is destroying this as it did forests in the nineteenth century. So far, in America, at least, no concerted effort of musical reforestation of the rapidly dying repertory of increasingly tired and worn-out classics is planned. (The mortality of the Francks, Regers, and Saint-Saëns is very high these years.) This improvident depletion of the repertory has gone on for years, while the twentieth-century composers were producing work after work that have been treated as seasonal novelties and dropped instead of being drawn in to replenish the failing repertory. The American public of symphony subscribers has not yet caught up with the Viennese music written fifty years ago, nor that of Varèse which is thirty or forty years old. However, there is evidently another public for such music as was proven by the success in New York of the all-modern music repertories of the BBC Orchestra and the Hamburg Opera in 1967. But the average subscriber has no part of this literature. For him the gap between contemporary music and his understanding has grown wider through the years, and it is ever harder for him to catch up. Unless this situation can be remedied it will have a severe effect on the future of orchestral music. Often in recent years, composers have felt that the future of the symphony orchestra was doubtful.

Needless to say, the artist who puts his faith in future recognition thinks a long time before he wastes a lot of time and effort on a medium which many think is dying. The contrast between this situation and that of chamber music, where contemporary music is welcomed, serves to emphasize that this plight is strictly a matter of the orchestral situation and not that of the composers as described in Henry Pleasant's book *The Agony of Modern Music.* The orchestral brontosaur staggers with inertia and ossification; its very complexity resists change.

Now let us look at that institution, the conductor (seldom an American) of an American symphony orchestra. He is involved in a complex of economic and social problems in his community and orchestra that threaten to draw his attention away from musical ones: in tea-party strategies to keep and augment his audiences, in making himself a public personality, in helping to raise money, in getting better pay for his performers through recording contracts, in maintaining and raising the performance standards without causing ill-feelings. Keeping the orchestra alive and functioning must often seem to be the primary issue, while the actual giving of concerts and learning new repertoire becomes almost a secondary responsibility. Yet these latter duties—the backbone of his role as conductor—form a very taxing schedule. The extended seasons of the major orchestras devour an enormous number of standard works, few of which can be repeated more than once every two years, none of which can be performed without rehearsal and, on the conductor's part, without restudy and rethinking of interpretation. Understandably, the conductor has little time left to study the few new scores he may have scheduled, none to look through the piles of new music sent to him every year, and, certainly, very little time to keep up with the progress of contemporary music by following new trends through scores and recordings. His impossibly demanding tasks naturally force him to find time-saving solutions and not do anything which will augment his problems. To satisfy the pressure of the progressive minority of his audience, he must inevitably find works that do not require much rehearsal, will not cause much dismay, or be too long or too unusual. He can hardly be blamed for not choosing more important scores under the circumstances. In fact, it is remarkable that as much important new music is played as there is.

The situation of the orchestral musician is not much better with regard to new music. The high cost of living in the United States naturally forces him to need high pay for his very skilled efforts. He must participate in as many higher-paid services as possible—concerts, broadcasts, and recordings, and as few lesser paid ones—rehearsals. This state of affairs limits the repertory of concerts drastically and, when combined with the extended seasons of many orchestras, results in overwork, fatigue, and tedium. When such musicians are faced with a new work which has been allowed a small amount of rehearsal time insufficient to produce a good performance, many players, otherwise sympathetic to new music, become disgusted while the unsympathetic performers are annoyed at being required to do many difficult and unfamiliar things that seem to lead to a pointless result. At a recent rehearsal of my *Piano Concerto*, an orchestral musician said to me: "Your music does not make sense unless the dynamic markings are followed." At most rehearsals and the majority of performances of new orchestral music, the players are so occupied with playing the right notes that they often forget to follow the instructions to play them softly or loudly. Music requiring careful observation of these distinctions needs extra rehearsals, therefore, in order to "make sense." A work like my *Holiday Overture*, in which the variety of dynamics is produced almost automatically by the addition or subtraction of instruments, can make sense without such care being taken although it makes better sense when it is. One can easily imagine the frustration of an orchestral musician who works hard to master his part only to discover that he is being entirely covered by a neighbor who, instead of playing softly as his part indicates, is giving all he has.

Often the blame for the growing gap between audiences and new music is laid at the door of the orchestra's board of directors or of the audience itself. Most of the time with both of these groups, there has been and still may be an interest in new music, in small amounts. However, if this curiosity is satisfied by poor contemporary music and not by the finest, a receptive attitude can readily turn to animosity, as has happened only too often. Many times when looking over the modern music played by orchestras for a certain period or season, one gets the impression of visiting an art museum where no examples of Picasso, Braque, Kandinsky, Klee, *et al.*, but only the works of the latest recipients of Guggenheim Fellowships, had ever been shown. Everybody concerned with music—composers and musicians, as well as the public—has constantly to develop a background of understanding based on the best works of the recent past if they are to come to terms with new compositions. Recordings and scores can and have helped the public and composers, but the conductor and performer must have had direct performing contact with these works in order to be able to make quick sense out of the welter of new musical methods developed over the past sixty years. Most practitioners do not have the time nor the encouragement from a good majority of those connected with music who are shortsightedly still milking the "masterpieces" dry.

As if all these practical problems were not enough to keep a composer from writing orchestral music, and they are not, the very instrumental make-up of the orchestra itself presents many serious difficulties in these years. Developed to play romantic music based on a common practice of standardized harmony, rhythm, and counterpoint, of singing themes, of widening sonority by octave doubling, the orchestra seems to require this kind of music to justify its existence. Since most contemporary composers do not wish to compose this way, the orchestra has to be forced to do things which seem to violate its fundamental nature. For example, the dry incisiveness and powerful rhythmic articulation of Igor Stravinsky's music since 1920 does not fit the sonority expected from the orchestra. Also the whole growth of the orchestra, intensifying its romantic character with Bruckner, Mahler, Strauss, and early Schönberg, made the works of these composers and others unplayable outside large cities, especially in the United

States where they are a drain on the budgets of orchestras. Many European composers still feel the need, today, to write for large orchestras and can get their works played because of state subsidies—the Stalinist symphonies of Dmitri Shostakovitch and quite a few recent Polish and German works. American composers ruled out this possibility long ago. Aaron Copland recently revised his *Symphonic Ode*, written originally for a large Boston Symphony Orchestra, for a smaller group of instrumentalists.

Aside from the enlargement and increasing technical demands made by composers in the late nineteenth and early twentieth centuries that limited their works to special situations which became rarer with each passing year, there came forth a realization which was expressed by many composers that the orchestra is no longer useful. Schönberg complained in 1928 to Erwin Stein, in an interview translated in the booklet accompanying the Columbia Records of the works of Schönberg, Volume II:

> If it were not for America, we in Europe would be composing only for reduced orchestras, chamber orchestras. But in countries with younger cultures, less refined nerves require the monumental: when the sense of hearing is incapable of compelling the imagination, one must add the sense of sight. . . . But disarmament is as slow here as it is in other areas; so long as there continue to be nations which, in art, have not yet won their place in the sun, so long will America demand large orchestras and Europe maintain them; Europeans will remain incapable of acquiring that finesse of ear that artists long to see generally acquired as long as they continue to maintain large orchestras.[1]

It is significant that quite a number of the twentieth century's best composers—Schönberg, Bartók, Webern—seldom wrote for the orchestra.

The orchestra's very instrumental make-up severely limits its possibilities of sound. All of the instruments of the usual orchestra playing a *tutti* can only be written for in a very few ways that will produce a balance of sound in which each element contributes

[1] Courtesy of Columbia Records.—E.C.

significantly to the whole and is not partially or totally blotted out by more powerful instruments. A flute, for example, as sometimes happens in the Ives scores, playing a theme in its medium-low register against a full, loud orchestra playing above and below it, is unlikely to be heard at all, and scarcely contributes anything to the total effect. The fewer the instruments that play, the more possibilities of combinations there are. Recent Stravinsky works, like *Agon* and the *Variations*, treat the orchestra as a storehouse for many changing chamber music combinations, avoiding its full sound almost throughout. This requires sensitive playing by the musicians and careful listening by the audience, which neither are prepared for, especially when many orchestral concerts take place in halls where acoustics prevent great delicacy of sound from being heard distinctly.

If there is still any point in composing for orchestra, it is to treat the medium with as much novelty of concept as one does harmony, rhythm, or any of the older musical methods, so rethought in our time. It is the compositions that are written for orchestra that will make it live. If these are dull and routined in the use of the medium itself, not consistent with the composer's thought, then the orchestra has to be left to the ever-diminishing repertory of the past.

To compose for the orchestra, as far as I am concerned, is to deal practically with the instruments, writing idiomatic passages for them, and, particularly, to compose music whose very structure and character is related to the instruments that play it. The entrance, register, sound of an oboe or a solo viola must be a matter of formal and expressive signification for the whole piece. The combinations of instruments are as much a compositional consideration as the material they play, even to determining the material, and all must reflect the over-all intention. The handling of the orchestra must have the same distinctiveness and character as the other components of the work. This concept of orchestral writing takes considerable imaginative effort, increased, as has been said, by the many built-in routines which the orchestra was developed to accomplish. The uses of any one of these would be as much out of character in my music as a passage of conventional four-part harmony.

It took me many years of experience and thought to arrive at this technique of orchestral practice. My first works, the *Tarantella* (1936) for men's chorus and orchestra and the ballet *Pocahontas* (1939), were orchestrations and amplifications of prior piano four-hand scores, while the *Symphony No. 1* (1941) and the *Holiday Overture* (1944) each began to move away from this procedure, the symphony dealing with orchestrally thought textures and the overture with orchestrally thought counterpoint. In fact the *Holiday Overture* began to use consciously the notion of simultaneous contrasting levels of musical activity which characterizes most of my more recent work. *The Minotaur* (1947), a ballet, is another step toward direct orchestral thinking which culminated in my *Variations* (1954), conceived as it is entirely in terms of the orchestra for which it is written. After this, each of my two concertos used a different approach to orchestral sound. The *Double Concerto for Harpsichord and Piano with Two Chamber Orchestras* (1961) makes the percussion the main body of the orchestra, the pitched blown and bowed instruments secondary, with the two soloists mediating between them. The *Piano Concerto* (1965) uses the orchestra mainly as an elaborate ambiance, a society of sounds or a sounded stage setting for the piano.

In every case, these works have taken into account the practical situation of the American orchestras that might be their performers at the times they were written. The complete change of aim and direction, amounting to a private revolution in musical thought, which went on through all these years in my chamber music, hardly found its way into my orchestral work until the two concertos. There was good reason for this decision since I was—and am still—made painfully aware with each orchestral rehearsal that the type of writing found in almost every measure of my chamber music could never come out under American orchestral conditions that I know or imagine. Orchestral passages of a far simpler structure have often proved serious stumbling blocks to musicians who always seem to face my scores with the belief that they will never make sense—although occasionally some performers find that they were mistaken. For these reasons, I have sought different goals in orchestral scores than in chamber music.

Up to now, although finding these were useless precautions, I have tried to fit the situations for which my music was written, carefully. The ballets used the size of the orchestra that would fit into the pit of Broadway theaters; the Martin Beck in the case of *Pocahontas,* and the former Ziegfeld with *The Minotaur*. The *Variations,* commissioned by the Louisville Orchestra, uses the exact number of instruments that comprised the orchestra—a very small number of strings (nine players of first violins, etc.) and the normal-sized brass section, which could cause serious problems of balance. My score allowed for possible enlargements of the string section in other performances. The *Piano Concerto,* partly to save rehearsal time, relegates much of the difficult playing to a concertino of soloists. Each of these self-imposed restrictions affected the form and plan of the work drastically, of course, and seem in no way to have helped the performance prospects of the work, as they have gone unnoticed. In the case of my *Variations,* when played by the Philadelphia Orchestra, the entire wind section was doubled through most of the work, as is sometimes done in Beethoven symphonies, without my knowing, until I arrived at the last rehearsal when the work was completely rehearsed. This resulted in a rather intense and coarse sound in fast passages, which I did not want. I realized, however, that this amplification of the orchestra was probably necessary due to the bad acoustics of the then recently opened Philharmonic Hall at Lincoln Center. When the work was performed there, one of the critics wrote that this work was seldom performed because it required such a large orchestra!

I made unusual orchestral demands in the score of my *Double Concerto* because the generous commissioner of the work, Paul Fromm and the Fromm Foundation, assured me of excellent musicians and sufficient rehearsals. Unlike my other compositions, this one presents many kinds of special performance problems, the main one being the harpsichord itself. The instrument is of always unpredictable volume which varies from hall to hall as well as from instrument to instrument—a fact that I was so aware of that during the work, all the other instruments usually stop altogether or play their softest in their dullest registers when the harpsichord is playing. These precautions do not prevent it from being lost and requiring amplification under many performing conditions but, as it is the soft member of a dialogue "pian e forte," it cannot be amplified very much. The balance and accuracy of the percussion, its damping, its sticking, have to be worked out with great care, otherwise the work will sink into a miasma of confusion, as it has on a number of occasions, especially when the hall is too resonant.

The work is built on a large plan, somewhat like that of Lucretius' *De Rerum Natura,* in which its cosmos is brought into existence by collisions of falling atoms, in the music by ten superimposed slowly beaten out regular speeds—five for the harpsichord and its orchestra on one side of the stage, and five for the piano and its orchestra on the other side of the stage. A musical interval is associated with the attacks of each of these and used in the introduction as if it were a percussive sound. The distribution of the speeds and intervals is given in Example II, 1a. As can be seen, the smallest ratio of speeds is 49:50, which is the one first presented. This fans out to the largest 1:2 in intermediate steps, reading from right to left, during the introduction. 49:50 is presented by alternating rolls of the snare drum on the piano side of the stage at metronomic speed 25, and of the cymbal on the harpsichord side at speed 24.5, starting in an ornamented way in measures 7 and 8 and resolving to the pure lengths combined with the associated intervals in 10–12. Then harpsichord speed 28, perfect fourth, and piano speed 21⅞, major seventh, appear in measures 13 and 14—piano speed 21, major sixth, and harpsichord speed 29⅙, augmented fourth, in measure 17—harpsichord speed 19⁴⁄₉, minor third, measure 20; piano speed 31.5, perfect fifth, measures 23 and 24—finally harpsichord speed 17.5, minor seventh in measure 31, and piano speed 35, major third, measure 36. During these measures some of the layers of speed that have

Example II, 1a

DOUBLE CONCERTO

RATIO BETWEEN SPEEDS							METRONOMIC SPEEDS	PIANO	HARPSICHORD
↓	↓	↓	↓	↓	↓	↓			
2					1/5	10	35 →	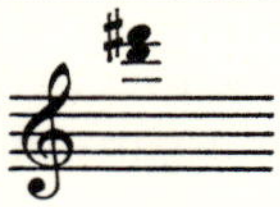	
	81					9	31½ →	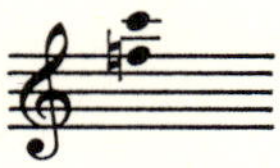	
		25			1/6		29⅙ →	→	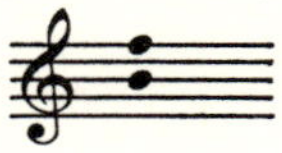
			32			8	28 →	→	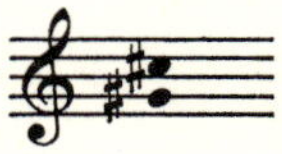
				50	1/7		25 →	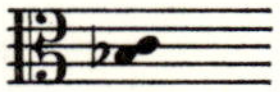	
				49		7	24½ →	→	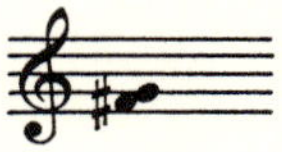
			25		1/8		21⅞ →	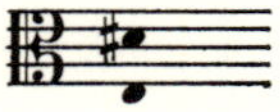	
		18				6	21 →	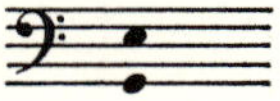	
	50				1/9		19 4/9 →	→	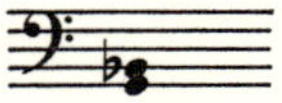
1					1/10	5	17½ →	→	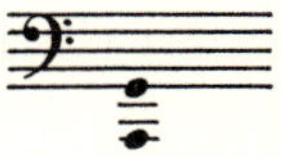

Examples II, 1–2, copyright 1964 by Associated Music Publishers, Inc. Used by permission.

been introduced drop out, but they all begin to be sounded as the two climaxes, made by rhythmic unisons, approach. Four of the speeds that fill in the ratio of 35:17.5 are in a ratio of reciprocals, as the chart shows, and these reach a rhythmic unison in measure 45, while the other four speeds fill in 35:17.5 in a ratio of whole numbers and come to a rhythmic unison in measure 46. The two systems engender a pattern of regular beats in the case of the reciprocals and a pattern of acceleration and retardation in the case of the whole numbers as shown in the diagram, Example II, 1b.

EXAMPLE II, 1b

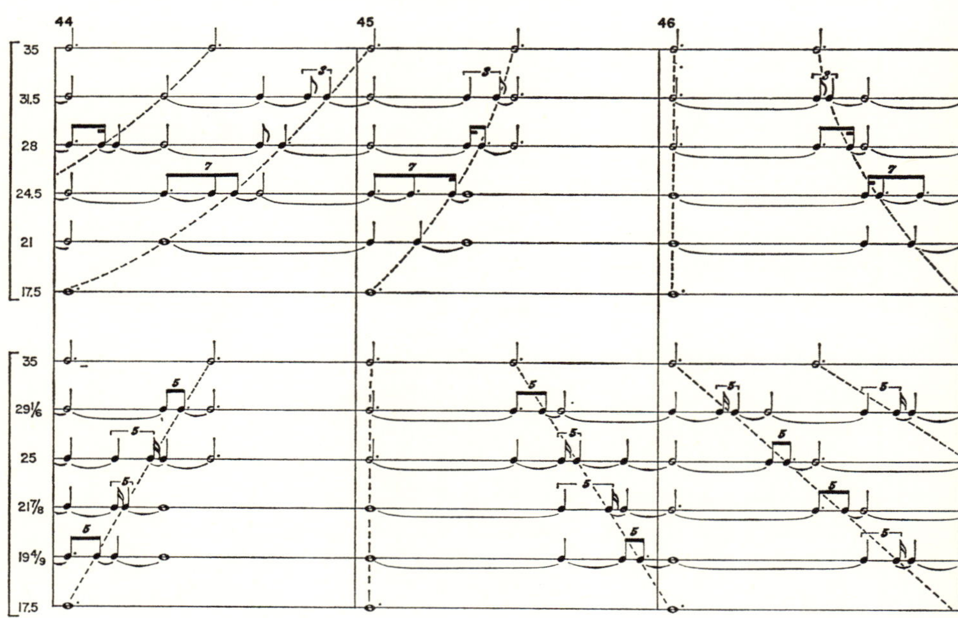

After the introduction, the various speeds and their intervals are joined together to produce polyrhythmic patterns of a lesser degree of density but a higher one of mobility and articulation, different combinations producing different sections. How this is done can be seen in the harpsichord and piano cadenzas in which almost the entire repertory of both parts is presented in aphoristic form. The slow movement which emerges from the previous fast one at measure 312 and continues to measure 475, overlapping the beginning of the next section, uses alternations of accelerating and slowing up in a pattern that runs around the outside of the orchestra counterclockwise (percussion 4,3,2,1, harpsichord, contra bass, cello, piano) when accelerating and clockwise when slowing up. The central part of the orchestra, the winds, play a slow piece not related rhythmically to these motions, but maintaining their interval identity in each orchestra. Until the coda, the two orchestras adhere to a system of interval interrelationships that is different for each, as indicated in Example II, 1c. In general the piano and its group specialize in rhythmic ratios of 3:5 while the harpsichord group uses that of 4:7. The coda extends these ratios over many measures producing long, slow waves of oscillating sounds, an orchestration, so to speak, of the sound of a tam-tam heard in 619, dying away over many measures. The piano group at this point has important attacks every seventh measure with subsidiary ones every thirty-fifth quarter, while the harpsichord group emphasizes every fifth measure and secondarily every thirty-fifth dotted eighth—all with many subsidiary patterns and accents. The coda is the dissolution of this musical cosmos—Lucretius' "Burning of Athens" or, perhaps, the triumph of Chaos at the end of Pope's *Dunciad*.

As in all my music such intervallic schemes provide a somewhat ordered substructure (like the triadic harmony of the common practice period, but more freely used because it is not adhered to so strictly) as a source of ideas of many degrees of interrelationship on several different levels at once.

With the many performances this work has had, I had a great deal of opportunity before the score was printed to try and get all its indications as foolproof as possible. There is a constant stream of unfamiliar ideas that can hardly be expected to come out "all by themselves" if musicians have never participated in a work that presented these particular problems before. It is a great advantage not to conduct the music myself, so that I can find out just how explicit the score is to the conductor and players. When it is not,

Example II, 1c

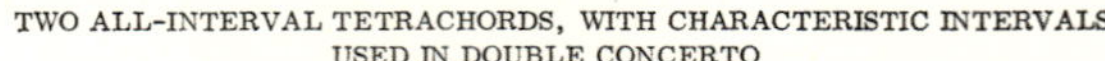

then I can make it clearer so it will come out well when I am not present. In it there are many problems of notation—the awkward dotted notations, used for quintuplets and septuplets in compound time that have bothered performers in Warsaw and elsewhere. In defense of them, I do not think many passages which use dotted and undotted notes simultaneously could have been notated as clearly.

If I had not had the experience of my *Variations* behind me, I do not think I would have ventured to write orchestral works of the unusualness of the *Double Concerto* or the more recent *Piano Concerto.* It is strange to have a work like the *Variations* over the fourteen years of its existence not only become easier and easier for performers to play and for listeners to grasp but also gradually to sound more and more the way I intended it to sound with each new performance. At its *première* in Louisville in 1954, the music sounded so confused, particularly in the very resonant gymnasium in which it was played, that I wondered if I had not gone off the deep end and written a score that would never sound as I imagined it. Although by far the hardest work the Louisville Orchestra had commissioned to that date, so I was repeatedly told, it was far simpler in performance demands than the chamber music I was writing at the time. The conductor, Robert Whitney, and the orchestra worked hard and well and made the fine Louisville recording of the *Variations.* After that, the work received, I think, no performances in the United States until 1964, although it was performed in the interim at Donaueschingen, Rome, Stockholm, Paris, and Liverpool. During its first years of existence, I was particularly eager to learn from live performances with different musicians in different halls, so that I could witness for myself just what was difficult, what was easy and why, what always came out well, and what was troublesome. I would have needed to hear lots of such performances by competent orchestras while the score was still fresh in my mind, in order to profit from its lessons in my next works. This did not happen, and by the time the score began to be played fairly frequently in places where I could be present, I had written my *Double Concerto* which approached the orchestra in an entirely different way.

Under present conditions in America, it seems to be very nearly impossible to develop a personal orchestral style that also takes into account the practicalities of the performing situation. Either a composer must use the standardized, "tried and true" orchestral routines, or he must suffer for years through misrepresentative, tentative performances, which teach him very little. In situations where new music is taken more seriously, as in Germany, Italy, Sweden, Poland, and elsewhere, the composers' contacts with orchestral performances have often allowed them to develop highly distinctive, yet practical techniques. In the United States, the prospect of troublesome situations is very discouraging—situations in which the performers assume that the composer does not know what he is doing, in which the score cannot come out as intended for lack of rehearsal time or because the conductor is unable to imagine how the score might sound if played correctly. These painful prospects which a composer must face every time he plans an orchestral work make it hard for him to follow his own ideas, and to take the whole operation of composing orchestral music with the seriousness that he might devote to chamber music, where the musicians are eager to discover precisely the composer's intentions and to play the work to his satisfaction.

My most recent work for orchestra, the *Piano Concerto* (1965), presents a number of quite different concepts in orchestral use that involve difficulties of balance and, to a lesser extent, playing. For conductors unfamiliar with the late scores of Charles Ives and others, the orchestral score presents a forbidding appearance with its pages that sometimes divide the strings into many single parts. These pages are hard for performers to grasp and interpret, too, since they comprise as many as seventy-two different parts that need to be balanced and co-ordinated—especially in the fast passages near the end in which the orchestra plays in 3/2 while the concertino plays in 12/8. The work consists in a different dimension of dialogue from the *Double Concerto*, the solo piano is in dialogue with the orchestral crowd, with seven mediators—a concertino of flute, English horn, bass clarinet, solo violin, viola, cello, and bass. These share with the piano its material and various characters. Like the *Double Concerto* it employs no pre-established form but is a series of short, usually overlapping episodes, mosaics of fragments that derive from parts of the basic material combined in different ways. This basic material is formed of the twelve different groups of three notes, triads, six assigned to the soloists and six to the orchestra. Each of the twelve triads is related to one or more speeds and characters as the chart shows in Example II, 2.

The triads, written in whole notes, show how each participates,

EXAMPLE II, 2

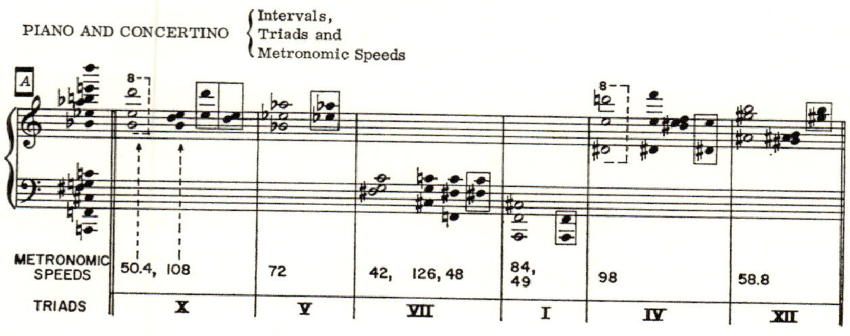

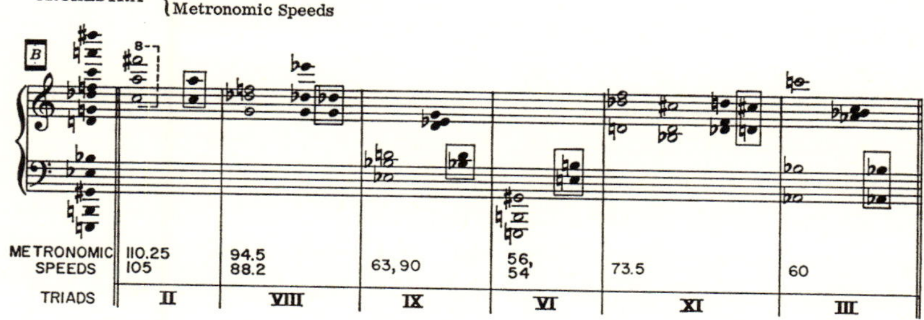

and in what register, in the two twelve-note chords: *a* for the soloists; *b* for the orchestra, which dominate the first movement and conclude it. The main triad for the soloists is VII, for the orchestra, VIII, both sharing the augmented fourth. This relationship is stressed in measures 19–22. After these, triads I and IX are frequently used. The black-headed notes in the example show the other spacings of the triads used, while the two-note intervals in boxes indicate the interval of the triad which is most frequently stressed. Each triad has its associated character or characters, and hence its own kind of continuity. Triad III, for instance, is constantly superimposed on itself in a way which leads to the large tone clusters in the strings that become thicker and more frequent as the work proceeds. The first movement stresses the similarities between the triads of both groups. After the opening of the second movement—its first thirty measures, 349–378, being a transition from the first to the second large section—the music stresses the difference between the two groups. The orchestra has a constantly changing series of slow, soft chords that gradually become denser over many measures. At the same time, it keeps up a web of accented beats in many different speeds between 105 and 10 5/13 in as many as eight different layers going on at once. The piano and occasionally the concertino play a series of rhapsodic, cadenza-like sections based on the chords and intervals used in the first movement with the addition of the perfect fifth and the major seventh. Sometimes these soloists play accelerandi and ritardandi against the regular beating of the orchestra. The many-voiced chords of the orchestra become thicker and the eight polyrhythmic, regularly beaten-out accents of the orchestra gradually approach a rhythmic unison as the piano dies away repeating a single note. At this point the slow accents of the orchestra become very emphatic, the piano and concertino take up their parts, and the whole leads into a kind of battle between the soloists and the orchestra, with the orchestral strings playing fast passages of twelve-tone chords. The music subsides with a short piano solo in which all of its chords and characteristics are stated in a brief summary of its entire part, recalling each idea with quiet insistence.

Before the first rehearsal of the *Piano Concerto*, I was presented with the alternative of signing away my right of refusal to allow the work to appear on a recording (allowing the conductor alone to make this decision) or not having the recording made at all. Reluctant as I was to give this right up, since I could not be sure whether on hearing the piece for the first time "live," I would be satisfied with every part of it—or, even if I were, whether the performance would present the piece adequately—I decided to take the chance and was fortunate to have had two unusually good first performances from which to make the tape. Naturally, this surprising request was connected with the record's financing and other aspects of commercial recording ventures. Nevertheless, such a curious lack of consideration for the composer's artistic rights only adds to the general reluctance to write for orchestra that he gradually develops.

For all these reasons and others which come to mind every time I plan an orchestral work, I hesitate a long time. My first conclusion usually is that given the large amount of imaginative effort, skill, and experience such a work as I am interested in writing demands, it will not be worth the effort (particularly in view of the disagreeable, absurd, and hypocritical situations that it will give rise to) since I always write music that cannot be expected to be a "hit" or a "scandal" with the audiences we know. The two or three thousand dollars (the Louisville was one thousand) I am paid for commissions recompenses my work at the rate of about twenty-five cents an hour. Artistically, there is not much to be said, either, for making the effort, given the inadequacies of most American performances, the apathy of most conductors and orchestral performers, and the consequent disaffectation of audiences. As the satisfaction of a personal artistic need to write for masses of instruments, there is perhaps more point. Although if the composer feels this need without the concommitant one of writing for the public situation, there is no reason why he should use the usual orchestral setup, considering it stereotyped, but invent his own combinations, which in the United States would, no doubt, rule out all possibility of performance. All in all, it is hard to understand why composers commit the folly of writing for orchestra in our country in recent years. They do. Is it quixotic? Certainly the answer cannot be expected to come from our orchestras, who are too busy with their own organizational and financial problems to bother seriously about the work of composers foolish enough to see something in the orchestral medium.

CHAPTER THREE: Ross Lee Finney

ROSS LEE FINNEY (born in Wells, Minnesota, on December 23, 1906) received early instruction at Carleton College, the University of Minnesota with Donald Ferguson, in Paris with Nadia Boulanger, and with Alban Berg in Vienna. Finney continued studies at Harvard University in 1928 and the following year joined the faculty of Smith College where he remained until he became composer-in-residence at the University of Michigan in 1948. During his tenure at Smith, he founded the Smith College Archives, a series of scholarly editions of old music to which he contributed the initial volume. He also founded the Valley Music Press dedicated to the publication of contemporary American music. For several seasons, Finney conducted the Northampton Chamber Orchestra. He gained international recognition when his *First String Quartet* was awarded a Pulitzer Prize in 1937. World War II sets apart the earlier compositions from the better-known works of the middle 1940's—the *Christmastime Sonata,* the *Pilgrim Psalms* for chorus and orchestra, and the *Fourth String Quartet.* Probably the most significant date in the career of Finney is 1950, the year he composed the *Sixth String Quartet* wherein he adopted the principle he described as a method of "complimentarity." The pitch details of the quartet were ordered on the basis of the twelve-tone technique while the larger form still adhered to the tonal tradition. Even though the serial devices and tonal schemes used in each work since 1950 have varied somewhat, the fundamental principles have remained intact. The next ten years were extremely productive. Toward the end of the decade (1959), his *Second Symphony* was commissioned by the Koussevitzky Foundation, and the *Third Symphony* appeared a year later. In addition to the Pulitzer Prize, Finney has received two Guggenheim Fellowships for study in Europe. He has been elected to the National Institute of Arts and Letters and was made an honorary doctor of humane letters by Carleton College. Several times Finney has traveled abroad as a lecturer for the Department of State, and he has also served as consultant to the Fulbright Commission, the Ford Foundation, and the U.S. Commerce Department.

My orchestral works belong to two periods of my career: the first composed in my thirties and early forties, and the second composed in my fifties. Since these two periods are separated by some fifteen years, a world war, the development of electronic tape, and many other cultural and social changes, they must be viewed separately, though I like to feel that my basic musical convictions have not changed over the years. When I began composing for orchestra again in 1956, I had to decide whether my earlier works should be destroyed, either totally or in part. Several earlier works were withdrawn at that time, but six remain in my catalogue: *Violin Concerto* (1933), *Bleheris* (1937), *Slow Piece* (1940), *Symphony No. 1* (*Communiqué*, 1943), *Hymn, Fuguing, and Holiday* (1943), and a *Piano Concerto* (1948). I felt that each of these works, in a small way, added something to the picture of my total musical personality and that each had some validity as a composition. It is not easy for me to discuss them for I am perfectly aware of their shortcomings and I have no desire to claim for them a virtue that they do not have.

I had almost no opportunity to hear these works. There was never any encouragement or hope that my orchestral works might be performed. It should also be remembered that I had never heard a real symphony orchestra until I was well into my teens. When I finally began to compose for orchestra in my thirties, there were two strong motivations: the first was a desire to deal with an emotional statement that a smaller group could not adequately express, and the second was an overwhelming desire to master the technical craft involved.

People today find it very hard to reconstruct the musical environment of the Middle West during the twenties in which a young composer shaped his early career. There were no recordings, there were no tapes, and there were very few scores of contemporary music. The fact that I had heard a little early Bartók and Stravinsky and some Scriabin and that I liked what I had heard made me a "radical" when indeed I was not a radical, but merely musically starved and musically ignorant. When I went to Paris at the age of twenty-one I was suddenly engulfed in a totally new world. It is probably my good fortune that a wonderfully vital group of fellow students of Nadia Boulanger and a genuinely understanding teacher kept me afloat and that I absorbed gradually those influences that I could properly digest. My insistence in keeping, rightly or wrongly, those qualities that were a part of my background and my slowness in absorbing new influences has shaped whatever musical personality I have.

My *Violin Concerto* was sketched in 1933 but was revised and reshaped for fifteen years. Melody and solistic brilliance were my major concerns; I wanted this work to be a violin concerto, not just an orchestral work with violin solo. The last movement is a medley based on fiddle tunes and songs that I had grown up with. There was a degree of chauvinism in using them, no doubt, but singing folksongs has been a genuine and unaffected part of my family background and I felt they added brilliance to the ending of the work. An early version of this work was presented by Gilbert Ross and the orchestra of the University of Michigan under Wayne Dunlap; otherwise it has never been performed.

Bleheris (1937) is a dramatic monody for tenor and orchestra, setting a fragment from *The Hamlet of Archibald MacLeish*. It was composed at the same time that I wrote my cycle of songs based on poems of MacLeish, and it is related to a choral work, *Edge of Shadow*, that I composed in 1959. It is a work of which I am personally very fond. I have not yet had the good fortune to hear this work.

At the request of Dimitri Mitropoulos, I composed a short work for strings called *Slow Piece* (1940), and it was given its *première* by the Minneapolis Symphony Orchestra in 1941. It was published by the little press that I started at Smith College with John

Verrall in Northampton, Massachusetts, called The Valley Music Press. The work is a very simple, uninhibited arch of melody, and was the expansion of an idea that I had originally used as a slow movement of a sonata for cello and piano.

The most substantial work of this early period is my *Symphony No. 1* (Communiqué, 1943). The *première* was given by the Louisville Orchestra under Robert Whitney in 1962, and even after twenty years it seemed to me to project the feelings that had motivated its composition. It was started immediately after Pearl Harbor and the heroics and humor and pathos are of that time, not of today. I could no more deny it than I could deny my service in that conflict. It sounds very much as I thought it would when I wrote it and seems to me generally firm and cohesive in its structure.

Hymn, Fuguing, and Holiday (1943) was originally called *Variations, Fuguing, and Rondo* and was first performed in 1947. It is essentially variations on William Billings' hymn *Berlin* though the variations become much freer as the work progresses. I have always thought of the work as a festivity—a work to be danced or at least to be heard in terms of dance. When I heard the final published version performed in 1966 by the Miami Symphony Orchestra under Fabien Sevitzky, it seemed to me to have the energy and brilliance that I thought it had when I composed it. It is unproblematical and direct, in other words, youthful.

My *Concerto for Piano and Orchestra* (1948) is a light work that I composed for Felix Witzinger to perform with the Berne Philharmonic in Switzerland. It has no great pretensions but affords the pianist considerable display within its neoclassic proportions. Though composed later, it was conceived before the war and rightly belongs to that earlier period. I always remember with a smile the criticism in a Berne newspaper that spoke of the sound of "*Buffelherden*"—buffalo herds—in the work. I suppose one has to pay some price for a free and wonderful childhood in North Dakota.

These six works were all concerned with the control of functional design. The only other factor of equal importance in my mind was the melodic-motival fabric. There was no conflict between the two for me at this time. The works that had the strongest influence on me were Sessions' early symphony and piano sonata, and his influence as a teacher in the mid-thirties fortified my concern for musical function and motival unity.

I lived for twenty years in Northampton, Massachusetts, and taught at Smith College. Men like Sessions, Jacobi, Josten, Duke, Leland Hall, and John Kirkpatrick were friends and colleagues, and the musical world of the twentieth century opened up as freshly there as anywhere in the United States. I studied with Alban Berg in the early thirties. The Kolisch Quartet visited the Jacobis, and in the evenings we heard them practice Webern and Schönberg. Kirkpatrick introduced me to the works of Ives. More important even than the friendships were the conscientious performances of my chamber music. It was a decade in which my work not only coalesced but my vista was enlarged so that after the interruption of the war years, my work turned inevitably in a new direction.

Nor can I speak of my later orchestral works without mentioning the change and the challenge that I faced in my new position at The University of Michigan where I have been in residence since 1948. In Northampton I had never taught composition; at Michigan I was involved in the development of a group of very talented young composers and they, more than anything else, made me aware of the aspirations of the postwar generation.

This is surely not the place to dwell on the shift that resulted by my use of serialization, a shift that took place because of the increasing chromaticism of my melodic thought after the war and the conflict of such melody with the formal concepts that had dominated my music during the thirties and forties. This conflict, however, has led me to a somewhat unconventional solution that will be apparent in all my later orchestral work. In all these works I feel closer to my teacher, Alban Berg, and to certain works of Schönberg and to the thought of men like Sessions, Dallapiccola, and Roberto Gerhard than I do to Webern and that postwar trend. Obviously, my technical solutions are shared by none of these composers and spring almost entirely from my different background.

I will deal with the six works that are purely orchestral, though the stage work *Nun's Priest's Tale* (1965) and the choral-orchestral works *Edge of Shadow* (1959), *Still Are New Worlds* (1962), and *The Martyr's Elegy* (1966) show the same direction of thought.

My more recent interest in the orchestra begins with *Variations* composed in 1957 on a twelve-tone row by Luigi Dallapiccola, to whom the work is dedicated. Some of the most interesting lessons I had with Alban Berg dealt with his concept of variations, and I was referring to these ideas when I composed my "Variations on a Theme by Alban Berg" (unpublished) for piano. Instead of a rigid unit that repeats itself, I thought of variations as being the systematic repetition of musical events with new and unexpected qualities. It seemed to me interesting to quote a fragment of music that I admired and to investigate its meaning to me. My *Variations* for orchestra is based on the row that Dallapiccola used in his *Canti di prigionia,* but it is stated in such a way as to remind one of a Wagnerian motif. The work unfolds like a round trip, reaching its destination in the middle and then returning to the point from which it began, but while we recognize the musical events on the return, they are presented from an opposite viewpoint, and the experience is entirely new since one cannot move backward in time. This short work was given its *première* in 1965 by the Minneapolis Symphony Orchestra under Russell Stanger.

No commission has meant more to me than the request in 1958 by the Koussevitzky Foundation to compose a symphony. Since almost none of my orchestral music had been performed by that date, it was inevitable that I should be considered a composer of chamber music, but my interest in the orchestra had increased rather than diminished, and the hope that I might at least hear a major work stimulated me greatly. I had also reached a point in my use of row technic where I felt the need of the large orchestra. I had just completed my *String Quintet* for the Elizabeth Sprague Coolidge Foundation, and the row that I had used seemed to me to contain all sorts of possibilities that I had not touched upon.[1] What is perhaps more to the point, an orchestral work had been forming in my mind for several years and this row gave a new direction to my ideas, especially in the way that it might control segments of time—harmonic and melodic durations and the like. It seemed to bring into focus several new tendencies in my music, and the large orchestra seemed the right medium for their solution.

While it does not interest me to analyze my *Second Symphony* (1959), I might point out a few details that must be considered by the scholar who wishes to make an analysis and might even be suggestive to a conductor performing this work. The row functions both in determining pitch and through the numbers implied, in durations of harmony, inner metrical segments, and sometimes, though rarely, note durations in melody (see Examples III,1–4).

This symphony was composed during January and February, 1959, in a house overlooking Glendora, California, that Scripps College had made available to me. It was orchestrated during the

EXAMPLE III, 2

Examples III, 1–10, reprinted by permission of the publisher, Henmar Press, Inc., 373 Park Avenue South, New York, N.Y. 10016.

[1] Ross Lee Finney, "Analysis and the Creative Process," *Scripps College Bulletin* (February, 1929).—R.L.F.

EXAMPLE III, 3

EXAMPLE III, 4

spring, and Eugene Ormandy asked for the *première* with the Philadelphia Orchestra when he saw the work during the May Festival in Ann Arbor, Michigan. The first performance took place on Friday, the thirteenth of November. It was scheduled for after intermission, but when the piano was being moved onto the stage for the concerto that preceded intermission, the legs collapsed with a great crash and my work had to be moved forward. Mr. Ormandy gave six performances of the symphony during the season. The following statement for program notes may give a few suggestions as to how I feel about this symphony:

> The dramatic beginning and ending of this *Symphony* seem to me to frame the work in a silence that is intense. Between these high points the work is sometimes tender, sometimes grotesque and bitter, sometimes humorous and capricious. It is futile to describe the emotional intention of this work, but surely the gradual relaxation of the tensions of the beginning into the boistrous confidence of the ending will be felt.

While the tempo markings are as nearly accurate as I could make them at the time, they tend to be a little slow. I don't like my music to drag nor to lose the forward thrust that is such an important part of my statement.

My *Third Symphony* (1960) was conceived in my mind while I was composing the *Second* and was something of a personal revolt against the demanding organizational process I was using in the *Second Symphony*. This *Third Symphony* is more lyric than dramatic, and its rhythmic organization is completely free. It was written while I was composer-in-residence at the American Academy in Rome in 1960, though it had to wait until I had finished my *Eighth String Quartet*. The *Third Symphony* was not commissioned, but it was written for Eugene Ormandy as an expression of gratitude for his fine performances of my *Second Symphony*. I know that it is not proper to dedicate symphonies to conductors, but when one realizes that I had never heard a major orchestral work of my own until 1959, my gratitude will not seem insincere. When I was finally able to work on the symphony, it was so clear in my mind that I composed it immediately in score and with almost no interruption. I have never enjoyed composing a work more, for I had the feeling that I could barely keep up with the long melodic lines.

In my *Second Symphony* I had been concerned with time-duration aspects of the row; in my *Third Symphony* I was concerned with the tonal-functional possibilities of the row. In both works my concern was practical and not theoretical though I was aware, of course, of the theoretical implications. The two works represent two tendencies that can be traced in most of my compositions, but I would not pretend that they are always clearly separated nor would I want too much emphasis to be put on technical matters since, after all, the final musical experience is a *Gestalt*—the total experience is larger than the composite of its parts. Whether the following analytical suggestions are of value to the scholar or the conductor I must leave to others' judgment.

There are three different aspects to the row from which my *Third Symphony* is constructed, all of them having a similar symmetry. The basic row is fundamentally melodic and is stated in such a way as to minimize its hexachordal structure (see Ex-

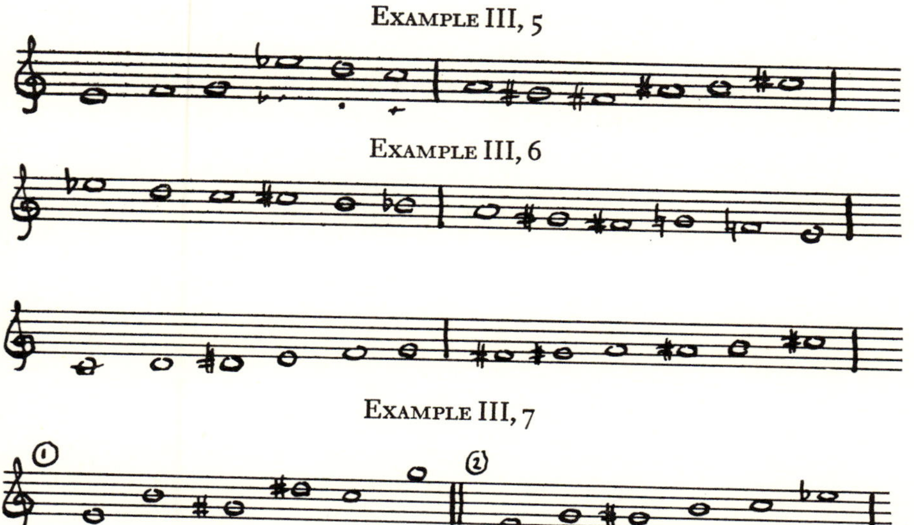

Example III, 5

Example III, 6

Example III, 7

ample III, 5). There are two scale-wise forms of the row that are used to increase the flow of the counterpoint (see Example III, 6). There are also two hexachords that furnish harmonic materials (see Example III, 7). All of these row forms are introduced in the first few measures of the symphony, and as the work unfolds they are developed and contribute their special musical functions to the form and statement.

Three Pieces for Strings, Winds, Percussion, and Tape (1962), the first work in which I have used electronic tape, is frankly experimental, not only in the use of tape, but also in a precise use of time-durations derived from the row on which the work is constructed. This interest in time which I have mentioned in connection with my *Second Symphony* may be traced in my *Second Piano Quintet* (1961) to these *Three Pieces* and the orchestral works that follow. The work is not related to my *Third Symphony*. It was composed in New York City during the summer of 1962 when I was most kindly permitted to work in the Columbia-Princeton Electronic Laboratory, and it is dedicated to that most gifted young composer, Mario Davidovsky, who was my teacher in this first timid attempt to work in the medium of electronic music. The structure of this work is so rigorous that I will not attempt to reconstruct it. If one examines the work in terms of the following row and the numbers that the pitches imply and then keeps in mind the title of each movement, one will quickly discover the structural process that I have followed (see Example III, 8). The first piece, "In lengths and densities," is primarily a

Example III, 8

counterpoint of controlled durations with the electronic tape freely commenting on the orchestral texture. The second piece, "In figures and groupings," is constructed in segments somewhat like the second movement of my *Second Symphony* while the electronic tape furnishes three cadenzas. The third piece, "In imitations," is something of a fugue in which, again, the duration of notes is dictated by the row numbers and the electronic tape is mood background for the orchestral texture.

Two works of mine may be mentioned together: *Three Studies in Fours* (1965) which was composed for the Poznan Percussion Ensemble and given its first performance in Poznan, Poland, in the summer of 1965, and *Concerto for Percussion and Orchestra* (1965) which was commissioned by Carleton College (Northfield, Minnesota) in celebration of its centennial and given its first performance on November 17, 1966, by the Minneapolis Symphony Orchestra under Stanislaw Skrowaczewski. *Three Studies in Fours* is written for a large percussion orchestra in which pitch is defined by such percussion instruments as bells, vibraphone, xylophone, and so forth. The *Concerto for Percussion and Orchestra* uses four percussion soloists with the orchestra as accompaniment somewhat in the manner of the conventional concerto. Since the earlier work was an exercise for the later work and the organizational process was somewhat similar in the two works, it will suffice to discuss the concerto.

The scoring of the *Concerto for Percussion and Orchestra* presented problems. I decided that I would have four percussion soloists dividing the instruments as follows: No. 1 performs the timpani and tubular bells; No. 2 performs the xylophone, lower drums, tam-tams, and so forth; No. 3 performs the marimba, slightly higher drums and cymbals, and so forth; No. 4 performs the glockenspiel and high cymbals and drums. I originally planned to divide the orchestra into four sections, associating each soloist with one of the sections. Two problems made me change my mind: in the first place it seemed to me essential that the soloists be placed where they could follow the conductor's beat, and in the second place the disrupting of the natural seating arrangement of the orchestra would present very great problems. The score, therefore, retains the normal positions for all instruments except the percussion. Solist No. 1 is at the far left of the conductor and front stage and often performs with the double basses and low instruments across the stage. No. 4 is placed at the far right of the conductor and front stage and often performs with the celesta, harp, piccolo, and similar high-timbre instruments across the stage. Nos. 2 and 3 are placed back stage and on raised platforms. The score is planned so that there will be considerable motion across stage or around the stage with a resulting visual effect.

As in the earlier *Three Studies in Fours,* the pitch row is used to determine many of the temporal aspects of the work. Without attempting an analysis in any detail, one illustration from the first movement, based on the first hexachord of the row, may be suggestive (see Example III, 9). The row and the scale form derived from the row dominate the orchestra very much, as they did in my second and third symphonies. Only in the solo percussion parts are the intervals limited to those derived from the three notes that control each section of each movement. Each movement, based on a different hexachord, follows the organizational pattern that I have shown for the first movement (see Example

EXAMPLE III, 9

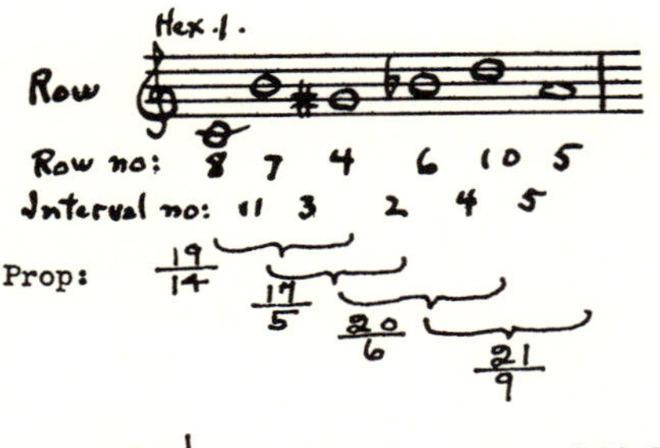

Tempi ♩=80,		204,	200,	136.5	
Duration:	40"	1'43"	1'36"	1'9"	Total 5'8"
Measures: (4/4)	13⁺	85	80	38½	Total 216½

Sect. 1. ♩=80, 13 measures (4/4)
Intervals: M7, m2, m3, M6, m6, M3.

Sect. 2. ♩=204, 84 measures (4/4)
Intervals: m3, M6, M2, m7, m2, M7.

Sect. 3. ♩=200, 80 measures (4/4)
Intervals: M2, m7, M3, m6, +4, °5.

Sect. 4. ♩=136, 35½ measures (4/4)
Intervals: M3, m6, P4, P5, m2, M7.

III, 10). Thus was formed a grid into which the musical batter was poured. This process may seem inflexible to the layman who thinks of the creative process in romantic terms, but composers have always formed their music according to some predetermined plan. There are always problems that have to be surmounted before a plan is transformed into music, and a composer is often challenged and frustrated as he works. There were certainly moments when intuitive-musical considerations forced upon me compromises that might puzzle the theoretician. The fact, however, that the orchestra was controlled and motivated in a different way than were the percussion soloists seemed to me to increase the concerto aspect of the work. Certainly there were many sparks of musical suggestion generated in this planning of the pitch-temporal design. But my concern—a concern that has dominated my musical thought for thirty years—to deal with the macrocosmic and the microcosmic aspects of music differently, to apply one controlling principle to large structure and a different one to the

Example III, 10

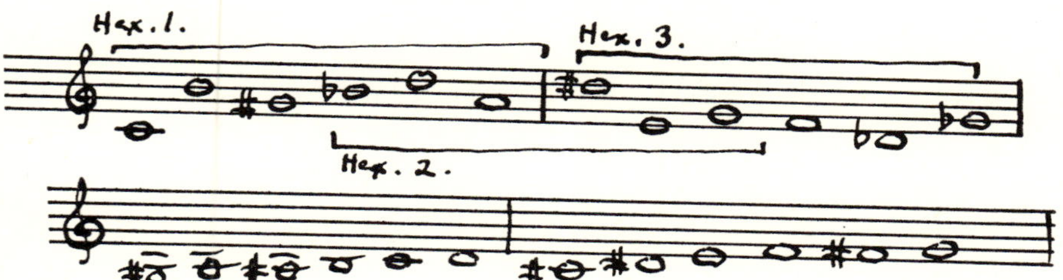

small details seemed to me to operate effectively in composing this concerto.

I would be unable to predict the direction that my future orchestral writing will take. Unlike many of my younger colleagues, I feel no distaste for the large orchestral organization, this in spite of the fact that I had to wait so many years before I could hear what I had written. Certain forces in the electronic medium direct my hearing towards greater freedom and an expanded, almost an excessive, use of instrumental articulation. Other forces direct my hearing to a greater control of the temporal design. Whether one direction will come to dominate the other will depend on how the work evolves in my mind, and I have very little control over that inner process. That other composers are facing the same issues that I am facing is surely true, but I have never given very much thought to the tendencies of other composers and certainly no thought to how my music fits into the over-all direction (whatever that is) of the music of this century. My tastes, my temperament, my personality were formed too long ago for me to hope to change them now.

CHAPTER FOUR: Peter Racine Fricker

PETER RACINE FRICKER (born in London on September 5, 1920) was educated at St. Paul's School in London. Advanced musical studies were started at the Royal College of Music, but these were interrupted by World War II during which Fricker served in the Royal Air Force in England and India. After demobilization he continued composition instruction with Mátyás Seiber and became associated with Morley College, first as accompanist, then as chorus director, and finally as musical director in 1952, succeeding Michael Tippett. The *First Symphony*, which won the Koussevitzky award in 1949 and was first performed the following year at the Cheltenham Festival by the Hallé Orchestra under Sir John Barbirolli, was the initial work to bring him to the attention of the music world, and firmly established Fricker as one of the most important English composers in the second half of the twentieth century. Following these successes, he composed a steady stream of compositions for all mediums, among them the brilliant oratorio *The Vision of Judgement* composed for the hundredth anniversary of the Leeds Triennial Festival in 1958. Fricker is a fellow of the Royal College of Organists, an associate of the Royal College of Music, an honorary member of the Royal Academy of Music, and holds an honorary doctor of music degree from Leeds University. Other honors include the Freedom of the City of London (1962) and the Order of Merit from the Federal Government of West Germany (1965). Since 1964 Fricker has resided in the United States, where he is professor of music in the University of California at Santa Barbara.

THE "TRADITIONAL" ORCHESTRA, consisting of double or triple woodwinds, horns, trumpets, trombones, tuba, timpani, percussion, and strings, has until recently been accepted by the public, by critics and writers of textbooks, and even by musicians themselves as being a natural phenomenon, the logical and only combination of instruments for a composer to use for his large-scale works, and for the transmission of his musical thinking on the most profound level.

In fact, many composers today have turned away from this "traditional" grouping, and I know of some who have stated openly that they have no interest whatever in the idea of writing for full orchestra. The emphasis is very often on smaller groups of mixed instruments, or divided groups of instruments used antiphonally. This immediately reminds us of the instrumental forces used by pre-eighteenth-century composers; the full orchestra, with its personality conductor, is in fact a nineteenth-century invention, and there is no law in music to say that this is the final solution to the production of sound for a composer's purposes. The full orchestra is an expensive item, rehearsal time for new works is usually far too short, finance demands far too many concerts for perfection of performance, and managements and audiences demand tried favorites by Beethoven, Brahms, or Tchaikovsky—not of course all of their works, but a few, well known to all players, and needing little rehearsal for what can usually be called an adequate performance, one reasonably sure of attracting an audience.

The composer, faced with these conditions, has very often preferred to write for a smaller select group: highly skilled individuals, especially gathered for a festival, or for a radio performance. Whether or not these works are commissioned (and they often are), the composer can be assured of a properly prepared performance, and the chances are that he will get a much closer collaboration with the players, and much more co-operation from them, than is possible in a rushed and routine orchestral concert.

Unless the composer is rewarded by a commission, or at least is stimulated by the promise of an adequate series of performances, he is, on the face of it, unlikely to choose to write a piece for full orchestra. The immense labor involved, and the uncertain and indeed unlikely promise of financial or critical reward, would deter anybody but a dedicated fanatic.

But then composers are, if not always fanatics, at least single-minded and often contrary individuals, and in spite of the obstacles, they do still write for orchestra. Illogical as this may seem, they have their reasons; this is a most satisfactory medium for expression, rich and full, expressive and delicate—any variation or inflection the composer needs, or is capable of, is there. To write for a restricted number of instruments can be a stimulating challenge, but often greater resources are needed, not to produce more noise but very often to produce the utmost variety, delicacy, and refinement of texture. The days of the really gigantic orchestra are probably past, except for special festival occasions, but the full orchestra is still a great instrument upon which the composer can work his imagination.

One perhaps unexpected difficulty which the composer has to face today is that it is no longer fashionable to use the word "Symphony"; in fact, a work with such a title seems to be suspect by some writers before a note of the music has been played. The preference in titling works seems to be for mathematical or scientific terms, and in many cases these have no more connection with the music than did the fanciful titles given to the weaker type of symphonic poem some sixty or seventy years ago—they certainly have no effect on the listener in helping him to judge the validity of the music. Sometimes the title is apt and descriptive—*Kontakte* or *Momente* of Stockhausen, *Structures* of Boulez, or *Atmospheres* of Ligeti—all these convey or describe something which is helpful to the listener. So, too, with some symphonic poems; in the cases of *Hunnenschlacht* of Liszt or *Don Quixote* of Strauss the form of the work is closely connected with the program. But I shall continue to use the word "Symphony" until there is a better one for a generally serious work, in one or more movements, for full orchestra. So far I have written four such works.

A further point is that a composer usually makes his first impact on the musical world with a large-scale orchestral work. It is not so common for a composer to become known widely through his chamber music. In my own case, I began to have some performances in 1948 and 1949—a *Wind Quintet, Three Sonnets of Cecco Angiolieri* for tenor, wind quintet, cello, and double bass, and my *First String Quartet.* It was my *First Symphony,* written in these same years and first performed in 1950, that was the biggest help to my career as a composer; it was awarded the Koussevitzky Prize in 1949, and within a few years after its *première* had been performed a number of times in Europe and in Australia. I would not write the same sort of piece now, perhaps, but probably many composers have felt the same way about their early works; an affection, and at the same time a feeling of some distance because of the other works that have been written since. (I should add that I have never felt the slightest desire to rework a piece after it has been completed and performed. In some cases I have withdrawn the work altogether—I would rather do this and start again than continue to patch a work that seems to me to be unsatisfactory.)

It would seem better to give a comparative analysis of the four symphonies, rather than an individual analysis of each one; that would perhaps be easier, but would have little value to those who can analyze for themselves, and would be of little interest to those who cannot. The symphonies were written, though not conceived, in pairs; the *First* in 1948–49, the *Second* in 1950–51, the *Third* in 1960, and the *Fourth* from 1964–66. This was more an accident of commissioning than of actual planning on my part, though with each odd-numbered symphony I have felt ready and eager to write another one.

The orchestra, basically the usual large symphonic one, shows some slight differences of details between the four works. The *First Symphony* is the only one to include piano and harp. The *Second Symphony* uses a fourth trumpet. The *Fourth Symphony* needs "normal" forces, except that extra strings might be needed in view of the considerable number of solo and *divisi* passages. The *Third Symphony* is perhaps the most unconventional in that the orchestra demanded is of classical, Beethoven size, with the exception of the addition of a bass clarinet. In both the *Third* and the *Fourth* the timpani player has a part of more importance than is usual; especially in the first movement and the scherzo of the *Third* and some sections of the *Fourth,* he has at times a solo role.

The *First* and *Third* follow the traditional four-movement pattern. The *Second* is in three movements; the *Fourth* in one, divided (in my idea of the scheme) into ten sections. It was interesting and amusing to watch, after the first performance in England in February, 1967, the critics trying to cope with such a form—which is after all not so unusual or outlandish; some made the work fall into more or fewer than ten sections, and one or two made valiant and quite unnecessary efforts to reduce it to a four-movement scheme, played without breaks.

To begin, the *First* and *Third* symphonies can be compared; they follow tradition in that each has the slow-movement second and the scherzo third. Both first movements are in sonata form; in the *First* the apparent slow introduction is a deception—the first section (M.M. 𝅗𝅥 = 66) uses quarter and half notes, and the second, at the same speed, eighths and sixteenths. The increase of speed is apparent, not real. The development of this movement is partly fugal, and the recapitulation is not, of course, an exact one; it continues to a certain extent the process of discussion and development, as is almost invariably the case in these days—very few composers are content with an exact recapitulation.

The first movement of the *Third Symphony* begins fortissimo and allegro, without any introduction. The phrases of the opening theme in the brass (see Example IV, 1) are important both in themselves and also because they generate motifs for later use. Compressed (see Example IV, 2), they form the chord pattern which accompanies the second group of subjects. Treated serially, they give a long chain of notes which produces the whole of the development and most of the last movement (see Examples IV, 3 and 4). The mood of the movement is generally angry, and it is largely dominated by the hammering of the timpani.

The slow movement of the *First Symphony* is simple in structure, an arch-form, with two main themes, and a big climax on an insistent brass rhythm. The end of the movement dies away, with isolated taps on the bass drum accompanying a solo flute. The

Example IV, 1

Example IV, 2

slow movement of the *Third Symphony* is more complex—a succession of themes, growing out of each other, and related in mood, and a more sustained climax, without the insistent rhythm of that in the *First Symphony*. Again, the orchestra is reduced at the end to a single flute, but this time the solo is cut off by the whole orchestra, fortissimo, diminuendo.

The third movement of the *First Symphony* is perhaps closer to a minuet than it is to a scherzo—not in rhythm, but in style. Entitled "Tableau and Dance," it has a brief introduction, which serves also as an interlude, and a coda. The equivalent movement in the *Third Symphony* is a presto, and generally very lightly orchestrated; the trio, for woodwinds, horns, and trumpets only, is in canon.

EXAMPLE IV, 3

EXAMPLE IV, 4

As for the finales for the two works, that for the *First Symphony* is in a kind of modified sonata form. There is an introduction, and three main ideas; a wispy and fleeting atmospheric section, a broader theme introduced by the violins, and a canonic section for the high first and second violins, supported by a cross-rhythm *ostinato*. There is no real recapitulation; the development uses these three ideas, and the material of the introduction is also important, particularly to bring in the coda.

The finale of the *Third Symphony* is in sectional form; it opens and closes with a *maestoso*, of which the chief features are a long broad theme (see Example IV, 4) and a chordal pattern, both derived from the first movement. Within this framework two allegros surround a central adagio, which has prominent solos for flute, bass clarinet, and viola. The moods alternate (as they do throughout the symphony) between furious outbursts and calm resignation.

These two symphonies, then, follow a fairly normal course, and are reasonably predictable, at least in over-all form. My other two symphonies offer different solutions to the symphonic problem. The *Second* is in three movements, and each one avoids the sonata allegro form. The first movement, Allegro moderato, is a kind of expanding rondo; the material is presented fairly briefly, and is discussed a second and then a third time, each time at greater length. The beginning of a fourth discussion forms instead the coda. Incidentally, this idea of expansion, of continuing growth, applies to the symphony as a whole; the last movement is the longest and most elaborate. The second movement, Andante, is more difficult to define, formally. It may be presented schematically as Introduction A B C A B A Coda; in other words, another kind of rondo. The introduction and the coda use the same short phrase (see Example IV, 5), and this also appears in the main body

EXAMPLE IV, 5

EXAMPLE IV, 6

of the movement. "C" is a short section inaugurated by a double canon for the four trumpets. However, since the different ideas are often closely related, the boundaries between the sections tend to be somewhat vague. The main theme, first heard on violins, retains its identity throughout (see Example IV, 6).

The third movement is again one which is not easy to classify formally. My view of it is another rondo, with the scheme A B A C A B A. However, a more detailed formal analysis will show that it can also be called a sonata-rondo—if such a strict definition is necessary or important. The opening section (in 2/4, though there is a deceptive and momentary impression of 3/8) uses several themes featuring wide leaps (see Examples IV, 7 and 8). The "B" section, first for trumpets and then for woodwinds,

EXAMPLE IV, 7

EXAMPLE IV, 8

is introduced by a brief phrase for glockenspiel, anticipating one of the phrases to come. This glockenspiel phrase acts as a kind of punctuation mark between the different sections of this first part of the movement. The next "A" section is a development of earlier material, and the glockenspiel again precedes and follows it. "C" is self-contained: a chorale-like theme with two variations, each using shorter note values (first half notes, then dotted quarter, then quarter notes). At the climax the time-signature changes to 3/8, with cross-rhythms briefly suggesting 2/4. The material of "A" and "B" is adapted to this new time-signature, and the movement is gradually dominated by a persistent chord pattern in the brass (see Example IV, 9).

The *Fourth Symphony*, in one movement, is in ten sections. These are to a very large extent interlocking, in that they share thematic ideas, in various transformations; the exception is section six, which is a self-contained adagio, an elegy with some variations of tempo. This symphony is dedicated to the memory of Mátyás Seiber, my teacher, colleague, and friend, whose death in a car

Example IV, 9

crash in South Africa in 1960 was a tragic loss to music, particularly in England, where his influence as a teacher was so great. My symphony uses some quotations from Seiber's own works (see Example IV, 10), which is the beginning of the row used in Seiber's *Third String Quartet.* Example IV, 11, shows a chord used in Seiber's *Permutazioni,* a chord constructed by increasing the intervals between the parts by one semitone, from the fourth at the top downwards. This and similar chords appear in section four of the symphony. However, the use of material from Seiber is rarely direct, and even more rarely recognizable. The rest of the thematic material of the *Fourth Symphony* shows perhaps a preoccupation with the intervals of the fourth and the second (see Examples IV, 12a and 12b), which show these intervals prominently. (Example IV, 12a, opens the work and appears in sections three and nine; Example IV, 12b, appears in sections two and eight, which is a brief scherzo.) Example IV, 12 c, shows another

Example IV, 10

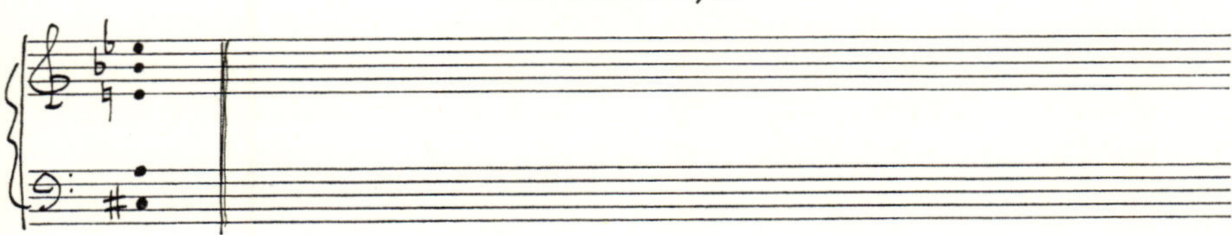

Example IV, 11

EXAMPLE IV, 12a

EXAMPLE IV, 12b

version of the additive process of Example IV, 11; the three-semitone groups follow one another at intervals which increase by one semitone each time—this is used in section three and five. There is no long self-contained theme, no "first" or "second" subjects. The ten sections are built up from these and other fragments, which combine, merge, and develop in a kaleidoscopic way. The sections are:

1. *Vigoroso*. Dramatic in mood, with strong contrasts of dynamics.
2. *Poco meno, ma scorrevole*. Flowing, with woodwinds mainly in the foreground.
3. *Allegro; Agitato*.
4. *Andante con moto*. Cadenzas, first for woodwinds, and then for solo violin, viola, and cello.
5. *Agitato*. Echoes of section three.

(Pause.)

6. *Adagio elegaico*. This is very free in rhythm, and generally

EXAMPLE IV, 12c

delicately scored, frequently with a light, almost chamber-music texture—there are several variations of tempo.

7. *Allegro*. Again free in rhythm, and like a recitative.
8. *Allegro molto*. A miniature, self-contained scherzo.
9. *Adagio*. Again in the style of a recitative, and free in tempo.
10. *Adagio*. At first in the style of a chorale, and then like a processional.

This form, incidentally, one of contrasting sections surrounding a central adagio, can be regarded as an expansion or development of the finale of the *Third Symphony*. The finale of my *Viola Concerto*, written between 1951 and 1953, is another version of this scheme, with alternating slow and fast sections.

If I have concentrated on the form rather than the matter of the four symphonies, it is because this is much easier to reduce to words, if one is to avoid flowery and imaginative writing that would be no great help to anybody. Let it suffice to say that they are generally serious in mood, that the *First* and *Second* have no program beyond a purely musical and symphonic one, that the *Third* is a study in contrasting moods, and that the *Fourth* is a tribute of respect and affection.

My shorter orchestral works need less detailed description. The *Rondo Scherzoso* of 1948 explains itself as far as form and mood go—a straightforward piece, rather early in my list of compositions. The *Prelude, Elegy and Finale*, Opus 10 (1949), for string orchestra, is a short work, dedicated to my wife—the opening is curiously (and unintentionally) like that of Brahms's *Symphony No. 1*. The *Dance Scene*, Opus 22 (1954), is conceived as a kind of *pas de deux* from an imaginary ballet; it has three sections all in dance rhythm, though not in any specific dance form. The *Litany*, Opus 26 (1955), for double string orchestra, is considerably larger in scale—a serial work, but using besides a note row a plainsong theme. The mood is generally grave, and partly processional. The *Comedy Overture*, Opus 32 (1958), is short and light—it was written for the opening of the new concert hall at Morley College, London. *Three Scenes for Orchestra*, Opus 45

(1966), were written for the California High School Symphony Orchestra. This does not mean, by the way, that I made any concessions to the youth or skill of the players, who are quite capable of accepting almost any challenge. The first movement, Nocturne, is atmospheric, the second, Danza, light and rhythmic, and the third, March-Ostinato, a study on a single theme—compare the *Bolero* of Ravel, or the Scherzo from Hindemith's *Symphonic Metamorphosis on Themes by Weber. Seven Counterpoints for Orchestra,* Opus 47 (1967), has a mixed origin—four of the seven movements are transcriptions of an early work, my *Four Fughettas* for two pianos, Opus 2 (1946). To these I have added three movements, canons of various kinds, one for woodwinds, one for strings, and one for brass.

This list of works constitutes the main body of my orchestral music. There are one or two very short works which I have not mentioned—works for the most part written for special occasions, which are unlikely in the normal course of events to be performed again. There are also about twelve film scores, and some for theater and ballet; these too are probably too closely linked with their originals to justify or warrant separate performances.

For the composer himself to produce such a survey as this is a curious undertaking. I have concentrated on formal matters—it would be equally possible to write on other aspects, such as the circumstances of composition, for instance, or recommendations for details and styles of performance. Whatever the point of departure, the reader—and indeed the writer—must remember that the last work discussed is not the end of the story; that this is only an interim report. Most composers must have plans for the future, and mine certainly include orchestral works, in spite of the apparent pessimism of my opening remarks. Not the least of my reasons would be the great pleasure I find in working with orchestral musicians. Their skill and experience, and above all their sheer professionalism, are equaled only by their helpfulness and interest when they are called on to present a new work. Perhaps this sense of collaboration is after all one of the biggest incentives to a composer when he comes to write orchestral music.

CHAPTER FIVE: Hans Werner Henze
(Translated by Willis J. Wager)

HANS WERNER HENZE (born in Gütersloh, Westphalia, on July 1, 1926) began music studies at the Brunswick State Music School. He was drafted into the army in 1944 and was taken prisoner by the British. Following his release, Henze gained experience as a chorus *repetiteur* at the Bielefeld Stadttheater, supplementing his income by playing piano at ballet schools. He resumed his studies at the Heidelberg School of Church Music where he worked with Wolfgang Fortner. It was during this phase of his development that Henze took an intense interest in the works of Igor Stravinsky, along with those of Alban Berg. Later, in Darmstadt and Paris, René Leibowitz guided Henze toward the music and theoretical writings of Arnold Schönberg which had a strong impact on the evolution of the young composer's personal style. It was at this time that Henze became artistic director of the ballet at Wiesbaden State Theater and also worked on the opera *Boulevard Solitude,* first performed in Hanover in February, 1952. Following this period, Henze withdrew to Forio on the island of Ischia near Naples where his compositional technics matured and mellowed in the seclusion of the countryside. Two works which were to bring him international renown were composed; the opera *König Hirsch* which had its world *première* at the Stadtische Oper in Berlin on September 25, 1956; and the ballet *Ondine,* commissioned by Frederick Ashton for England's Royal Ballet and presented at Covent Garden on October 24, 1958. After these triumphs, there appeared an amazing list of works in all medias year after year, each more novel and more successful than the former. Undoubtedly, Henze is one of the most prolific composers of our time and deserves the accolades of his admirers who describe him as the "greatest hope among German composers of the postwar generation." Italy, however, still holds a special charm for

Henze—he lives in Marino near Rome, often taking part in the artistic life of the capital.

ONLY BY RECOURSE to inferences and similes is it possible to recognize and judge the relationship between the art of these years and that of the past and future.[1] What we see in the course of ten years lying behind and anticipate in that of ten years lying ahead is still too close to us: it lacks the distance which would make clear recognition and cool observation quite possible. That which has just now been crowds near, almost still graspable, beside us. As yet it has no name. Later it will be called "past," will perhaps belong to history, and will be less and less disturbed by the ongoing of life—less and less affected by the fickleness of taste, by blindness, and by overexposure. We cast ourselves down before the unknown that arouses our curiosity. How good it is to know that, as time continues to recede farther into the background, by its crystallization it furnishes us with a point of reference, firm ground where experience has been corroborated. The retrospect on times that lie behind offers intensification, stimulation, and connection, provides parallels with the present, similarities, and reveals something which rests in itself crystalline, emitting a phosphorescent glow—a light which shines on into the present.[2]

In our world, with its self-destructive tendencies, there seems to arise at the very core of its music an inclination to deny the time for which it was purposed, to work from within against its

1 This chapter was copyrighted in 1964 by B. Schott's Söhne. It is reprinted here by permission of Associated Music Publishers, Inc., agents for the U.S.A.—R.S.H.

2 "We dwell with satisfaction upon the poet's difference from his predecessors, especially his immediate predecessors; we endeavour to find something that can be isolated in order to be enjoyed. Whereas if we approach a poet without this prejudice we shall often find that not only the best, but the most individual parts of his work may be those in which dead poets, his ancestors, assert their immortality most vigorously. And I do not mean the impressionable period of adolescence, but the period of full maturity." (T. S. Eliot, "Tradition and the Individual Talent," in *The Sacred Wood* [London, Methuen & Co., Ltd., 1928], 48.)—H.W.H.

manifest and stable aspects, and to focus on renunciation. To music in our time there is given scant opportunity of glorifying situations and of shedding light over men. The fire of Hiroshima has overshadowed everything. The continuing threat to life and individual freedom puts the artistic-creative on the defensive. In the sixteenth and seventeenth centuries music could realize and glorify itself and the time given it, for the one supported the other. Later, more and more deprived of ties linking it with the social context, it turned into an individualistic activity. And today, although it really wants to speak out and be open, it almost resembles a secret cult—assailed, often really persecuted, fleeing from dangers such as those of miscalculation and vulgarization under dictators and elsewhere before the commonplaces of aesthetic orders of the day.

I, too—so far as I can think back—have been used to looking on free music, the music of freedom, as something mysterious and anti-authoritarian. In the very last years of the war when I started to compose, that free and hence forbidden music, which was to be heard only over forbidden wave-lengths and secret stations, seemed to me a symbol of isolation, an idiom that under all conditions was exposed to senselessness and trivialization and that later would be supplanted, though the fragility of its material was not inherent but was to be brought to it by destructive misinterpretation and profanation from without.

The end of the National Socialist domination meant the beginning of a new era, in which those who had been innocent, pure, or purified by repentance would be permitted to receive what was free, what had been taken away, the humanly unrecognized latent possibilities of *noblesse,* the manifestly unseasonable, and that which was farthest removed from crudeness. This was a situation filled with a sense of new beginnings and joyous anticipation, scarcely to be blighted by disappointments, temptations, and offenses. It would have continued so for years—until it then seemed necessary to take up a position anew, namely against phenomena that had been thought dead and that now, in remarkable variants of fascism, rose up against the new image that man had made for himself of the world. It was a disappointment to see that not many years after the dictatorship had been overthrown in my native land impulses revived which indicated that the evil spirit had not died. The disappointment not only continues but also increases, and brings with it anger and shame. It also compels me, in my work, more consciously than ever before to swim against the tide, and with, in, and through this work to plead for a life in which brutality and neglect of love for one's neighbor are excluded and intellectual and social freedom are guarded.

From the tension between my wish to live and work actively and positively in our time and the impossibility of encountering much in it that is worth affirming, there has apparently arisen a relationship of resistance. This involves certain internal and external contradictions. This does not matter. Yet a foolish answer to the nineteenth century, a bemused Puritanism, characterizes a great part of the musical life of our time and brings forth a plebian result in comparison with past epochs. For it tries to confine the efficacy of art by mechanization and depersonalization to the provincial circle of consumers. This simple-minded decorousness of the progressives! With the aid of new technical achievements—they seem to think—the life of music is once again to be spared. All this leads me to assume that I shall continue my journey even farther alone.

Of me it is not—or not yet—to be learned how I for myself conceive of the presence of music in this time. My own music gains distance, absents itself, in so far as men with sanctioned intentions of murder or an unpunished murder-record can listen, discuss, and judge it.

I have certain conceptions, indispensable to my existence or the existence of my music, of what music can do, what it is good for in the world, what it consists of, and what in it is lasting. But for the moment I confine myself to speaking of fictions, of uncertain outlines, and of conjectures. With what I know, what I have experienced and learned, with what I am, think, and do, I have placed myself in distinct opposition to the prescriptions of the popes and the rules of the monks. Nothing among the newly arising prescriptions and theories, under which the liberated threw themselves with joy into the arms of the technical era, has interested me other than out of curiosity. Scarcely, it seemed to me, was a thesis advanced, the first notes written out in their series, really the end always determinable, before the breath of its validity gave out in the course of the season. For the end lay already contained in the beginning of the thesis. Proclamations and orders of the day swept through the provinces. Every stirring of music, every workshop secret that was still to be kept confidential (i.e., of things that concern only the one who is himself writing), every new discovery relating only to the finder himself, was trumpeted forth. Jurors stood around and conducted the necessary business, commented, noticed this and that, wished to instruct, advise, write up further manifestoes. They exercised a sort of supervision —back-slapping, looking this way and that, never missing a trick, always ready to disavow the idea of the year before the moment it seemed to be established in favor of something new. Really they produced in their writings unconscious self-analyses; for when they spoke of inability, of failure, they set up demands, approved this and rejected that, discouraging the possible and encouraging the impossible—these fussy, bourgeois-reactionary fans!

In its urgency music has to become sonority. In its haste it has to come into the world, to manifest itself. Its property is always to make the manifestoes relating to it superfluous. The road which it takes is never the one expected, requested, or prescribed. It ignores the theoretical corrective and dissolves the dogma whenever it wishes. Its purlieus are neither materialization nor chaos. Between these so opposed poles it operates—knowing of both, but existent only in the tension between them, and excited by this tension.

One needs knowledge of the urgent, hidden formulas, formal ciphers, idioms, to become master of chaos, of a chaos that would be boring and quite as ugly as a totally materialized creation; and one needs unlimitedness, limitlessness, explosions, and chaotic images to resist the oppression of the mathematical, which belongs to the aboriginal material of music quite as much as does the disordered and chaotic. Everything that has to do with mischance, doubt, and the extremely ancient pains of music-making is comprised in an awareness of this polarity. The composer takes his place between the two, to maintain the possibility of his writing at all. He who feels the haste and urgency of his writing—as though every day might be his last—will find his way, establish himself, will pay no heed to the noise of the socially marketable, to keep his ears open all the more alertly for the as yet unknown sound which awaits him. Only that which remains open, which has not yet become analyzable, not yet written out, can fascinate him.

Wherever the by-products of physics have been applied to music to permit it to arise mechanically in itself (as if this were not otherwise a mathematical matter so long as it continued in its state of lethargy), tendencies have been carried to their ultimate conclusion. Thus a new sense of freedom, breaking with previous rules and usages, has been able to endow music with new life. Renewed, it transformed this life into one opposed to physical nature and belonging to the world of imagination. This too has happened in these years: after so much technologically induced materialization, there was heard the cry for a more powerful thematic basis for the possible generation of new forms. The question is posed anew: whence are we to get the power through which music can be brought to live on, whence a fascination and therewith everything comes full circle, at the beginning of which stood the cry for the utter demolition of the figural work that was making up music. The demand is for a new beginning, after everything has obviously played itself out. And yet, in all this time, the quiet, inner pulse-beat, this almost ineffable but most essential feature of the tonal art, was never for a moment interrupted, with whatever temptations and offenses it has been charged. Actually this is what happened: even in the last ten years of breakup, disorganization, annulment, and leveling, there have arisen important works here and there in the world: and the result of these efforts, the successful and the not so successful works, have been pitched out like fodder to a brood of imitators everywhere, while the works themselves, already having become independent of their momentary fate, stand there in isolation, not trying to be exemplary—just music, polyvalent, already far distanced from its creator.

What emerges in the academies and studios as learnable modern is a colloquial language which can no longer serve even the purposes of current *Gebrauchsmusik*—a colloquial language in which no single particular word is still possible. Every corrective in the form of a reaching backward into older tonal structures seems all the more enlivening and promising. Was it to be foreseen, was it intended, that a tonal language, which at the beginning of this century in the hands of some few was able to express the heights and depths and was something exceptional, should now become everybody's simple stock-in-trade so that the cry for something new and different *as such* is understandable if it mainly proceeds from the mouths of those who have collaborated industriously in bringing on the dilemma? I do not know. At all events, the different and the new, for which such a literary cry was raised, certainly has quite a different musical look from what those who raised it might have liked it to have.

One must accustom oneself to the realization that music, though it may be handled with ever so much technical knowledge and ability and may be interlarded with fine and progressive-sounding vocables, takes on no meaning if its necessary relationship to the ancient beauties is forgotten. It will live by the same or yet a related body of ideas as those which animated it in the past centuries. It will not make out apart from those old requisites, such as idea, imagination, excitement. In these very respects it is perhaps not so different from music of earlier times, which wished to represent, symbolize, address. Bits of knowledge and chains of reasoning in modern ways of thinking—whatever that means—cannot be injected into it directly. There is a need of refractions, perhaps of a childlike faith in realities and ties, of a culture-feeling that consciously relates itself to the past events and adventures of music.

Every new piece is the first that has ever been written. The entire area of feeling is cleared and directed toward receiving messages from one's own subconscious. Composing is a process of selection, of decision. What, from the universe of immanent possibilities, do I adopt for the work—only a selection therefrom can I indeed master. What I hold fast to is but a small part of the whole. The state which I produce is limited in time. How is the selection, how is the image to be constituted? What is to be clear? What must remain inexact, that what is to be understood exactly may stand in contrast to it? What I compose is basically one single work, which was begun fifteen years ago and which will end sometime. The beginnings and the endings of individual works are only make-believe. Perhaps, more modestly, one might also say that the beginning lies five or six hundred years back. Between the one piece and the other there lie stretches of time that can be called rests only in the sense that during them no music was written down. The joy in transforming traditional models—or the pains taken to enter into the conventions of these models and to see them in a new light as a newly effective means—crops up from time to time in various forms, perhaps as a change of masks, but also as a formative corrective which uncovers relationships. Composing consists of self-confrontation—which means something that could be glossed as communication, message, and expression. In its strongest impulses it also achieves the highest degree of transfer and surrender, as what is to be kept quiet can no longer do. Accordingly, formulations that are especially simple and opposed to thematic imbroglio must be introduced, with special clarity of gesture. Where insight into difficult matters is to be conveyed, one must make use of likenesses, must have a key. I consider it inadequate to present tightly locked music as such, like a riddle without an answer. The being that suffuses all things indeed lies behind their outward shapes and will yield itself to recognition; and its master, as soon as the force of this pressure compels him, will do everything to give out the key.

I was never sure that the things which I dealt with were to be made manifest in only the one way that I had chosen. But I have always striven to give the most difficult musical proceedings the simplest formulation that I could devise. My music, despite its intercourse with pre-existent forms and figures, is not explicable in a literary way. It is direct. Only with effort could one find something yet to read between its lines. It has quite as much for the naïve listener as for the expert who can probe the ciphers and appraise objectively. And yet where it seems to be quite accessible and graspable, it is quite remote, meaningless to the normal secondary-school ear, yet acceptable only in such masquerade. Where, on the other hand, it seems to be more modish (that is, takes on the manner of the contemporary festival vernacular), it contains relatively simple things of a pastoral and bucolic character. Thus there exist in all the pieces, not only in the instrumental but also in those intended for the theater, passages of transition, indecision, allusion, seriousness, evanescence, anticipation, recall, presentiment—contrapuntal dramas.

The work of every composer may sometimes appear discontinuous when it is examined quite superficially or when it cannot be subjected to continuing analysis. Yet in it there is an uninterrupted development, a growth, upon which ever new external influences and inner discoveries operate, enriching and transforming it.

As for instrumental composition, chamber music signifies something intended for dealing with what is intimate, and accordingly can attain to the very limits of what is nameable. Chamber music is understood as a sounding world which, to be sure, has outer boundaries, but no inner ones. It is a music for reflection and further thought—far more so than that which resounds in great concert halls and theaters. The latter is intended and obliged to produce a more direct effect than does the music which is really addressed to the players, and which is to be worked out slowly and through much practice. Ever since chamber music began to be written for distinguished virtuosos instead of for distinguished dilettanti, it is mostly hard to play, and often borders on the limits of the performable. There is an idea—easy to understand—that things difficult to conceive of in the mind are also difficult to play. But that ought not to mean that one should have to call for the ultimates and extremes of instrumental technique. On the contrary, it should be kept in mind that still today there are difficulties of interpretation in, for example, Mozart's instrumental music or Verdi's handling of the voice-parts that make phenomenal demands on the performers and in particular instances are even unsolvable and insuperable. One must guard against assuming that achievements with great demands attendant upon them can go on increasing forever. For records there is a limit, on the other side of which dwells nonsense. Besides, everything is still hard enough as it is, and what is easy turns out in actuality to be hardest of all.

Everywhere in my instrumental compositions there is interplay between counterpoint and chordally supported *cantabilità*. Some characteristic features, first to be encountered in *Apollo et Hyazinthus*, are developed from one piece to another. Naturally, in the chamber music the contrapuntal aspects remain more complex; but they have also quite filled out the orchestral pieces such as the *Symphonische Etüden* and the *Antifone*. At other points, as for example in the *Cinque Canzoni Napoletane* and the *Nachtstücke und Arien*, the *cantabile* aspect prevails, and counterpoints are avoided. Yet there is no consequent abandonment of the "thematic work," the development of the composition from germinating motives. The continually changing relationship between contrapuntal and *cantabile* pieces (the North German and polyphonic natural disposition in the *arioso* South) could be interpreted as indecision, but also as an artistic means of clarifying tension and relaxation, strictness and ease, light and dark, as something theatrical, perhaps even as an intended juxtaposition of irreconcilables. A synthesis is not attempted. This feature carries over from work to work in varying forms of evident friction.

Everything moves toward the theater and returns from it. In the orchestral pieces it is noticeably closer at hand, although what is typical in certain symphonic traditions is also kept in view. This is chamber music in larger dimensions, oriented outwardly and strengthened. With the growth of the means of personal expression, the formulations become more succinct, and the successful transmutation of conventionalities occurs more readily. My orchestral pieces had so far always been planned as symphonies or as preliminary steps thereto. Works such as *Quattro Poemi, Antifone, Nachtstücke und Arien, Ode an den Westwind* always embody certain overt attempts to attain the greatest Middle European form of instrumental music, the sonata. My first effort in this direction, the *First Symphony* (1947), quite missed the mark. I have now made a new version, reorganized the material, and tried to reconstruct what I then intended, like a teacher helpfully correcting his pupil. The *Second* and *Third Symphonies,* both in three movements, written in 1948 and 1949, have more in common formally with the pre-Classical than with the nineteenth-century symphony. They contain *chaconnes, ostinati, ariosi.* The *Second* is serious and dark; the *Third,* more clear, dance-like, hectic. In the *Fourth Symphony,* written in 1955, the preoccupation with the traditional form is clearly recognizable. It contains five movements in one. There is a prelude, in which the material for the whole is prepared. Then follow a sonata, some variations, a scherzo-like A B A form, and finally a rondo-finale. It was in the beginning thought of as the conclusion to the second act of the opera *König Hirsch* (*Stag King*). But later I extracted it from the opera, incorporating also the voice-parts somewhat as Alban Berg had done in the symphonic suite from *Lulu.* (See Example V, 1.) In the *Fifth Symphony* (1962) the first movement is a further attempt at the sonata, the second a sort of song with variations, and the finale (*Moto Perpetuo*) could be considered a rondo, but is in the last analysis the thirty-two-fold variation on the *arioso* of the second movement.

Thus in these five orchestral pieces that are to be understood as symphonies those great forms were attempted which our tradition has taught us to consider receptacles for the broadest and highest of absolute music. Now—as we know and yet do not wish to know, however abundantly the evidence may pile up—these receptacles are shattered. The expansive power of the Late Romantic era has burst them open. For the past fifty years and more the symphony, as the nineteenth century understood it, exists no

EXAMPLE V, 1

4. SINFONIE
(in einem Satz)
HANS WERNER HENZE
1955

Example V, 1, copyright 1963 by B. Schott's Söhne. Used by permission of Associated Music Publishers, Inc., agents for the U.S.A.

EXAMPLE V, 1 (continued)

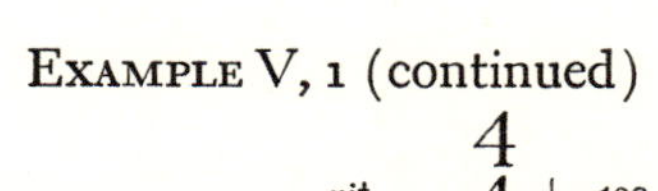

EXAMPLE V, 1 (continued)

Example V, 1 (continued)

more. Between Stravinsky and Webern everything which still passes for symphony seems to be rejoinder, obituary, or echo. It is as if today's musical language has no mastery over the old forms, or as if the old forms no longer had power over the new language.

However this may be, I have in this connection forsworn an all too available pessimism. Mahler's *adieux* suited his own lyre, not the European symphony's as such. We ought further to think his music through: It contains—beyond its indisputably necrological qualities—many new starting-points, challenges, and impulses.

Every artist has the idiosyncrasy of making a picture of things for himself, of setting up his own world, without regard for the facts, *mores,* and modes that stand outside this world. Only through the disregard or transformation of such circumstances into images that occur to his imagination, through paraphrase, reinterpretation, or redesignation does it become possible for him to give an answer to his surroundings. His world is filled up with freely discovered arrangements of magnitudes.

In my world the old forms are intended to recover a meaning, even where the novel sonority of the music no longer allows it to appear entirely or partially on the surface. Some have felt that in modern man there is insufficient emotional power—the only kind of power that can master these forms. It has been shown that the constructive resources, the tonal state of music today will still produce only illusions of the forms. Even so, they serve—precisely in view of such misery—to delineate things that determine my world.

In my world these figures raise their voices and wish to reveal themselves: Mercury and Jupiter, Vergil, Faunus, Harlequins, Tritons, Leonce, Touchstone, Hamlet, and Gloucester. Old forms, I might say, appear to me as classic ideals of beauty—no longer attainable, but visible from afar, stirring memory as dreams. But the road to them is filled with the very great darkness of the era. The road is most hard or utterly impossible. To me it seems the only folly making life worth living.

CHAPTER SIX: Ernst Krenek

Ernst Krenek (born on August 23, 1900) studied in his native city of Vienna and also with Franz Schreker in Berlin. Between 1925 and 1927 he was an opera coach under Paul Bekker in Kassel. The phenomenal success of his opera *Jonny spielt auf*, often described as a jazz opera, brought Krenek international fame at twenty-six. The work was translated into eighteen languages and performed all over the world. In 1928, Krenek returned to Vienna and turned his attention to literary work. He also traveled extensively throughout Europe lecturing and accompanying recitals of his songs. By 1933 he had adopted the twelve-tone method of composition—a natural evolution in view of his inquiries and interest in tonal areas beyond the late Romantic spirit of his early works. Twenty years later Krenek entered into yet another realm of composition with *Spiritus Intelligentiae, Sanctus* (1957) for electronic sounds and voices. Like many intellectuals during the 1930's, Krenek found the European political climate intolerable and migrated to the United States in 1937. He became a citizen in 1945. From 1939 to 1942 he was professor of music at Vassar College, and until 1947, dean of the School of Fine Arts at Hamline University in St. Paul. Since then Krenek has resided in California, devoting himself to composition and traveling throughout the world, lecturing, and conducting his works.

At the time of this writing—August, 1967—I have completed about forty-five works for orchestra, in about as many years, among them a number of works including solo voices or choral ensemble, and several concertos. My discussion of this output shall be limited to compositions for orchestra alone, for introduction of linguistic elements poses problems that would by far transcend the scope of this paper, and the concertos may generally be regarded as marginal works in which I exploited stylistic resources arrived at and developed in the purely orchestral works.

It seems to me characteristic that among the first four items on the list of these works are three symphonies, all of them created in 1921 and 1922, when I was twenty-one and twenty-two years old. I now remember very well that at that time I was filled with the ambition of becoming the successor of Gustav Mahler in the field of symphonic music. Apparently I did not have enough of a truly revolutionary temperament or enough critical insight in order either to reject the traditional concept of the symphony, or to recognize through historical and sociological analysis that the age of the symphony had passed. Probably the subversive streak in my nature is not strong enough to try to overthrow the Establishment, and I was too young for the wisdom that might have resulted from critical examination of the issue.

What I wanted was to write bigger and better symphonies. But I was intelligent enough to realize that this could be attempted with a hope for even a minimum of success only if I would try completely new, different tracks. In this light my *First Symphony* appears to me even today as a fairly novel solution. It is in one movement of about thirty minutes' duration, consisting of a freely organized sequence of contrasting thematic statements and development sections derived therefrom. Especially the fairly long introduction that presents cascading string passages strikes me even now as a remarkably original idea.

The *Second Symphony*, written only one year later, has remained the most ambitious of my orchestral works, at least as far as duration is concerned. It takes about fifty minutes. The idiom is typical of the vocabulary I tried to develop after shedding the eggshells of post-Romantic and Impressionistic mannerisms of my school years. Closer acquaintance with Arnold Schönberg, or perhaps even more so with Béla Bartók, led me to use a fairly ruthless dissonant style which once in a while would enclose isolated remnants of traditional tonality like debris left over from a bygone age.

In my memoirs (which I have deposited at the Library of Congress) I wrote on the occasion of a performance of this work under the direction of Dimitri Mitropoulos in Minneapolis in 1943 (it was the second time that I heard it, twenty years after its *première*):

> Analyzing the impression which I have gathered so far from objectively listening to the work, I feel that the first two movements evoke very much the picture of a giant moving about in a cage, or cave. The first movement is full of terrific efforts to break the walls of the cave, or the bars of the cage, defiant stomping and pounding seem to be the dominant expressive qualities of the music, sorrowful resignation being the only lyrical detail coming to the fore. At one place the narrow intervals that open the movement in the pianissimo of celesta and violins, indicating a sort of hazy, misty atmosphere, are repeated in fortissimo by strings and brasses: it sounded to me like the cries of the poor souls in purgatory [see Example VI, 1].
>
> The second movement sounds like the result of such a resignation: indulgence in the narrowness to which the giant is confined, a sort of desperate dance, making a virtue out of the deficiency, madly hopping around in the cage, or cave.
>
> The third, slow movement, is quite different, based as it is on strongly expressive patterns of great expansiveness. It . . . sounds like the passionate prayer for freedom uttered by someone who has finally broken down the inhibitions that prevented him thus far even to burst out in such a prayer . . . . The climax at the end . . . has, as I feel it now, more uplifting than crushing quality, but does not act as solution of the conflict, it rather sounds like a delirious attempt to accept the contradictions as ordained by a supreme power and to integrate the conflicting elements into a sort of cosmic pandemonium [see Example VI, 2].

The above quotation is offered as a historical footnote rather than a definitive interpretation of the "meaning" of the symphony. It is indicative of my mood and frame of mind at the time

EXAMPLE VI, 1

Ob. I. II.
I. II.
Klar. (B.)
III.
Fag. I. II.
Kfag.
I. II.
Hörn. (F.) III. IV.
V. VI.
I. II.
Trp. (C)
III. IV.
I. II.
Pos.
III. Tub.
Pk.
I.
Viol.
II.
Vla.
Vcll.
Cb.
a 2
ff

EXAMPLE VI, 2

103
Largo.
Kl. Fl.
Fl. I. II.
Ob. I. II.
Es-Klar.
I. II. Klar. (B.) III.
Basskl. (B.)
Fag. I. II.
Kfag.
II. Hörn. IV. (F.) VI.
I. II. Tr. (C.) III. IV.
I. II. Pos. III. Tub.
Kb.-Pos.
Pk.
cresc.
a 2
simile
Schall.
Schalltrichter hoch bis Schluss.
sempre
103
Largo.
I. Viol. II.
Vla.
Vcll.
Kb.
div.
sempre
cresc.
simile

of its writing. Of course, the work supplied the cues for it. Today, another twenty-five years later, I might stress quite different aspects of the symphony if I had to explicate whatever is implied in the music. May it suffice to point out one more rather unusual detail of the last movement: a very long passage played by all first and second violins in unison.

According to my records, I wrote my *Third Symphony* during that same year, 1922. As it was in the case with the *Second Symphony*, again some sections of it were conceived during a railroad journey from Vienna to Berlin. I remember that at that time the railroad was one of my favorite places for writing music. From Franz Schubert I had learned to date all manuscripts. Thus I can see that the sketching of a good-sized symphonic movement took me about one week, its orchestration another week. Today it seems quite mysterious to me how I was able even physically to put on paper such masses of notes in so short a time—not to consider the creative process involved. For in that year 1922 I seem to have written also my first opera, *Zwingburg* (*The Tyrant's Castle*), a chamber symphony, and a major piano work. From music history we know that the tempo of writing has little bearing on the artistic quality of the product. One might say that fast, carefree writing promotes overextended, loosely knit works while slow, deliberate creation favors brevity and concentration.

I remember that I wanted my *Third Symphony* to be significantly different from the *Second*: smaller in scope, lighter in vein, and for small orchestra. I succeeded in the last two respects, but when I recently was asked to conduct this work I introduced many substantial cuts. In the *Second Symphony*, which lasts about twice as long, I have never felt the necessity of such cuts. The general style of the *Third* is, of course, rather similar to that of the *Second*, as may be seen in the imitatory development of one of the secondary themes of the first movement (see Example VI, 3). The middle movement is somewhat unusual because I had decided to write, for a change, a violent, fierce Adagio. I believe that at the age of twenty-two one does such things just "for the heck of it," not being aware of implications, or significance. Today I

Example VI, 3

feel that this movement with its vehemently expressionistic gesticulations is the most valuable part of the symphony (see Example VI, 4). A new stylistic feature is an element of levity, as manifested in the distortion of the secondary theme quoted above (see Example VI, 5), or the lilting tune of the last movement (see Example VI, 6). Such heterogeneous items were intentionally left isolated in the more or less atonal language of the whole work in order to produce a shock—as if one would suddenly look at a completely different world through some crack in the wall. In such procedures one might detect a touch of surrealism.

It was my last venture in the grand style for a long time to come. As if to make sure that I would not miss any trend, I already had written *Symphonic Music* for nine instruments. This work has retained much of its original vitality through its relentless rhythmic drive. It suffers somewhat from an overdose of contrapuntal imitations such as emerged at that time as a dominating feature

EXAMPLE VI, 4

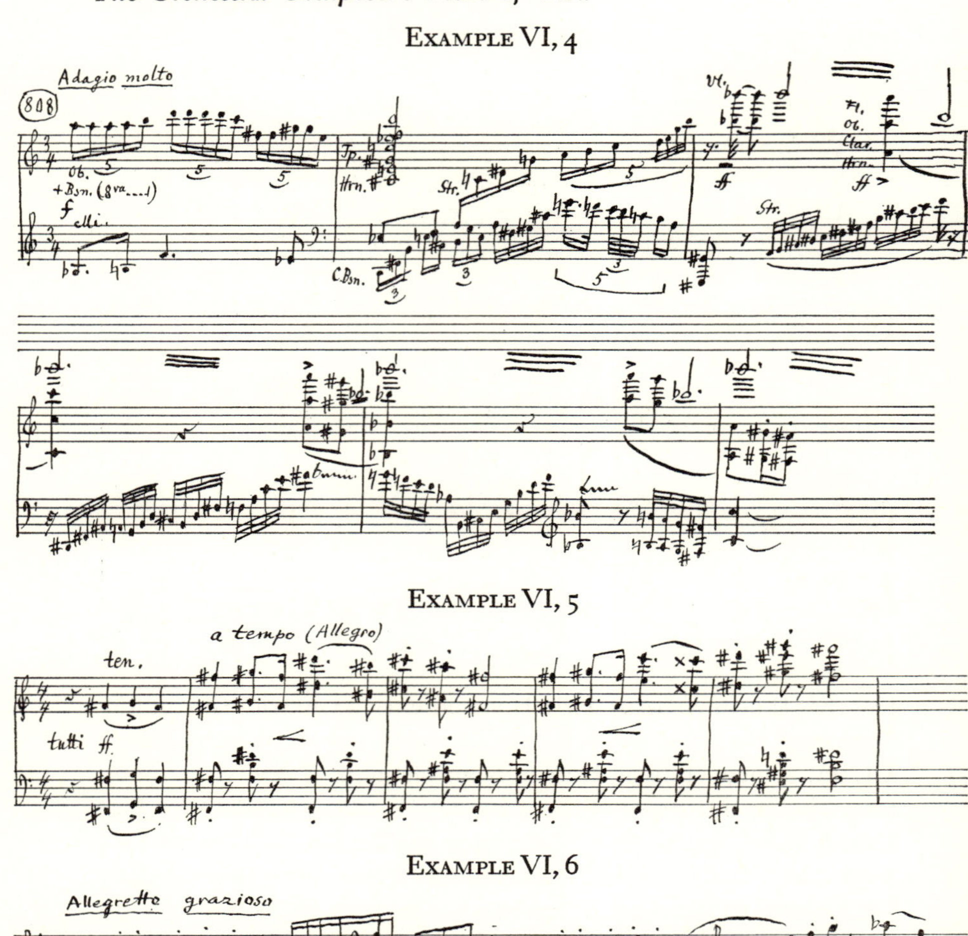

EXAMPLE VI, 5

EXAMPLE VI, 6

Allegretto grazioso

Clar. (A)

p Str. pizz.

of Hindemith's style. The temptations of neoclassicism beckoned more strongly as soon as Igor Stravinsky had opened up this avenue. As early as 1923 I wrote a *Concerto Grosso* with a concertino group of six against a string ensemble. Later I found this piece so unsatisfactory that I withdrew it from circulation. Its only noteworthy feature was that the first theme, played by the *tutti* in unison, imitated in melodic outline the profile of a mountain range that I observed looking south from the deck of an excursion steamer on one of the Bavarian lakes—some time before Villa-Lobos' skyline inspiration.

A *Second Concerto Grosso*—this one of more durable quality—and a *Concertino for Harpsichord* followed shortly. In retrospect it now appears to me that in my flirtation with neoclassicism I soon became tired of its serious and somewhat ponderous Germanic variety, and more interested in the playful and jazzy approach of the French composers. Instead of following the line of modernized restoration of the Baroque concerto I was more attracted to whimsical juxtaposition of heterogeneous materials quoted from earlier vocabularies out of context and mixed up with morsels of pop art (which, at that time, meant elements of moderate jazz character).

This, of course, is also the *ambiente* of my opera *Jonny spielt auf*, which was written during this period, at the mid-twenties. My preoccupation with the theater was so strong that in other media I devoted time to smaller projects only. I mention here a symphony for wind instruments and percussion, which I adorned with the French title *Symphonie pour instruments à vent et batterie*, probably because of its particularly obvious Stravinskyan flavor. For the Donaueschingen Festival, which for a while had been transferred to Baden-Baden, I wrote *Three Marches* for military band in the spirit of the old Austrian army marches. The closest approach to the entertainment music of the period materialized in the *Potpourri*, in which I tried to imitate somewhat satirically the conglomerations of dashing and sentimental tunes on the repertoire of outdoors orchestras, and the *Little Symphony*, in which the jazzy character was already evidenced in the orchestration by substituting for the viola section an array of banjos and mandolins.

At the end of the twenties I felt that I had reached a dead end in my compositional endeavors, and I began seriously to consider the possibilities of the twelve-tone technique. *Theme and Thirteen Variations* shows some, if ever so faint, traces of this turn. The idiom of the work is still entirely tonal, but the piece is not as entertaining as its predecessors. When I immediately afterwards decided to embrace the twelve-tone technique, my first work in that style was again a major theatrical venture, *Charles* V. Apart from more profound motivations, it may be that for purely practical reasons I did not write any larger orchestral works during those years of my most intensive dealings with dodecaphony. The most productive outlets for contemporary Central European music had been the German orchestras and broadcasting stations, and since the Nazi government had outlawed atonal and twelve-tone music in 1933, there was little incentive for writing such music. In other countries it was not received with much enthusiasm either.

Thus I produced another substantial orchestral work only ten years later, after I had settled in the United States where I had come when I felt that my freedom and perhaps my life were endangered by the Nazi regime. This work is a set of variations on what is known as a folk tune from North Carolina, "I Wonder as I Wander." It is not as characteristic of my most elaborate and closely reasoned twelve-tone procedure such as I employed in the *Sixth String Quartet* and the *Twelve Variations* for piano (1936 and 1937), for in 1942 I was already experimenting with somewhat relaxed treatments of the tone-rows. The orchestral variations are based on a twelve-tone series, one-half of which comprises the six tones of the folk tune, D, E, G, A, B, and C. According to the nature of the resulting six-tone groups many stretches of the work exhibit a sort of bimodality.

For the *Symphonic Elegy* for string orchestra, which I dedicated to the memory of Anton Webern when the shocking news of his violent death reached me, I set up a twelve-tone row of the symmetrical type so frequently used by Webern (see Example VI, 7). The compositional treatment of the row, however, does not produce the astronomical, quasi-abstract image of Webern's

EXAMPLE VI, 7

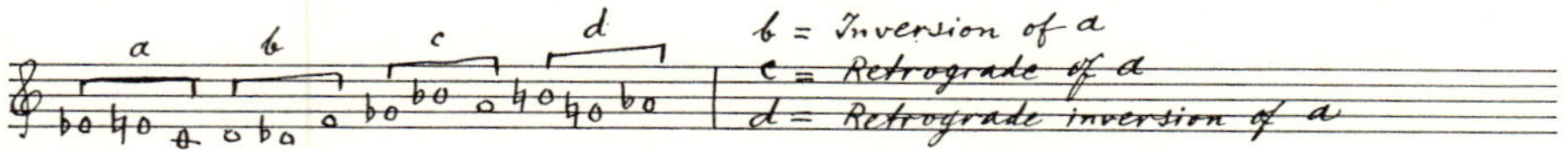

music, but leads to a more emotionally charged manner of expression, perhaps more reminiscent of Alban Berg. Here is the beginning of the final section (see Example VI, 8). Although I had developed special admiration for Webern's style even before everybody else discovered him, it took me a long time to acquire similar constructive discipline and elegance.

In 1947, following an outside suggestion, I took up once more the concept of the symphony and wrote my "Fourth Symphony." It seems to me that I was too conscious of problems and implications and tried too hard to achieve profound "significance" in all directions so that this work did not live up to my expectations. The "Fifth Symphony," completed two years later, is a symphony only in name. It is rather a suite of loosely related movements. This experience confirmed my earlier conjecture that symphonic form and style as they were known until the period of Mahler were, at least for me, not compatible with the new idiom.

EXAMPLE VI, 8

Examples VI, 7–8, used by permission of Elkan-Vogel Co., Inc., Philadelphia, Pa., copyright owners.

A forthcoming change in my general attitude toward writing music announced itself through my growing interest in short pieces, wherein the musical utterance had to limit itself to succinct statement of an idea without relying on further elucidation in development or variation. In 1954 I wrote *Twenty Miniatures* for piano, which, in the orchestral field, are paralleled by the *Eleven Transparencies*. The title does not suggest a literary program. It only indicates that interpreter and listener likewise are free to assume the existence of conceptual meaning residing behind the music and coming to light through it. The pieces are consistently dodecaphonic, but the tone-row is put into the service of freely articulated expression of mood.

When I at that time began to work in the electronic medium I also became aware of some preliminary attempts at serial thinking in earlier twelve-tone compositions of mine, that is, predetermination of elements other than the succession of pitches, and I decided to develop these procedures systematically. The first result was an orchestral piece called *Circle, Chain, and Mirror*, with the subtitle "symphonic design." Here is the tone-row of the work (see Example VI, 9). In the course of the composition I employed twenty-four derivatives of the row (and its inversion) obtained by successively retrograding any two adjacent tones, alternating between even and odd pairs (in the following example the tones in their original succession are numbered from 1 to 12). (See Example VI, 10.) After twelve such operations one arrives at the complete retrograde form of the original series; after twenty-four one returns to the original. This arrangement suggested the "circle" part of the title. The sequence in which the forty-eight

Example VI, 9

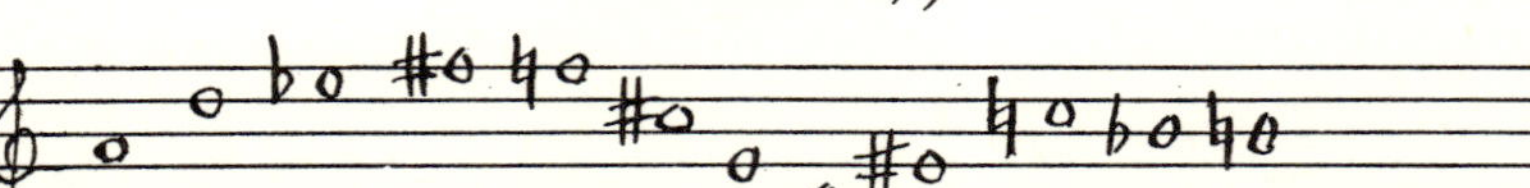

Examples VI, 9–17, used by permission of Bärenreiter Publishing House, Kassel, Basel, London, Paris.

Example VI, 10

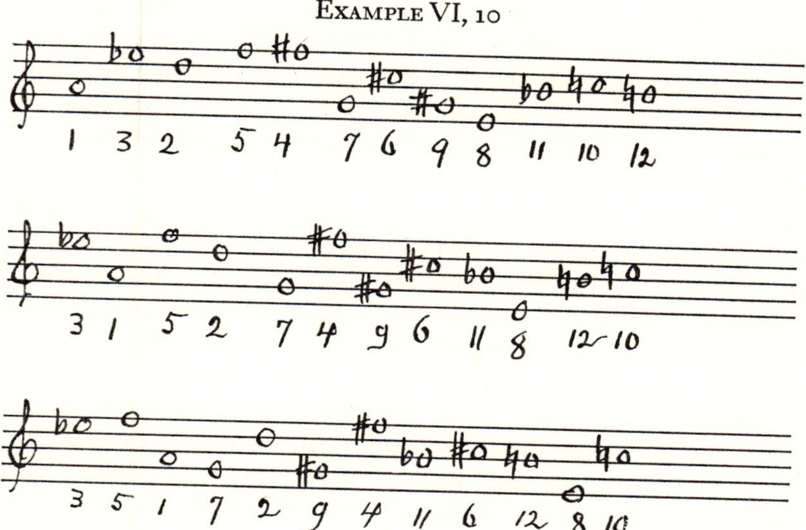

rows thus obtained were used in the work was determined by the decision to have each original form followed by one of the two forms of the inversion which would have for their first tones the last tone of the preceding original, while this inversion in turn would be followed by an original form beginning with the last tone of the preceding inversion. This interlocking arrangement is meant by the term "chain" in the title.

The term "mirror" refers to the fact that the musical configuration that opens the work appears later in inverted, retrograde-inverted and—at the conclusion of the piece—in retrograde form. No other parameter beside the succession of pitches was serially ordered. In this respect the work belongs to the province of "classical" twelve-tone technique. It transcends that province in that it allows its structure to arise from the serial arrangement of the rotational derivatives of its tone-row.

A totally serialized work (the only one in my output apart from the *Sestina* of 1957, for voice and ten players) is *Quaestio temporis* (*A Question of Time*). Here all parameters (pitch succession, durations, dynamics, timbres, densities, distribution of octave registers, etc.) are regulated by premeditated serial statements derived through very complex computations from the succession of the magnitudes of the intervals in the basic tone-row measured in half-tone steps (see Example VI, 11). The piece has eleven sections. Their lengths are proportional to the sizes of the intervals in the above series. The tempo of the music varies between ♩ = M.M. 20 and ♩ = M.M. 210, in six steps taken from the so-called Fibonacci series of numbers in which each member is the sum of the two preceding members (2, 3, 5, 8, 13, 21, etc.). Examples VI, 12 and 13, show the contrast of minimum and maximum densities. Comprehensive discussion of the considerable compositional consequences of serial procedures would far exceed the limits of this paper. Suffice it to say that especially the predetermination of the dimension of time prevents establishing themes and developments thereof in the traditional sense; that the over-all structure of the piece becomes a function of factors other than inspirational impulses; and that details of the design, while being preordained through the serial mechanism, become largely unpredictable because of the latter's complexity.

The concept of unpredictability is a main feature of *From Three Make Seven*. The music consists of two blocks, A and B. Each of these is presented in three versions of different lengths (or speeds). In other words, the musical substance is available in forty-two measures, or condensed (speeded up) in twenty-one, or further condensed in fourteen. Each of these variants is available in three different orchestral colors: one for strings, one for wind instruments, and the third for percussive instruments. Consequently, the substance A exists in nine different versions, and so

Example VI, 11

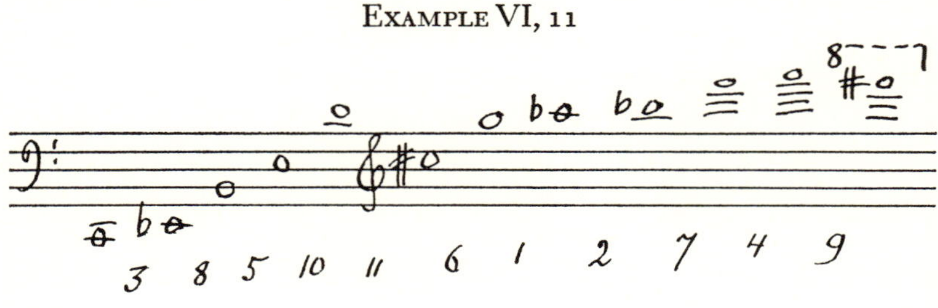

EXAMPLE VI, 12

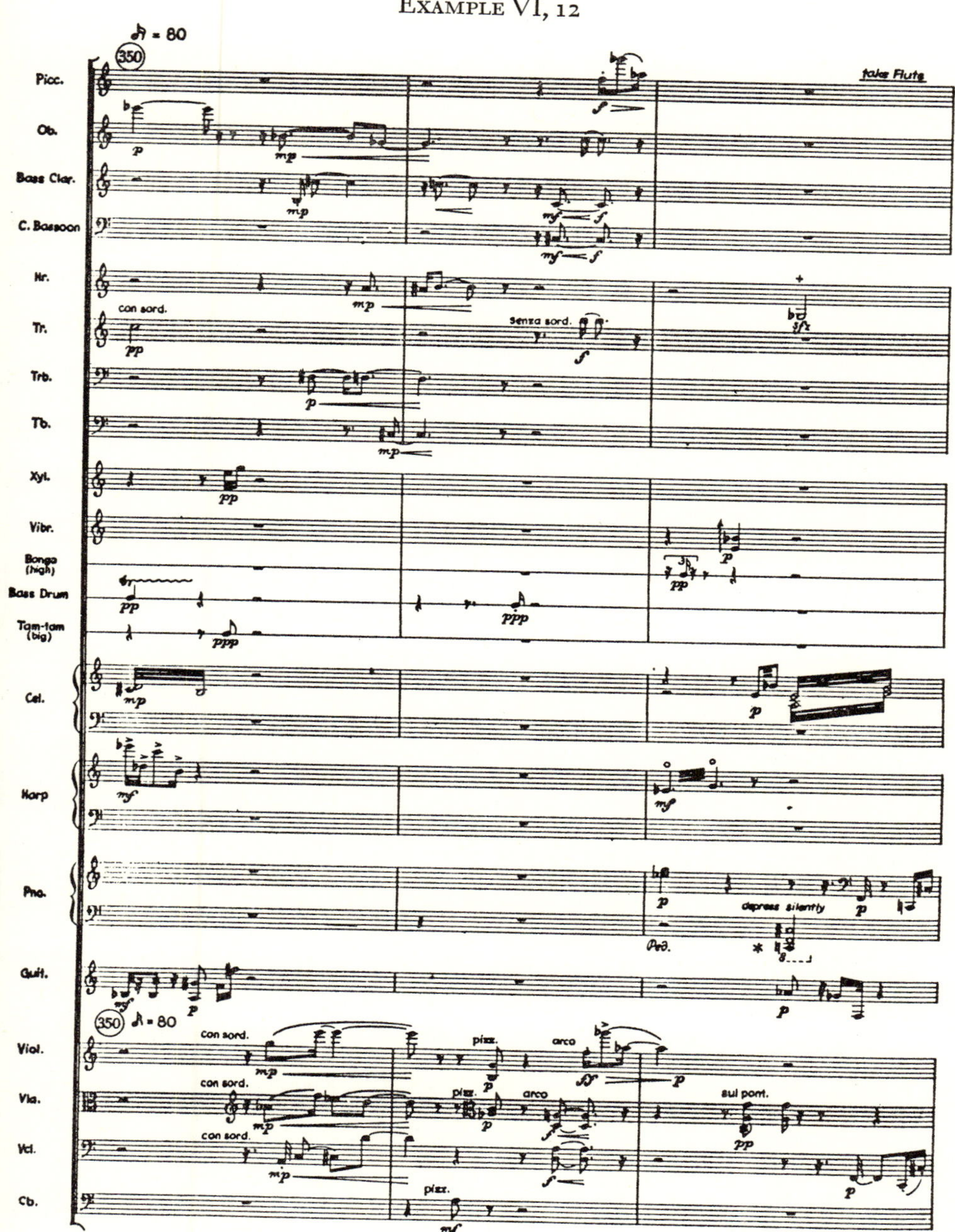

EXAMPLE VI, 13

does the substance B. All of these eighteen objects may be so combined that they will coincide at seven predetermined points (hence the title of the piece). They may start or end together, or meet at five other points. The following diagram shows two of the combinations for A. (1, 2, 3 refers to the degrees of speed, from slow to fast; *a* means wind instruments, *b* percussion, *c* strings.) (See Example VI, 14.) Still other co-ordinations are possible, and versions of A and B may be combined too.

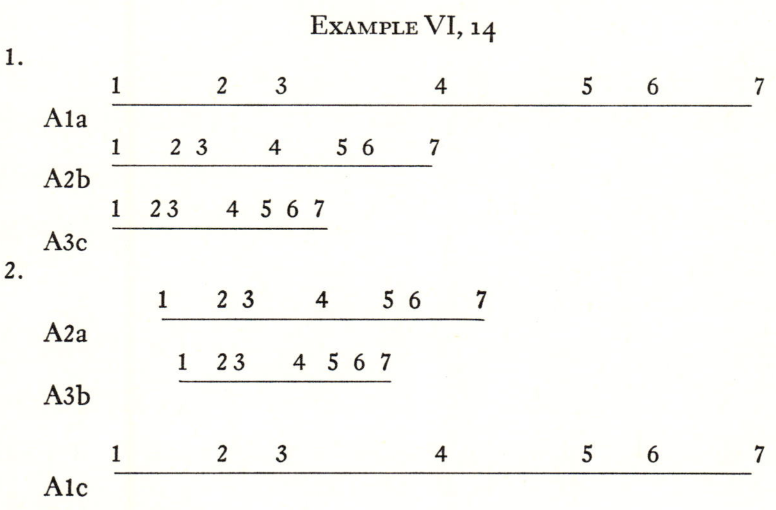

SCALE: 1 bar = 2 mm
Numbers indicate points of coordination. In Ex. VI, 14, 1., the three layers start together (on point 1); in 2., they coincide at their points 2.

Obviously, simultaneities of sounds are not any longer controlled in such ways as traditional or even advanced theory of harmony would require. The over-all "fittingness" (if this term may be improvised for what is designated in German by the well-nigh untranslatable term *Stimmigkeit*) of the whole results solely from the fact that all details of the design are derived from the same basic set of patterns so that whatever happens simultaneously will automatically fit into the general concept.

A recently completed orchestral work is called *Horizon Cir-*

Example VI, 15

I. azimuth

ERNST KRENEK
1967

Units=72

Sec. 1/2 ⟶

Picc. 1 2

Oboes 1 2

Clarinets 1 2

Bassoons 1 2

Horns 1 3 / 2 4

Trumpets in C 1 2

Trombones 1 2

Tuba

Tympani

ffp — ff

non legato

a2 non legato

flutter

gliss. as high as possible

p

ff

1) hold 𝄐 until the vibration of the gong has reached the dynamic maximum
2) trem. on all strings behind bridge, for ½ second
3) lowest tone that may be held in ***ff***
4) highest possible tone (not necessarily the same for all instruments of the same species)
5) 12-tone group to be repeated as many times as indicated, slowing down to fill approximately the time spans indicated
6) repeat the 12-tone group at the same speed

cled. It has six sections subtitled *Azimuth, Elevation, Meridian, Inner Circle, Parabola,* and *Zenith.* These subtitles do not suggest any program, but hint at the imagery of astronomy implied by the circular form of the piece. It starts with a musical representation of chaos (see Example VI, 15) to which it returns, for the final section is an exact retrograde of the first (see Example VI, 16). There is an object (not explicit enough to be called "statement") which appears four times (straight, inverted, retro-inverted and retrograde—an idea lingering on since *Circle, Chain, and Mirror*). The "inner circle," 180 degrees away from the starting point, is a four-voice canon by inversion—symbol of a very high degree of order.

At several points of the work a certain degree of "aleatory," or not precisely determined playing is required, as for instance in the slowdown of winds and strings in Example VI, 15 (or the cor-

Example VI, 16

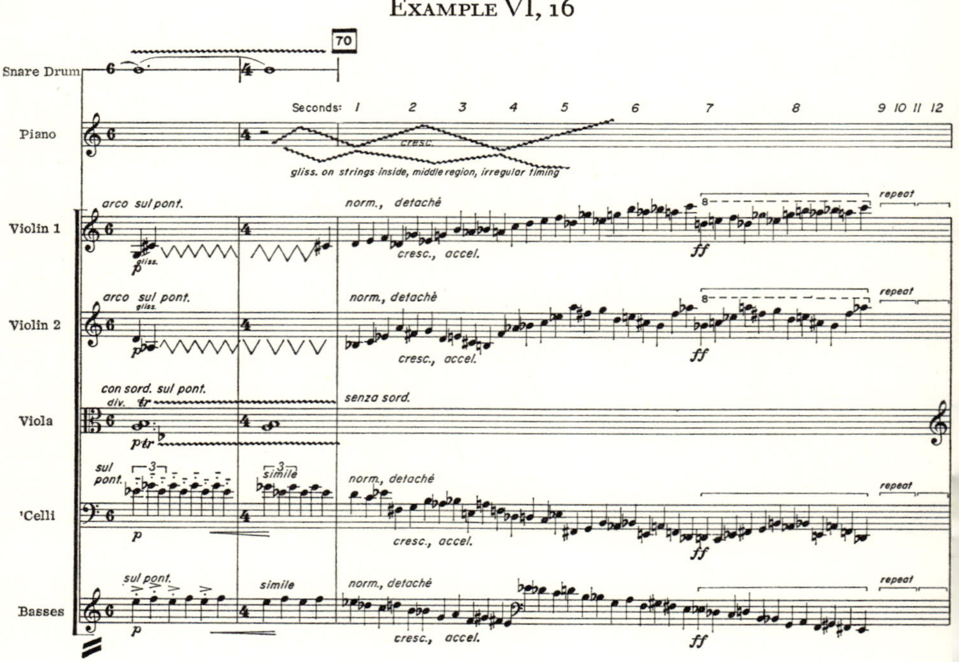

Example VI, 16 (*Continued*)

responding speed-up in Example VI, 16) where the individual tones of the several players do not have to fit into any regular subdivision of meter.

Another instance is the fifth movement, *Parabola.* The piece is divided into time segments (bars) comprising from one to eleven time units of equal length (units about M.M. 100, i.e., each unit about 0.6 seconds). The number of units in each segment corresponds again to the magnitudes of the intervals of the basic tone-row. All twelve tones of this row (or of one of its rotational derivatives) are played in each segment, which causes the density to vary considerably, for in a segment with only one time unit the twelve tones will be very crowded, while in a segment of eleven units they will be spread out thinly. The time points at which the tones are to be played within each segment by the individual instruments are not precisely defined, but only indicated in relation to other tones. The instrumentalist is instructed to place his tones approximately according to the graphic position of the notes within the segment. The purpose is to achieve a weightless, floating quality, as far as possible removed from "squareness" (see Example VI, 17).

In my early orchestral works I tried above all to get away from the late Romantic, neo-Germanic pseudo-contrapuntal hubbub of the Straussian type as well as from the mistiness of Impressionistic mixtures. I took my cue from Mahler and used orchestral color rather to set off melodic lines against each other in dry and harsh textures.

In the later works, especially since *Quaestio temporis,* I have tried to re-create with traditional instruments some of the sounds so characteristic of electronic music: the sharp, percussive attack, the reverberation of the echo chamber, the accelerated or retarded tremolo. Hence the predilection for vibraphone, marimba, electrically amplified guitar, and the recently discovered unorthodox ways of treating the piano. Timbre takes on a new significance. Since in serial and post-serial music polyphonic continuity appears only exceptionally, color becomes frequently the essential vehicle of design.

Example VI, 17

To speculate on the future of orchestral music is a thankless job. Some devotees of electronic music have predicted, and probably wished for, the demise of the symphonic orchestra. This has not kept them from writing time and again for just that orchestra. Why should both media not exist side by side since either one has potentialities that are out of reach of the other? Furthermore, their modes of reception are so different that the idea of competition is purely illusionary. We should rather hope for interesting results from a mutual exchange of inspirational impulses.

CHAPTER SEVEN: Witold Lutoslawski

WITOLD LUTOSLAWSKI (born in Warsaw, Poland, on January 25, 1913) studied music at the Warsaw Conservatory where he obtained a piano diploma in 1936 as a pupil of Jerzy Lefeld and a diploma in composition a year later under the direction of Witold Maliszewski (a pupil of Rimsky-Korsakov and Glazunov). For two years, Lutoslawski studied mathematics at Warsaw University. His intention to continue his composition studies abroad was frustrated by the outbreak of World War II. In 1939 he was mobilized and attached to one of the Polish units as chief of a military radio station. Lutoslawski spent the years of the German military occupation in Warsaw where, in spite of obvious difficulties, he made every effort to continue his work in musical composition. After the end of the war, Lutoslawski took an active part in the committee of the Union of Polish Composers, in Polish Musical Publications, in the committee of "Warsaw Musical Autumns" festival and in the Radio Council—all in addition to intensive work in composition. Several times Lutoslawski has been a member on panels in international music contests. He was awarded Poland's First Government Prize in 1955. There have been two visits to the United States: in the summer of 1962 as guest instructor of composition on the faculty of the Berkshire Music Center at Tanglewood, and in the summer of 1966 as composer-in-residence during the "Fourth Congregation of the Arts" at the Hopkins Center at Dartmouth College, Hanover, New Hampshire. The summer of 1963 was spent teaching composition in England at the Summer School of Music at Dartington, Devon; and the spring of 1964, in Sweden at the Stockholm Conservatory. Lutoslawski was honored in 1962 by being elected to the Swedish Royal Academy of Music. He was elected an honorary member of the Freie Akademie der Künste Hamburg in

1966 and extraordinary member of the Akademie der Künste Berlin in 1968. In 1964 he was awarded the Koussevitzky International Recording Award, and the Léonie Sonning Music Prize in 1967.

Is THE SYMPHONY ORCHESTRA as such no more than a museum piece, a relic bequeathed to us by the generations that came before us? Or is it perhaps a living organism, showing no signs of age, with years of development still lying ahead of it? These questions cannot be answered by one general statement for the simple reason that composers hold a diversity of views on the subject. The problem does not exist for composers whose musical language and sound ideas are inseparably bound up with tradition. Their creative inventiveness has been shaped to such an extent by the music of the past that conventional instruments and ensembles are to them an ideal tool for carrying out every musical idea. To others, the sound of old instruments evokes such strong feelings of tedium that they have banished them from their composing techniques forever and have found new resources which are capable of producing the desired sounds. In view of this wide diversity of views, I shall not attempt to provide an answer that would even pretend to be objective on the subject. Being one of the group of composers to whom the problem is not only real but one of the most burning issues at hand, I seek to resolve it for my own purpose. I find that this is indispensable in my daily work and in the process of composing itself.

I must confess that I entertain greater respect than enthusiasm for the instruments that compose a symphony orchestra. True, we have not developed anything that can approach the rich and noble timbre of old instruments, yet the limitations which the old instruments impose on the contemporary composer are gallingly restrictive. The strings and the wind instruments alike are, owing to their very construction, closely identified with music that is now a thing of the past. They are not even chromatic instruments in the true sense. It is more difficult to perform nondiatonic than diatonic sequences on the piano with its keyboard arrangement, on the harp with its tuning in the scale of C-flat major, or on the wind instruments based on the principle of harmonic series. Although it must be conceded that string instruments are capable of playing both diatonic and chromatic sequences as well as sequences of tones that do not belong to the twelve-tone scale of equal temperament, yet a completely new technique of playing would have to be devised to make this possible. Development of new techniques comes up against a twofold obstacle: the preponderant demand for performers of old music and the greater earnings possible in this profession. The situation is worsened by the absurd system of notation, where for the twelve tones of an octave we have only seven positions on a five-line staff. This is a serious drawback to nontraditional music, which often looks unnatural and is incomprehensible when written with these seven symbols.

For various reasons, therefore, the instruments of a symphony orchestra satisfy the requirements of my composing technique only in a limited sense. A great many composers find themselves in a similar predicament. Each one in his own way is compelled to look for a way to break the stalemate.

One way out is simply to ignore the limitations of the instruments, to idealize them, to treat them abstractly, in a manner unrelated to actual practice. This fact may lead to uncompromising, logically constructed scores which are not bound by the restrictions inherent in tradition. The bad thing about these compositions is that they are often difficult to perform. Much worse, however, is the fact that these difficulties are incomparably greater than the resultant effect would warrant. Consequently, I find this method entirely impractical to my purpose. Unlike composers who employ this particular method, I hold to the principle that compositions must be made as easy to perform as possible, despite the fact that this places an additional burden on the composer. For everyone knows how extremely difficult it is to write works easy to play without sacrificing something important. Nevertheless, I on my part do try to write simply not only because I firmly believe that music that is easy to play sounds better than difficult music, but also because in this manner I hope to have some part in helping musicians recapture the sense of pleasure that the playing of music can provide. It is my contention that only that musician who derives pleasure out of playing can interpret a musical composition in the fullest sense. If, however, he is given a difficult and unrewarding text, if he is asked to perform functions that can better be required of a machine, it is ultimately the composer and his composition that are made to suffer.

Experimenting with new ways of playing old instruments is still another way of trying to find a solution to the problem under discussion. This method, like the preceding one, is of no use to my particular purpose. The prepared piano and use of strings and winds as if they were percussion instruments enlarges the range of these instruments by decidedly second-rate and marginal attributes. Furthermore, this particular treatment of musical instruments has a jarring effect on me. I find it not only exceedingly unnatural, at variance with the true designation of the instruments, but above all brutal in relation to these delicate objects which are often great works of art in themselves. The sound of prepared instruments, their use as percussion instruments, is gross. The method may be compared to apings, parrotings, and mockery but never to natural speech. As such its uses are very limited indeed.

My critical remarks regarding some of the ways in which instruments are used have bearing solely in relation to the applicability of this method to my composition technique; they are not meant as criticism of the composers who employ these methods. The most ridiculous creative methods can be defended when they produce an outstanding work of art, in the same manner as the most convincing methods are compromised when they are used to produce a worthless piece of music.

Although the various methods of using instruments here described are of no use to my particular purpose, yet the very existence of these methods strengthens me in my conviction that the instruments of a symphony orchestra are indeed obsolete and that the contemporary composer can make only limited use of them.

Irrepressible in my mind is the thought that new instruments will be designed, that they will fully meet the demands of contemporary musical ideas. The new instruments will, so I like to imagine, retain all the fine qualities of conventional instruments while at the same time they will be able to produce with equal facility all the sequences that lie within the twelve-tone scale of equal temperament as well as the sequences that lie beyond it, while being capable of producing noises and tone-mixtures and finally, a fact which could put a new feature on music as a whole, produce tones of pitches which vary in a continuous manner.

Experimental studios working on new ways of producing sound will, I feel, make this possible. Although the results so far achieved cannot as yet compete with traditional instruments as regards acoustical richness and expression, yet the fact that they can be expected to develop in the future is definitely an advantage in their favor.

Since at present there are no new instruments which would fully meet the new demands, and since I do not wish to use old instruments in a manner which would be inconsistent with their natural attributes, I must perforce seek other solutions to the problem under discussion.

The experience acquired in employing the element of chance in musical composition has afforded me the opportunity to achieve certain results in this realm which may perhaps be far from perfect and not very lasting. In this very restricted and strictly controlled aleatorism, old instruments do at times sound in a fresh and stimulating way. I shall return to a lengthier description of my experience in this area in another part of the essay. At present it may suffice to state that this experience has enabled me to reach once again to what had seemed like an exhausted store of sound contained in the symphony orchestra without the slightest twitch of aversion or that dull sense of weariness and, I may even venture to say, with a dash of enthusiasm.

My *Symphony No. 2*, another in the series of symphonic works which I have recently completed, is also another of my "farewells to the orchestra." My first farewells were made in 1958 with a set of compositions for the orchestra. At that time I had already realized that the symphony orchestra has no prospects for further evolution, that its heyday had long since passed. This next of a series of "farewells" is obviously not to be the last. New instruments, which must give at least as wide and as noble a range of tone as the instruments we now have and which will at the same time faithfully mirror the sound ideas of contemporary composers—that is a possibility that still lies, I am afraid, in the dim and distant future ahead.

The term "symphony," in the same manner as the terms "sonata," "variations," and others, refers to the concept of a closed form. Such a form owes its existence to the ability of the listener to remember the music he has heard and to integrate its individual sections while he listens so that after he has heard the composition to the end (no matter how many times) he is able of perceiving it as an idea that, like a painting or sculpture, exists outside the limits of time. But to reduce the idea of a closed form to a "timeless" existence would amount to simplification. Composing closed forms, we also take large advantage of the fact that music is a form of art which does take place in time. Consequently, one of the reasons why we compose music is to evoke in the listener a series of specific reactions whose sequence and development in time is of essential importance to the final result, that is to the perception of the composition as a whole. In other words, composing a closed form, we assume that in the course of its performance the listener is led, so to speak, by the composer through the various stages of the composition and to its final conclusion. (I have used the term "listener" in the sense of an "ideal" listener rather than to denote a specific type or even an "average" listener.) In order to get a better idea of what is meant when we say that the composer "leads" the listener through the performance of his composition, we may recall the familiar stratagems and tricks, some of them infinitely subtle, that have been employed by the classic composers. One of them, to take an obvious example, is to break up a given motive, to repeat its fragments in various positions of the musical scale *ad nauseam* in order to prepare the listener for the introduction of a new musical theme. Without this preparation, in which a kind of "vacuum" had been created by the weariness, or perhaps even impatience which the tedious repetition of the same motive generates, the introduction of a new theme might have gone almost unobserved by the listener. It would not have been anticipated or expected with such impatience. Another typical stratagem employed by classic composers is to evoke in the listener—most frequently by harmonic means—the impression that the composition or one of its stages is drawing to a close, only to introduce slight changes which successfully annihilate the initial impression that the movement is ending and replace it with the certitude that no conclusion is to be expected at the given moment but that, on the contrary, the form will continue to unfold itself.

The examples provide evidence that there is a psychological aspect to the creation of musical forms. Account is taken of such listener attributes as musical memory, ability to foresee, ability to react in the desired manner to the different densities of musical substance. Thus the closed form is a complex phenomenon, for it is based on the concept of a dual role that time can play in a musical composition. The composition evolves in a given period of time, it is true, but once it has been performed it begins an independent existence of its own in the consciousness of the listener due to the faculties of memory and to the ability of the listener to integrate impressions. Unrestricted by time, the composition can be conceived in its entirety in one brief moment.

Open-form compositions do not possess this quality of "timelessness." Before this form became the object of interest of contemporary composers who belong to our cultural sphere, it had existed in its primitive state in folk music and specifically in the music of primitive peoples. The object of this music quite often is to induce a state of excitement similar to the effects produced by certain stimulants. One cannot speak of a definite length of a musical composition in this case and even less so of an impression made by the composition as a whole after it has been performed.

To simplify the problem somewhat, we might say that the closed-form composition is an "occurrence" while the open-form composition is a means of inducing a certain psychological "state" in the listener. The simplification applies primarily to the open form because it is the object of interest of a large faction of composers and is now undergoing an exciting evolution. The closed forms, which were at their peak in the Baroque and Classical periods, are today cultivated mostly in their ossified and degenerate form. Personally, I cannot see how or why the closed form, like the "sonata," "rondo," and others, should be revived. The principle of the closed form, however, is not, in my estimation, obsolescent in the least. Listening to music, I too react to it in the manner described here, that is by involving my memory by integrating and responding to every impulse communicated by the composer, who is fully engaged in the process. Everything I have written so far is inseparably bound with the closed form. I feel that a long process of evolution may still lie ahead of the closed form.

My *Symphony No. 2* is an expression of this conviction. In the light of what I have written here, it must be obvious that *Symphony No. 2* has very little in common with the classical or with the neoclassical symphonic form. The reason I decided to use the term "Symphony" for my composition is that it is a work for a symphony orchestra composed in a large-scale closed form.

Symphony No. 2 is composed in two movements that are not separated from each other by a pause. The last phrase of the first movement still echoes when the second movement has begun. The composition, therefore, constitutes an indivisible whole. There is a close interdependence between the two movements though they stand in sharp contrast to each other in many respects. The first movement is composed in such a way as to prepare for the second movement while the second movement is a natural consequence of the first. To put it in the most general terms, the first movement is designed to involve the listener in the musical "action"; it is the kind of music that makes the listener receptive to the musical "occurrence" presented by the second movement. On the other hand, the second movement would not

Example VII, 1

be a musical "occurrence" in the full sense if the first movement had not prepared us for it. Using a trivial comparison, if I may, the first movement is an appetizer before the main course. The first movement performs its role in the following manner:

It is comprised of a series of episodes performed by various small instrumental groups. The introductory episode is played by the brass alone. The next five are played by:

1) two flutes, five tom-toms, and a celesta (see Example VII, 1)[1]
2) four stopped horns, a side drum, a parade drum, a bass drum, and a harp
3) three clarinets, a vibraphone without a motor, and a piano
4) two cymbals, a tam-tam, a celesta, a harp, and a piano
5) three flutes, three clarinets, three horns, five tom-toms, a celesta, a harp, and a piano.

The last and slightly longer episode composed of several stages is played by a succession of various small groups which finally give way to the percussion.

All the episodes unfold in the same way: a short phrase emerges tentatively and then subsides for a brief moment. Only then does the true beginning of every episode follow. None of the episodes has an actual ending. The growing boldness and mounting momentum of the musical action is followed by a pause, as if the energy had been spent. Then a few tentative attempts are made to take up the episode again. All the attempts are in vain and the theme is abandoned. Despite the clear distinctions between them, the episodes are united by certain common traits: an analogous construction which invests each of them with something like diffidence, indecision (that is why the movement is called "Hesitant"); no single moment of "full expression"; the use of chamber

[1] In this score accidentals affect only the notes to which they belong. Notes without accidentals are always to be understood as natural.—W.L.

groups and solo instruments, which inevitably give a defective, deliberately fragile sound; and finally a lively tempo.

Each of the episodes is followed by a slow, short refrain which is always played by three instruments. The refrain is heard in a slightly altered version every time it is repeated. It is played by instruments which do not take part in the episodes, for example, two oboes and an English horn, an oboe and English horn and a bassoon, three bassoons. As the refrain ends, a new group of instruments takes up a new episode. Always, however, the initial attempt seems tentative. It is followed by the central "musical action" of the episode.

The last episode is the pivotal point of the first movement of the *Symphony No. 2*. It is longer than the preceding ones, and the different instrumental groups are heard in it in succession. It seems to accumulate more momentum than the preceding episodes, but as it approaches the point which seems to bode the climax it stops abruptly. As in the preceding episodes, the pause is followed by an attempt to take up the theme once more. This time the role is assigned to the percussion. As before, the attempt to take up the theme is ineffective and the dying sounds of the percussion conclude the last episode. Thus the first movement of the *Symphony* does not have a climax and it therefore leaves one with a sense of unfulfillment. In this sense, the movement is intended as an introduction, involving the listener and building up for the central "occurrence"—the second movement. The incomplete nature of the first movement is further emphasized by the fact that the string orchestra does not take part in it, with the exception of three, almost percussive pizzicato chords placed at specific moments of the form (e.g., to interrupt the introduction and the closing episodes).

The refrain is heard again after the last episode has been played. The final version is considerably developed, forming a bridge to the second movement. This time the trumpets, trombones, and a tuba join the oboes and the bassoons in the refrain. The last statements of the refrain are distinctive by their raw and deliberately ugly sound, which serves to heighten the contrast with the double-bass arco pianissimo, with a totally different subtle tone color as it comes in at the beginning of the second movement.

As I have already said, the second movement is intended as a contrast in many respects to the first movement. The listener is expected to accept it as a natural and anticipated consequence of the first movement. The second movement, unlike the first, unfolds continuously without any pauses. Individual musical ideas overlap one another frequently, creating uninterrupted discourse. This development heads straight for the final solution without any digressions. That is why this movement is called "Direct." The sound of the string orchestra is heard here for the first time. The strings are joined soon afterwards by other groups of instruments. The solo and chamber-group character is superseded by the full sound of a large-scale sound mass. The lively tempo and the prevalence of short notes in the episodes of the first movement give way to the slow, sustained, and at times lyrical melodic lines of the first stage of the second movement. In the most general outline, the form of the second movement corresponds with its agogic plan. The plan is simple in itself. It is composed of five successive evolutionary stages of the form. Sustained notes and a slow tempo prevail in the first stage already described. Individual melodic lines are tightly meshed, creating a thick, as if gummy, sound-mass. Due to the lengthened motion and mutual pervasion of sounds, the first stage appears massive, as if "languid" in character, unaffected by the sporadic moments of some liveliness or of sudden bursts of energy which finally lead to a broadly developed cantilena intoned by the mass of string instruments (see Example VII, 2). The second stage is comprised of a superimposed cantilena of the string instruments begun earlier with initially short and then increasingly long interventions of instrumental groups playing in a fast tempo. The moment is significant with regard to tempo because two contrasting kinds of tempo are manifest here simultaneously. The growing length of the interventions of instrumental groups which play a fast tempo, the briefer and briefer distances between the interventions, and the subsiding action of the strings—all these factors taken together

EXAMPLE VII, 2

give critical meaning to this stage of the form. The fast tempo triumphs ultimately, gaining full control of the situation. At this moment the form enters the third stage of its evolution: the fast tempo prevails, the tension mounts (see Example VII, 3). One small step takes us to the fourth evolutionary stage with its fast tempo and steadily rising vehemence. The fourth stage is distinct by the fact that it is the only fragment of the composition where the orchestra is conducted in the traditional manner. I shall come back to this remark to explain it at greater length when I come to the subject of the rhythmical aspect of the composition. It is necessary for this part to be conducted because of the acceleration of tempo and of the increasingly close succession of sound "occurrences." The steadily heightening tempo and tension resolve ultimately into an elementary and deliberately primitive result, that is a persistent repetition of the same rhythmical values performed at an accelerating tempo. An abrupt pause and a brief "contest of forces" are followed by the fifth stage which marks the high point of the work. Here the primitive rhythm gives way abruptly to collective ad libitum, with the whole orchestra playing at full force. Then every instrument goes on to complete its culminating phrase on its own. The three final accented notes constitute the culminating point for each instrument. Thus the sound of the culminating phrase is resolved into a series of independent solo parts and into a series of moments which succeed each other at irregular intervals. It takes the individual instruments some time to finish the culminating phrase. In the background for a long while now, the wind instruments have been conducting a soft and quick "babble" which will embrace a wide range of the musical scale before the final instrument completes its culminating phrase. When this has been accomplished, the pianissimo "babble" runs on for a while, then gradually by means of a few steps is shifted to the middle register as it gains in force. What follows is an attempt of sorts to end the composition with a fortissimo accent. This attempt is "unsuccessful," for in the pauses between the repeated triumphal enunciation of the E-flat–F ninth by the entire orchestra, one can already hear four cellos and four double basses preparing the background for the epilogue that is to follow in a moment. Two double basses, playing solo, intone pianissimo a shy interrupted phrase (see Example VII, 4). It ends with F–E-flat, the same notes which began the composition and which resounded a moment ago in the *tutti* by the full orchestra. When the two double basses complete the phrase, the background sounds begin to fade gradually and the composition draws to an end.

As in a few of my earlier compositions, so in my *Symphony No.*

Example VII, 3

Tba.
Timp.
Pf.
(2es)
SOLI
Vni.
Vle.
Vc.
Cb.
f molto espr.
pizz.
Tutte Viole
Tutte V.C.

Example VII, 4

2 the rhythmical physiognomy is closely bound with the technique called in general usage "controlled" or "limited" aleatorism. Without going into the pros and cons of the fitness of the term, I should like to explain what the term means to me. It signifies a composing technique in which the element of chance does play a certain role. The role it plays, however, is strictly limited by the composer so as not to allow the element of chance to affect in the slightest degree the architectural order of the composition or the pitch organization. This treatment of the element of chance consists above all in the abolition of classical time division which is common for all the members of an ensemble. This is accomplished by having a certain, frequently large, number of performers playing ad libitum simultaneously. The sections constructed in this manner do not have the same pulse, the same meter, or even the same tempo for all the performers and cannot be conducted. It is evident from this very brief outline that the technique of "controlled" or "limited" aleatorism has nothing in common with improvisation. Nor do any of my compositions contain parts that may be improvised by the performers.

It may be assumed from the above that the technique here described has a decisive influence on the rhythmical physiognomy of the musical composition. We may distinguish two kinds of rhythms which appear simultaneously. One is the rhythm within each separate section performed ad libitum, which may be called the "microrhythm." It is often very complex, for it consists of many parts superimposed one upon the other, in that each of the parts is subject to fluctuations of tempo which remain independent of the other parts and which allow individual treatment of the pauses and others (see Example VII, 5). The second rhythm is produced by the sections as a whole, or rather by their beginnings. In contrast to the first, the rhythm of large sections, hence the "macrorhythm," is extremely simple. It plays a singular role in the second movement of my symphony. Here the sections grow gradually shorter the closer we come to the end until finally we are but a short step from the kind of music where the tempo, meter, and pulse are the same for all the performers, the kind of

Example VII, 5

music which has to be conducted in the traditional manner. From here on, the rhythm gradually grows simpler until it is reduced to the elementary, primitive form. This transition from highly complex structures, the result of ensemble playing ad libitum, to the primitive repetition of the same rhythmic values at an accelerating tempo, occurs slowly and almost imperceptibly during the long development of the second movement. A swing back to the ensemble playing ad libitum is abrupt, occurring at the culmination point of the composition. One common pulse does not emerge again to the end of the composition and, what follows, neither do we go back to traditional conducting.

It is apparent, therefore, that the rhythmical construction, or preferably the organization of time, is closely bound with the formal structure of the composition as a whole and plays an important role in shaping this structure.

The basic element of pitch organization in my symphony is the twelve-tone chord, or the simultaneity of twelve different tones, hence a harmonic creation. As in a number of my other compositions, so in my *Symphony No. 2*, the twelve-tone chords appear in a wide variation. The frequent use of elementary twelve-tone chords—that is, those whose structure is based on one, or at most two, kinds of intervals—enables me to make frequent use of sharp harmonic contrasts. When the instrumental composition is reduced to a few one-part instruments, the twelve-tone chords appear in their defective forms and are completed within a certain sector of time. This "summing up" of the twelve-tone chord occurs in the mind of the listener. At such moments, however, the succession of intervals in time acquires greater importance. Consequently, depending on the density of the texture, the oscillation between hearing the "horizontal" and the "vertical" is a typical phenomenon on which the pitch organization in the composition is based.

In addition to tones of a definite pitch, percussion instruments of indefinite pitch take part in my *Symphony*, as they do in every composition written for the traditional orchestra. I often try to treat them independently and in the same way as other instruments, as far as the position which they occupy on the musical scale is concerned. In many instances, certain ranges of the musical scale are reserved exclusively for percussion instruments of indefinite pitch while other instruments are used in other ranges of the musical scale. At other moments the ranges may intersect, permeate each other, and so on. In this manner, the percussion instruments of indefinite pitch are promoted to the role of an element which co-operates in organizing pitch to the same degree as other instruments whose tones belong to the twelve-tone scale of equal temperament. In using the instruments that compose the traditional symphony orchestra, I was guided by the following principle: to make full use of the chief properties of the instruments according to the purpose for which they were constructed and with a view to the technical possibilities of performance and characteristic attributes of sound. The string parts are therefore not deprived of a clearly lyrical sound in the same way as to a certain extent the wind instruments. I tried to write the more lively sections for all instruments in such a way that they would be easy to perform. I was compelled to go in for certain simplifications regarding details of individual instrument parts. But I did this deliberately, and I do not feel that this will detract in any way from the composition. The ensemble ad libitum technique is distinctly helpful in making my composition easy to perform while at the same time enhancing its sound qualities. For the performer is able to play with an expressiveness which cannot be attained in music with a common time division for all the performers.

I have described here only one, the external, aspect of my composition. It is only a façade which hides the true life of this as it does of every other work. It is the inner life, however, which is the more important, the more essential part of the musical composition. What can I say about it? How would I describe it? What is it supposed to express? Fortunately, I cannot possibly have anything to say on the subject. Fortunately, for if the essence of music could be expressed in words, then the music would be unnecessary in the composition. One could then simply take a few minutes to read the verbal description. Writing this essay, I was aware through the whole time that I was only skimming the surface of the subject which the music alone can communicate fully.

I began to work on *Symphony No. 2* in the summer of 1965 and completed the work in the spring of 1967. Happily, my decision to write a symphonic composition coincided almost precisely with the moment when the Norddeutscher Rundfunk asked me to compose a work to be performed in October, 1966, at the gala hundredth concert of "Das Neue Werk" series devoted to contemporary music. Unfortunately, I was unable to complete the work on time. But desiring to meet my obligations to Norddeutscher Rundfunk, I had to relinquish the idea of having the complete composition performed at the hundredth concert of "Das Neue Werk" and decided instead to have only the second, the principal movement of the *Symphony*, performed on October 18, 1966. "Direct," as the movement is called, was performed as an independent composition by the orchestra of the Norddeutscher Rundfunk of Hamburg, conducted by Pierre Boulez. The warm reception accorded the piece by the Hamburg audience and by those who had come to the gala concert from many parts did not however relieve my deep sense of regret that I was able to present merely part, merely the torso, of my work and therefore did not give the audience a full picture of what I had undertaken to do. I am writing these words on the eve of the *première* of *Symphony No. 2*. Rehearsals are to start in a few days. The composition will be performed by the orchestra of the Polish Radio, which I shall conduct myself.

Out of the series of questions addressed by the editor to the contributors to this volume, one in particular seems important to me—the one which asks what suggestions the composer would give to the future performers regarding the interpretation of his work. The editor has given the composers a chance to express thoughts which may exert a decisive influence on the future of the compositions described by them. As we all know, the system of musical notation used currently is not precise. At best it expresses the composer's sound vision imperfectly and only approximately. In order to see this, one need do no more than contemplate for a moment the relativity of such terms as "ritenuto" and "piu forte." Even less exact are terms like "espressivo," "appassionato," and others. Yet, we must of necessity take recourse to these terms in order to provide at least a sketchy idea of the kind of interpretation we have in mind as we write the given work. Despite this, the composer always takes the risk that his score may be misinterpreted by a performer of small insights and no intuition. The risk is the greater the farther the composer's style departs from tradition. Introduction of new techniques of conducting and of performance in an ensemble leads almost inevitably to misunderstandings. This problem has assumed a particularly acute form in my experience as a composer, and that mainly owing to the ensemble ad libitum technique here described. It is practically impossible to score music composed in this manner because of the cardinal principle according to which notes placed in a vertical line on a score are understood as simultaneous. This rule does not hold in the case of music played ad libitum. Consequently, when writing this music in the form of a score, essential for the performance of an orchestral work, I fully realize that my system of notation must give a false impression of the music I have composed. It has been my experience that the score can be misconstrued by some conductors who add bars, meters, and others to the score. Needless to say, this distorts the composer's intention and reduces the work to a sad caricature. That is why, despite a certain reluctance, I am compelled to add numerous comments and explanations to my scores and even to give detailed instructions regarding interpretation. *Symphony No. 2* has been annotated in the same manner as several of my earlier compositions.

Though it is true that my "controlled aleatorism" may meet with lack of understanding or even aversion on the part of certain conservative performers, this does not mean that this reaction is universal. I have the good fortune to belong to that group of composers whose ideas, even those that are most diverse from the accepted conventions, have captured the imagination of a number of performers and thus provided confirmation of the effectiveness of my experiments. Interpretations of my *Jeux Vénitiens* and *Trois poèmes d'Henri Michaux* (the orchestra part) by the Polish conductor Jan Krenz and the interpretation of my *String Quartet* by the American La Salle Quartet display a profound understanding of my intentions. My experience of these interpretations is of immeasurable value to me, not only because it has provided me a more rewarding satisfaction than anything I have known, but also because it has stimulated me to carry on along the path of my choice.

CHAPTER EIGHT: Frank Martin

(Translated by Willis J. Wager)

FRANK MARTIN (born in Geneva, Switzerland, on September 15, 1890) played and improvised on the piano at an early age before attending school. He was ten years old when he began to compose. After two years as a student of mathematics and physical studies at the University of Geneva, he devoted himself entirely to music and studied piano and composition with Joseph Lauber. From 1918 to 1926 he lived and worked independently in Zurich, Rome, and Paris. Many years were spent reaching his own personal musical language, which is a synthesis of chromaticism and twelve-tone technique. When he returned to Geneva he founded a chamber-music society in which he was pianist and harpsichordist for many years. Martin became professor of harmony and improvisation at the Jacque Dalcrose Institut in Geneva (1928), director of the Technicum Modern de Musique (1933), and professor of chamber music at the Geneva Conservatory (1940). He was president of the Association of Swiss Musicians (Schweizer Tonkunstler Verein) from 1942–46. But soon after World War II, he felt that he needed more tranquility for his work than he could find in Switzerland, where everyone knew him, so he moved to Holland (1946) where he lived in Amsterdam for the next ten years. The composer now lives in the country in a wooded area some twenty-five kilometers east of Amsterdam. In 1950 he was appointed professor of composition for the master-class at the Cologne Conservatory, where he traveled from Holland every two weeks for three days of teaching. While at the Cologne post, he received the Grosser Kunstpreis für Musik des Nordrhein-Westfalen in 1953—the first time this prize was awarded. The Philadelphia Orchestra honored Martin for the best new work (*Concerto for Seven Wind Instruments*) performed in its 1959 season. Earlier, in 1947, the Schweizer Tonkustler Verein presented him with its coveted prize for composition—Schroeck and Honegger being the only Swiss composers previously honored with this illustrious award. Martin was the first person to receive the Grand Prix des Semaines Musicales Internationales de Paris in 1964. Other honors include honorary doctorates from the University of Geneva (1949) and the University of Lausanne (1960), and the Mozart Medaille Vienna (1965). During the summer of 1967 Martin visited the United States for the first time as composer-in-residence at the Hopkins Center, Dartmouth College, where he performed and conducted many of his compositions.

THE *Petite Symphonie Concertante* and *Les Quatre Éléments* are two singularly different symphonic works. At almost all points they differ, one from the other—in their instrumental means, in their form, and finally in the spirit animating them. All they have in common is that they were both born of the same composer and accordingly share some relationships of musical idiom, of harmony, melody, and rhythm—of, in other words, style. So one can say, using a formula that has become famous, *Le style, c'est l'homme*; and I do not think that there has ever been an example of a man, a composer, who has jumped out of his skin, even if he has wished and tried to do so. It would no doubt be most interesting if we could see wherein these two works differ in spirit, but that is a matter we cannot very well grapple with directly. Before approaching it, we must envisage how and whence they have reached the composer's mind, what their instrumental means are, and how they are constructed.

First let us consider their age. The *Symphonie Concertante* was written in 1944–45, and *Les Quatre Éléments* in 1962–63. They are thus separated, the one from the other, by eighteen years and by a number of other instrumental or vocal works, operas, oratorios, concertos for various instruments, and still other compositions. But let us look at them a little more closely and see more in detail the circumstances of their origin.

Early in 1943 Paul Sacher, the conductor of the Basel Chamber Orchestra, asked me to write him a work for string orchestra augmented by the instruments which would have served in the eighteenth century to realize the *continuo*—such as the harpsichord, lute, or other plucked strings. Modifying this first idea slightly, I decided to utilize the plucked or struck strings that would have been in ordinary use at that time. I then chose the harpsichord, the harp, and the piano. The sonority of these three soloistic instruments I opposed to that of two string orchestras, and thus was constituted my instrumental ensemble. I hasten to add that never before in my life had I heard a harpsichord, a harp, and a piano playing together, and the mingling and contrasting of their diverse sonorities with those of the string orchestra was for me an exciting exercise of inner auditory imagination.

Les Quatre Éléments were written to celebrate the eightieth birthday of Ernest Ansermet, and it seemed to me that properly honoring the famous conductor of the Orchestre de la Suisse Romande called for a work which might display all the resources of his large orchestra and particularly his skill in subtly administering just the right amount of the various sonorities. It is then a sort of portrait that I have tried to make, a portrait of Ansermet the master of the orchestra playing iridescently with Debussy or Ravel—as I have so often heard him do. And to compass my ends, I conceived of a suite of pieces evoking various landscapes and various phenomena, under the title *Les Quartre Éléments*—"La Terre" (Earth), "L'Eau" (Water), "L'Air" (Air), and "Le Feu" (Fire). If then the *Symphonie Concertante* is rather a piece of augmented chamber music, *Les Quatre Éléments* is essentially symphonic music in the post-Romantic sense of the term. In chamber music, as also most often in the Classical orchestra, the different instruments converse, answer each other, interrupt, or let their partner go to the end of his phrase; they are individuals, sometimes soloists and sometimes accompanists, as well as in the strictly contrapuntal style all soloists, individuals juxtaposed or superposed. But in the large symphonic orchestra the instrumental mass constitutes a sonorous palette whose multiple colors the composer can utilize at will. Though nothing prevents his using an instrument in the Classical manner and entrusting a whole melodic phrase to it and to it alone, this is but one particular possibility among a thousand others; for example, a phrase begun in the strings may be continued in the wind instruments, a harmonic series may in its course pass through various sonorities and all that may therefrom ensue. Thus the *Symphonie Concertante* on the one hand; thus *Les Quatre Éléments* on the other.

In form, the first of these works is related without break to the Classical epoch. Of its two movements, the first is the only piece in which I have deliberately adopted the "sonata" form, with two themes (see Examples VIII, 1 and 2); after a slow introduction, based on a dodecaphonic melody (see Example VIII, 3) which will reappear in the development, the allegro is laid out rather exactly according to the rules, except that at the moment of the recapitulation it is the second theme that bursts forth alone, followed by a rather long coda. The second movement by itself plays

EXAMPLE VIII, 1

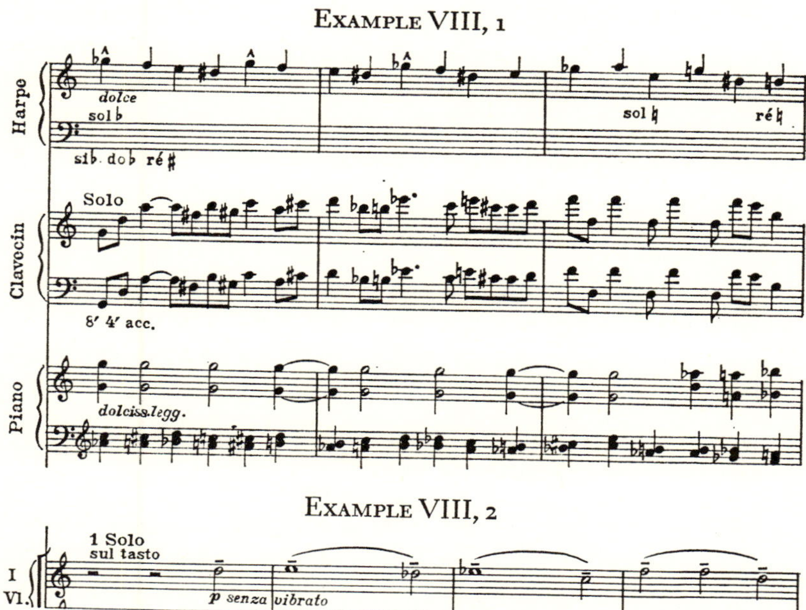

EXAMPLE VIII, 2

Examples VIII, 1–9, used by permission of the original copyright owner, Universal Edition, Vienna, and its U.S. representative, Theodore Presser Co., Bryn Mawr, Pa.

EXAMPLE VIII, 3

the role of both the slow movement and the finale, dominated here and there by the same melodic theme. Exposed as a rather mournful phrase by the harp against a chordal background of the harpsichord (see Example VIII, 4), this element will become through a progressive accelerando a sort of lively march (see Example VIII, 5), which, passing from the harpsichord to the instrumental ensemble, ends in a burst of joy. In its entirety it achieves a form connected most closely with that of the Classical sonata.

EXAMPLE VIII, 4

EXAMPLE VIII, 5

Les Quatre Éléments I have called "*Études symphoniques,*" not daring—out of deference for Debussy—to call them *Images*, a title that would have suited them better; for, in fact, they are images where the music develops freely without being connected —at least intentionally—with any scheme that the Classic era has bequeathed to us. (Only the third piece, that of "Air," assumes the traditional form of the scherzo, admitting of a trio followed by a more or less exact repetition of the opening.) This does not imply that there is here any absence of musical form, but simply that this form takes its origin from the music itself, as was at one time usual in what the Classical composers called a "fantasy." In the same way, these four pieces—each forming an image—balance each other and constitute a whole which I hope is coherent.

So far these two works have been considered only from the point of view of their technique—selection and working-up of sonorous material, musical form—to the exclusion of their meaning, of the musical thought which animates and governs them. Now an attempt must be made to approach as closely as possible this meaning, the place of these works in their author's mind, and his wishes for what they may be able to be for others who perform or hear them. It is very simple and quite tangible in inner and unformulated thought, as quite often the composer, before beginning to compose a new work and even before having taken in hand a single musical element, can have a sort of global vision of it, a presentiment which can be formulated only in the work itself but which, all the time he is engaged on it, will orient his efforts, reject what is foreign, and give the work its proper shape. This shape, when it is a matter of existing works, is scarcely less easy to describe, even when the inner vision that has guided it has already been set down.

Let us begin with *Les Quatre Éléments*, which exhibit the simplest instance. Desiring to represent these four elements— solid, liquid, gaseous, and heat produced by fire—I chose to draw my inspiration from the vision of various landscapes or natural phenomena. But I have hardly used means that are peculiarly descriptive—or, we might better say, that are imitative. What I have tried to express in this music is the impression arising in me from the view of certain landscapes; for the "Earth," I have had in mind the piles of bare and immovable rocks I have seen around

Example VIII, 6

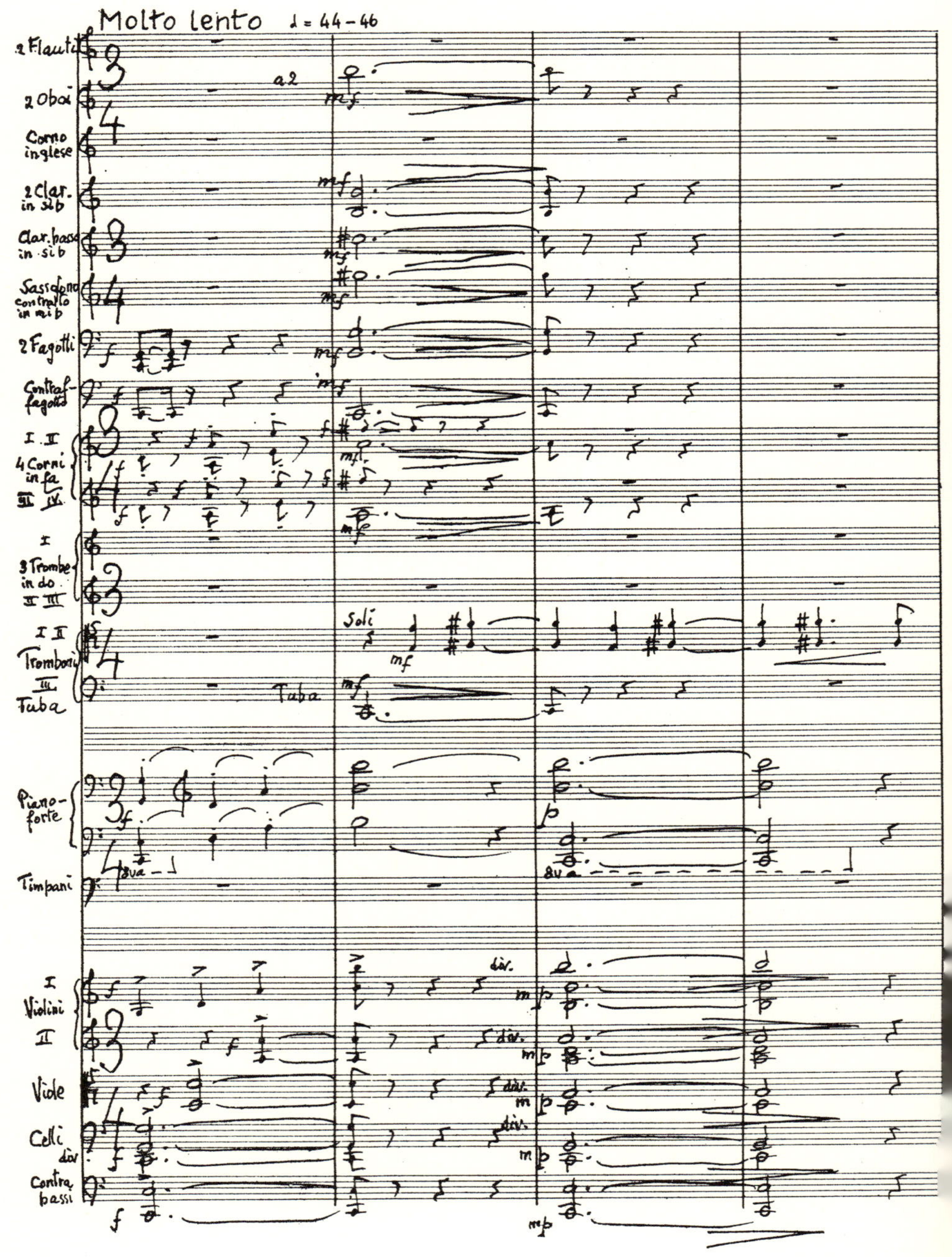

the North Cape or the endless plains in the middle of Iceland (see Example VIII, 6). For "Water," I have recalled—still in Iceland—the peaceful and strangely blue rivers, the immense cataracts, and the broad lakes where all is still (see Example VIII, 7). For

EXAMPLE VIII, 7

Example VIII, 8

"Air," I have thought only of lightness in itself, or—less frequently—of a breath of wind in the trees (see Example VIII, 8). "Fire" has been for me the vision of coal burning red and of clear flames rising from it (see Example VIII, 9). These are then some visions such as may have been impressed on me and have oriented and directed my musical efforts. It was only a matter of there being nothing in "earth" that could suggest fluidity, nothing in "water" that might give a rigid impression, nor anything ponderous in "air," even though everything there might for a moment stand immobile. One of the characteristics of fire, along with its brightness, is its eagerness always to rise. It is then my inner feeling of these phenomena that has suggested the four pieces and has given them their shape. One may say, in one sense, that it is only a part of myself that I have there expressed—this self which is moved on contemplating a landscape, breathes the air sweet after

Example VIII, 9

rain, is excited on seeing great flames dancing above live coals—a partial self, certainly, but quite important as well, for each of these visions reacts in depth and represents in fact a state of the soul. Even if this sort of contemplation, however, can lead me to a feeling of adoration, this adoration, which one can call pantheistic, does not involve me completely, does not touch the human and religious chords that are touched, for example, by the account of the Passion.

Of the *Petite Symphonie Concertante*, it is difficult to speak other than in negative terms: the feeling for nature does not—at least consciously—play any part there, and the composition has no more than a slight tendency to express any human or religious sentiments. I cannot connect it with anything external or personal, except possibly for the very positive and joyous ending, which was written soon after the close of the last war. At the time, however, this joy was manifested in my work quite unconsciously. Faced then with the difficult problem of the instrumental means —a harp, a harpsichord, a piano, and two string orchestras—I simply set to work making music, without calling up in my mind anything other than the sonority of these different instruments and what I could elicit from them. The lack of power in two of them, the harp and the harpsichord, necessarily obliged me to exercise great economy in sonority and, as a result, great concentration of musical thought—as occurs when genuine chamber music is written. I thus had only two ends in view: to use as well and as diversely as possible the sonorous means at my disposal and to try therewith to write some good music—that is, a kind of music that is self-contained and that, so far as possible, might be an organic whole in which each element flows from what has preceded and calls for what will follow.

Quite obviously, a musical work should offer us, in the first instance, those elements, those particular events, which arouse something in us, which take on a shape for our spirit, and which in our memory we can evoke individually—which we can envisage as some successive "wholes." In the same way we can recall a beautiful line or two of some poem, but these lines are not the poem. In music, in poetry, in every art that unfolds within a time-continuum, the ideal is then—I repeat—that each element should flow from what has preceded and call for what will follow. This invites some reflections on the way in which we can feel the whole of a musical work; and as it is a matter of a whole which manifests itself in duration, let us briefly see how this duration is manifested in our psyche. It is generally recognized that each of our present moments has a certain duration; a phrase read or heard constitutes a whole which we grasp as a whole and not as a succession of words which, themselves, would be only a succession of syllables, themselves a succession of various sounds and noises. A phrase understood in its context should then be considered as a single moment in our mind. This moment may be very brief; thus when I hear someone say "It's raining," the moment of comprehension lasts scarcely a second, although it connects in my mind with a whole series of auditory, visual, or olfactory associations. It lasts much longer if I hear someone say (from Baudelaire's "*L'Invitation au Voyage*"):

Mon enfant, ma soeur,
Songe à la douceur
D'aller là-bas vivre ensemble.

My child, my sister,
Think of the sweetness
Of going there and living together.

Here the moment of comprehension needs to last to the final syllable. Again, it is the art of the poet to make that moment last in us through anticipation of the course of the poem and, if possible, right through the whole poem to the end. It is the same thing with music: a musical phrase is heard as a whole, not as a succession of notes or of intervals, or as a succession of chords. This whole, felt as a moment in our existence, as a present moment, can here likewise be of very brief or of almost indefinitely long duration. At the extreme, I remember having heard, once in my life, all the first movement of the Beethoven *Violin Concerto* as a single present moment. This is a very special example, for a piece of some ten minutes extended as a single whole constitutes an extremely rare phenomenon, unless one falls into sort of a bemused reverie, rocked in the cradle of the music—but a state in which one is no longer in fact listening. One says then, "I don't know how the time has passed." Though it is also a form of the continuing present, it has something in common with the present of sleep, while my experience with the music of Beethoven happened at the very apex of musical consciousness. This continuity, which makes a musical work seem to us a single moment, is usually realized only in short pieces; in the largest forms it is extremely rare. At all events, it presents itself to the composer also as an ideal which he tries to approach, as a limit toward which he can strive rather than as an end which he must attain.

One should not make a mistake, however, on the meaning of this continuity in music. It is a question here of an organic unity and, even as our biological organism is made up of various substances—bones, muscles, nerves, and billions of cells endlessly differentiated—so a musical whole can be made up of elements extremely varied. Also, the impressions that these musical elements can evoke are quite diverse: impressions of joy, of sadness, of contemplation, of eagerness for the future or of return to the past. All this psychological play which music evokes in us has an active part in making us feel true musical form—not that revealed to us by analysis but the organization of a duration into an irreducible whole. I intentionally use the word "evoke," for I do not think that music expresses precise sentiments, whatever they may be; it can do that only when associated with a text which makes its meaning explicit—save perhaps when it frankly expresses joy or sorrow.

There is then a great difference between a music the very meaning of which happens to be bound up with a text or an image, as in *Les Quatre Éléments*—a text or image which, at all events, it may not contradict—and a music that follows no laws other than its own proper ones. And when music in its pure state is obliged to adapt itself to such and such instrumental means, even there the problems and the laws are simply of musical order. It will then not be any explicit sentiment that it is going to express, but only the most intimate self of its author, that self absolutely interior, unformulated, unformulatable, which can find expression only in a gesture, in the sound of a voice, in what one can divine from a person's demeanor—and sometimes, after all, in a work of art. For this reason, when these two symphonic works are considered, the *Petite Symphonie Concertante* seems to me a more intimate expression of myself than do *Les Quatre Éléments*. The latter, while seeking again the same musical continuity, are centered on a view of the world which is essentially aesthetic, on impressions felt in contact with nature, while the *Symphonie Concertante* has come from the most profound, from the most intimate level of my being.

CHAPTER NINE: Vincent Persichetti

VINCENT PERSICHETTI (born in Philadelphia on June 6, 1915) began piano, organ, and theory studies at an early age and showed remarkable facility in each. As a teen-ager, he played in orchestras and was frequently employed as organist and choirmaster in Philadelphia churches. By the time he was sixteen, he was presenting organ recitals. Full-time music study was undertaken at Combs College of Music, where he received his B.Mus. in 1936. For the next two years he studied conducting with Fritz Reiner. Two scholarships at the Philadelphia Conservatory enabled Persichetti to study piano with Mme Olga Samaroff Stokowski and composition with Paul Nordoff. The next two summers were spent at Colorado College, where he continued compositional work under Roy Harris. Persichetti received an M.A. in 1941 from the Philadelphia Conservatory and a Ph.D. in 1945 from the same institution. After 1939 he served as head of the composition department of Combs College, until he resigned in 1942 to accept a similar post at the Philadelphia Conservatory. Since 1947, Persichetti has been a member of the composition faculty at the Juilliard School. The National Academy of Arts and Letters awarded him a grant in 1948. He received an honorary doctorate in music from Baldwin-Wallace College in the fall of 1966, and a Citation of Merit from the National Catholic Music Educators in the spring of 1967. During the 1967–68 season he held a grant from the National Foundation on the Arts and the Humanities. Each year Persichetti travels extensively, lecturing, conducting, and performing his works with his pianist wife Dorothea.

MOST COMPOSERS who believe that their music is relatively successful in saying what it has to say dislike discussing it.

They have said what is to be said musically, and to attempt a verbal translation is like doing it all again, less satisfactorily. Even poets caught or freed in a lingual art are sometimes loath to undergo verbal analysis.

The problem of using words, a more precise but limited medium of communication, to rephrase feelings, emotions, and thoughts containable only in the larger vessel of musical expression, is a redundant problem for which the composer is both unsuited and unenthusiastic. But composers are very pleased when people listen to their music and recognize in it something of their common experience. Contrary to popular opinion, the contemporary composer is as anxious to reach his audience and to contribute musical enjoyment as the composer of any other age. The problem of communication is no greater in our time than in many other periods of history.

It is very likely that we live in the growing stages of a tremendous renaissance of musical activity. More than "renaissance" —it may be an apex surpassing any other high point in Western cultural growth. Composers of this century have discovered, rediscovered, inherited, and accumulated a wealth of musical resources. These raw materials are only beginning to be used in an unselfconscious manner. Ours is a period of great diversification but, paradoxically, it points to a multi-common practice in which composers may create a solid literature—a literature speaking of now. It is easy from a too-close view to see stylistic variety as a splintering of musical vocabulary; the long-range look may reveal this diversity as a rich fabric of common expression.

With an increasing ferment of creative activity there is a growing interest in performing contemporary music. Performance groups throughout the country are technically and aesthetically ready to play the literature—the chamber literature, not the orchestral works. Among the most active in this country are university chamber ensembles and bands. In contrast to most major symphony orchestra personnel and management—not to mention conductors—chamber groups and bandsmen are happy if a composer writes for their medium, and often set up elaborate commissioning plans for new music.

Generally, I accept commissions when they coincide with the medium ideas forming at the time. My first four symphonies were written during a period when few commissions of any kind were forthcoming. Those that did appear were for chamber pieces and were refused. Although my *Serenade for Ten Wind Instruments* of 1929 is listed as Opus I, a great deal of orchestral music was discarded before that date. There were orchestra pieces with the economy and severity of Stravinsky, some with Ravelian grace and some as comprehensive as Honegger. None of this music was performed—nor was it my music.

The first piece to use the orchestra in a personal way was the *Concertino for Piano and Orchestra* written in 1941. It is a terse work with a mixture of chromatic and diatonic materials; melodies tend to be diatonic and harmony, chromatic. Formally, the *Concertino* is evidence of a subconscious process involved with thematic growth and derivation. This is best seen if the piece is analyzed from the end, backward to the beginning. It is as though themes appearing late in the piece had been taken apart and presented in fragments retrogressively.

In the following year three orchestral works were written: "Symphony No. 1" and "No. 2," and the *Dance Overture,* but no orchestral work of mine was heard until 1945 when Eugene Ormandy presented the *Fables for Narrator and Orchestra* with the Philadelphia Orchestra. In this work the music parallels the Aesop text and looks for clarity through direct expression. *The Hollow Men* for trumpet and string orchestra of 1944 is a mood piece after reading the T. S. Eliot poem.

The *Third Symphony* was begun in 1942 but not completed until 1946—a leisurely process when compared to the earlier symphonies which were both written in the first half of 1942. Not until 1951 did the *Fourth Symphony* appear. The initial impulse produced two symphonies and seed for the third. The *Fourth* was written almost involuntarily, as a matter of instinct.

Certainly, the *Third Symphony* is a much more fully conceived piece than the preceding symphonies. The first movement, motivated by a dotted-note figure, is dark and inhibited music. A brighter melody is overtaken by a return to the somber spirit of the beginning, and the movement ends ambiguously on a twelve-note woodwind chord, with most of the instruments arriving at different conclusions about what has gone before.

There is a gay, almost naïve, second movement. The dance rests momentarily in a quieter middle section, and returns.

The third movement begins hesitantly with a slow rhythmic string figure which becomes background for a sustained English horn melody. This is interrupted by the trombones in a mood reminiscent of the first movement. There is a climactic development of all the material, and an ending much like the beginning.

The fourth movement is a virtuoso piece which sees each instrumental section taking its turn alone and in combination with the others in variations of the fast theme. Each exceeds the last in exuberance until a chorale in the woodwinds is presented and developed. The symphony ends with the chorale in the brass, combined with the opening thematic material.

Between the *Third* and *Fourth Symphonies* I wrote *Fairy Tale* to be played at a Children's Concert of the Philadelphia Orchestra, conducted by Alexander Hilsberg. Each member of the audience was asked to supply his own story to my musical narrative, and a prize was given to the winner. The story apparently didn't help; *Fairy Tale* has not been played since.

Work on the *Fourth Symphony* overlapped the writing of *Harmonium* for soprano and piano. It was a refreshing breather during the hour-long Wallace Stevens cycle, and the symphony came easily and quickly. I scarcely remember writing it; it was almost an automatic act. Its music is bright and light, and its form tight and classic in feeling. It winks at Mozart and Mussorgsky, and opens with a Haydnesque introduction.

Movement I

Adagio (Introduction) B^b center. Source motive is an ascending melodic 2nd, embracing a 3rd (meas. 1–2). Brass chorale (meas. 4) and pizzicato figuration (meas. 6) of the interval of the 3rd. Tonality moves to a low register B minor (p. 5, meas. 5) with the opening B^b motive (p. 5, meas. 6) above, projecting the major-minor quality of the symphony.

Allegro (Sonata Form)

A a sparkling 6/8 version of the source motive; 2nds and 3rds in changing directions.

Intermediate theme (from A) (p. 13, meas. 1).

B converting the triadic 3rds to 7th and 9th chords (p. 15, meas. 1).

Transition (p. 17, meas. 3).

Development of Intermediate theme (p. 18, meas. 2).

Figuration of A added at p. 21.

Transformation of A combined with Introduction brasses (p. 22, meas. 3).

Development section (p. 25, meas. 1). Two-note idea of Introduction.

Development of head of A and Intermediate theme (p. 28, meas. 4).

Transformation of B (p. 30, meas. 1).

Introductory brass chords and pizzicato motive (p. 33, meas. 2).

Development closes on first-measure motive (p. 35, meas. 3) in brasses.

Transition (false start) (p. 37, meas. 1).

Recapitulation (p. 37, meas. 5).

Solo string section of modified A.

2nd motive hint (p. 40, meas. 7).

Intermediate theme modified (p. 41, meas. 7).

B (p. 45, meas. 5) including modification of introductory, first, and intermediate themes.

Steam release (p. 50, meas. 4) before Codetta (p. 52, meas. 1).

Movement II

Andante. C center (Rondo form).

A aria with accompaniment of introductory 2nds of first movement (G–B^{b}).
B harmonic 3rds (p. 55, meas. 5).
A development (p. 56, meas. 11).
C (p. 57, meas. 13).
A (p. 58, meas. 14) solo strings.
D variant of A melody and accompaniment.
Transition leading to A (p. 61, meas. 1), anticipation of accompaniment idea (p. 63, meas. 3).
A (p. 64, meas. 2).
Hint of B (p. 65, meas. 2).
C (p. 65, meas. 5).
A extended and transformed (p. 67, meas. 1).
D modified (p. 70, meas. 3).
Coda A augmented (p. 72, meas. 3).
Brass chords of first-movement introduction in strings (p. 73, meas. 7); final horn solo on A of second movement, resembling A of third movement.

Movement III

Allegretto (Song form, Trio).
A a flowing sixteenths in strings.
  b flowing sixteenths in woodwinds.
  a brief return.
B Trio motivic 2nd of first movement introduction (p. 84, meas. 3).
  a strict augmentation of A in cellos (p. 84, meas. 5).
  b extension of motivic 2nd of first movement introduction (p. 86, meas. 5).
  a trombone solo.
Transition on accompaniment figure of second movement opening (p. 88, meas. 2).
A shortened (p. 88, meas. 5).
Hint of Trio (p. 92, meas. 4).

Movement IV

Presto (Rondo Sonata Form).

A (p. 94, meas. 1) release of sixteenth-note figures of first and second movements. Motivic 2nd of first-movement introduction in trombones.

B (p. 98, meas. 1) woodwinds.

A (p. 101, meas. 3).

Development of A and accompaniment figure of second movement (p. 104, meas. 3). Mozartian section.

C built on introduction motive of first movement.

Development of D of second movement (p. 112, meas. 8); augmentation of C (p. 113, meas. 4).

Development Section (p. 116, meas. 2). Pizzicato motive of first-movement introduction.

C of fourth movement with accompaniment of second movement (p. 120, meas. 1).

Brass of first-movement introduction (p. 121, meas. 4).

A of first movement (p. 123, meas. 6).

Transition to A (p. 130, meas. 9).

A A of second movement in piccolos and A of fourth movement in violins (p. 132, meas. 3).

B woodwinds (p. 136, meas. 5).

A solo violin (p. 138, meas. 7).

Development of A and accompaniment figure of second movement (p. 139, meas. 5).

C in pizzicato transformation (p. 145, meas. 5).

Return of two-note idea of first-movement introduction (p. 150, meas. 4).

Brass chords of first-movement introduction (p. 150, meas. 4).

Coda (p. 153, meas. 1) C with contraction of opening two measures of symphony.

Eugene Ormandy and the Philadelphia Orchestra played the *Fourth Symphony* brilliantly many times in various cities in this country. Ormandy then took the work with him on his midwinter tour (1955) and conducted it with the BBC Symphony in London and with the Concertgebouw in Amsterdam. He made a stunning recording of the work with the Philadelphia Orchestra.

Public reaction to the *Fourth Symphony* was varied, to say the least, and the extreme of one reaction made it impossible to take the extreme of the other too seriously, regardless of which I might have felt was justified. Philadelphia liked the work; Washington loved it. Amsterdam enjoyed it; and New York tolerated it. Baltimore scarcely heard it—and who can tell what the British think?

A Dutch reviewer was one of the few to find the fun in the piece and said that parts of the last movement sounded like "the favorite music of the Salvation Army—with refinement and skill!"

A heavyweight work, in spite of its curtailed symphonic instrumentation, the *Symphony for Strings* (*Symphony No. 5*) is essentially emotional music. In this respect it is consistently a part of a literature which has a strong human element and is basically more occupied with what people feel than with what they think. It was the most fully realized version of my concept of the single-movement form to appear by 1953. The music is a constantly changing, growing organic structure for which frequent tempo changes are necessary. Some of these indicate obviously separate sections, and others are inadequate notational means of indicating the evolutional process of the piece.

Part I

The piece begins with a long, pregnant viola melody (made of two germinal elements: #1, notes 2, 3, 4; #2, notes 11 and 12) ascending to a high C, supported by cellos and basses. The arrival has an edge of hysteria which becomes the emotional norm for the piece. The viola pitch is so high at measure 16 that, when the violins enter (five measures later), a 4th above the high viola C, the increased tension produces a sound-shock felt through the orchestra. The succeeding few measures tear open the initial melody line and clear a path for the entering solo violin. The solo violin is used here (meas. 26), at measure

246, and again at measure 316, as a separating line of demarcation between sections of music.

The Piacevole music at measure 29 develops the gentle aspects of germ #1 and moves through an Affrettando (meas. 41) in a crescendo section of great intensity, to a cadential expansion of germ #1.

Part II

The cadence becomes a place to gather more energy, and the Allegro agitato continues the climb to the next plane of intensity. This section releases the melodic germ #2 into its contrapuntal, then harmonic, pursuit of germ #1; the two tangle briefly at measure 165 in a web of solo strings, then break into the pursuit again, eventually stating the opening line of the symphony in a positive rhythmic frame (meas. 198).

A stubbornly unruffled solo violin (used for the second time as a halt to a crescendo section) is prolonged from measure 234 through violently declamatory strings and, clearing the hubbub, sings a serene and lovely introduction to the Adagio sereno at measure 247.

Part III

(a) The Adagio section is a gentle polychordal transformation of germ #1. A frightened, pizzicato crescendo at measure 259 threatens the quiet mood.

(b) The section is extended by five solo strings in a dissertation on germ #2 (meas. 268).

(c) The various transformed thematic motives are temporarily congealed, harmonically, at measure 289.

Stalled to a Lento (meas. 312), the third solo violin transition at the Andante (meas. 316) prepares for this composer's inevitable chorale, another version of the opening melodic line.

Part IV

The chorale, entering at measure 329, is not the blue-nosed

variety that shakes its finger in some of my music, but a simple and elegant tune of great repose. It is interrupted at measure 357 by cellos and basses playing a facsimile of the opening line, but answered—sometimes antiphonally—by overbearing violins, which rise from their controlled chorale to an agitated tremolo.

Part V

At measure 377, a strong melody (still from the opening melodic line) is sung (Molto appassionato) by the second violins and cellos, interrupted at measure 392 by the chorale, tried again at measure 396, and disrupted at the Allegro agitato (meas. 412). From this point on to measure 582, any element of the opening line that has succeeded in making its sound pattern felt tries to steer the tonal course. At measure 467 there is a free canonic version of germ #1, and at measure 537, the Molto appassionato melody makes its third try, still with violas and cellos, but is interrupted by what are now completely corrupted bits of the chorale.

Part VI

A triumphal augmentation of germ #1 begins the concluding section which is a continuation of the rising intensity of the music. Here all the germinal elements and their transformations are used together in a contrapuntal mold. At measure 612, three lines (a: top line from germ #2; b: middle line from germ #1; and c: bottom line, the Molto appassionato melody) are stated three times in triple counterpoint: first as a–b–c, then b–c–a, finally c–a–b. The orchestra is shaken energetically at measure 639, and with the triumphal augmentation of germ #1 at measure 657, the music heads into a coda which closes the piece with the strings in the rhythmic sound of snare drums.

St. Louis, like Louisville, Rochester, Tuscaloosa, and Berea, is a smaller city which, over a period of time, has evidenced real interest in my music. In such towns there is usually a nucleus of people interested in the literature; they introduce it publicly and it catches hold, resulting in performances and commissions by various groups throughout the city.

In St. Louis it was the interest of teachers at Washington University in my works for band which led to the University's commission of the *Symphony for Band* (*Symphony No. 6*), the American Guild of Organists' (St. Louis Chapter) commission of the *Sonata for Organ*, and the commission by the St. Louis Symphony of the *Seventh Symphony*. It was the first work the eighty-year-old organization had commissioned and was sufficiently successful for the orchestra to plan commissions as an annual project. The Junior Division Women's Association of the orchestra raised funds for the commission by presenting a concert of contemporary music at which the commission was announced. The project became a city-wide enterprise, involving performing organizations of Washington University and the city's young composers. The commission became an ideal kind—one which contributed what they hoped would be a good piece in the orchestral literature and also one which increased interest and acceptance of the city's own musical groups and composers. The week of the *première* was proclaimed by the mayor as St. Louis Symphony Orchestra Week, and the commission fund was miraculously oversubscribed, the remaining money being donated to the orchestra's general fund.

The *Symphony No. 7* (*Liturgical*) consists of five distinct, but continuous, movements. All are built of material from my *Hymns and Responses for the Church Year.*

I *Lento*

Introduction—prayer in low strings suggesting the profile of the *cantus firmus* of the *Symphony* and presenting a minor-major 3rd indecisiveness that functions as a harmonic irritant throughout the *Symphony*.

A *Cantus firmus* (meas. 13) horns state "Who art One God, One Lord; not One only Person but Three Persons in One

Substance. For that which we believe of the glory of the Father, the same we believe of the Son and of the Holy Ghost without any difference or inequality." This response does not appear in the published collection, *Hymns and Responses,* but it contains the motivic substance from which many of these hymns and responses are constructed, and is basic to this *Symphony.*

First Kyrie response (meas. 23), No. 29 in *Hymns and Responses* slightly intimated.

Expansion of *cantus firmus* "Who art One God" (meas. 27) in cellos and basses with harmonic elaboration above.

B *Second Kyrie response* (meas. 37) (not from *Hymns and Responses*) barely suggesting the rhythm of "Lord, have mercy upon us." Combined with *cantus firmus* "Who art One God" and intensified in a climactic arrival at the broad tutti at measure 117.

C Quiet entrance in low strings and woodwinds (meas. 132) of "The Lord is in His Holy Temple" (another response not included in the *Hymns and Responses*). This contemplative section reveals a thematic affinity between this response and the opening *cantus firmus.*

B Complete statement (meas. 156) of the *Second Kyrie* in muted strings, pianissimo.

D Transition (meas. 169) a tuba solo on the *cantus firmus,* leading, at measure 171, to the Padraic Colum hymn (No. 12 in the *Hymns and Responses*), "Now in the tomb is laid." This section predicts the Passiontide and welds the Kyrie, *cantus firmus,* and the Colum hymn into a tentative close, from which the *cantus* emerges as a recitative complaint in the violas. The movement snags on a string cluster and releases, in a fierce crescendo, the turbulent second movement.

II *Allegro*

A development movement that brings the *cantus firmus,* minor-major elements into tonal conflict. The strength of the response, "The Lord is in His Holy Temple," is tested canonically at measure 231 and elements of both responses combine and rest momentarily, at measure 264, on the Amen from the Shakespeare Response, No. 23 in the *Hymns and Responses.* The movement bursts suddenly and violently again as the minor-major elements of the *cantus firmus* are given a severe percussive treatment. The only voice of compassion during this section of Crucifixion is the first trumpet at measure 293, which manages to make harmonic room for a barely audible statement in the pizzicato strings of the Peter the Venerable hymn (No. 14 in the *Hymns and Responses*), "The gates of death are broken through." The mood of the movement continues to fluctuate from violence to despair, and from a deceiving lightness to genuine hopefulness.

Transition—the movement is finally dominated by the Shakespeare response, "My ending is despair, Unless I be relieved by prayer, Which pierces so that it assaults Mercy itself and frees all faults."

III *Andante*

The flute solo over four muted horns at measure 500 unravels the *cantus firmus* material revealing, at measure 508, the true melodic core and heart of the work, the e. e. cummings hymn (No. 5 in the *Hymns and Responses*), "purer than purest pure whisper of whisper so (big with innocence)"—a recollection of the Nativity and of promise. The hymn is expanded and transformed, then played simultaneously with the Padraic Colum Passiontide hymn. The sadness of the Nativity-Passion combination fades as the materials are converted to the clear and hopeful variant of the *cantus firmus* upon which the P. B. Shelley response (No. 27 in *Hymns and Responses*) is founded, "Heaven's light forever shines, Earth's shadows fly; Life, like a dome of many coloured glass, Stains the white radiance of Eternity." The movement closes on echoes of the first Kyrie with horns repeating "Lord have mercy upon us."

IV *Vivace*

The fourth movement, built on Wallace Stevens' response (No. 26 of the *Hymns and Responses*), "We say God and the imagination are one—how high that highest candle lights the dark," opens with a fugal passage in the flute, piccolo, and drums, over a divisi string chordal background that covers five octaves. Against the string chords, the woodwinds develop their fugue until the string figure is made to coincide with that of the woodwinds. A tutti expansion of the fugal material begins with the trombones at measure 655. There follows an inventory of the text connotations and the musical meaning of the material of the first three movements. A new fugue begins in the strings at measure 750 with a composite picture of the previous movements' thematic elements. A restless, pianissimo collection of motivic commentary forms an accompanimental background for the string fugue. A tempestuous section of defiance hails (at meas. 925) the triumphal entrance of the eleventh-century Easter words of Peter the Venerable (No. 14 in the *Hymns and Responses*).

V *Adagio*

The final movement consists of a succession of Amens (Nos. 36, 37, 33, 34, and the Sevenfold Amen, No. 40, of the *Hymns and Responses*). Short references are made to the earlier movements, and the minor-major question is resolved by the jelling of the minor and major 3rds in the next to the last measure. Both 3rds fade, leaving unimpassioned open 5ths on the *Symphony's* tonal center, F sharp.

Three works using the full orchestra followed the *Seventh Symphony*: the *Piano Concerto, Stabat Mater,* and *Te Deum.* The *Piano Concerto* was commissioned by the pianist Anthony di Bonaventura, was completed in 1962, and was first performed with the Hopkins Center Symphony at Hanover, New Hampshire. The conductor was Anthony's brother, Mario.

Horns begin the concerto with an enunciation of a motto theme which contains the seeds for the material of the entire work. (See Example IX, 1.) Although there are three distinctly separate

EXAMPLE IX, 1

movements, the work is essentially a one-movement concept with cadenzas that unite rather than separate the various sections. In the cadenza of the finale the solo piano supports a long passage for the cello section.

If it is true that some of my music comes easily and quickly, it is equally true that most of my writing is a slow and endlessly laborious process of selecting materials, discarding most of them, comparing possibilities of transformations, refining and giving meaning to inner lines, testing the projectional capacities of sections and segments, considering thematic unification of movements, and most important, making judgments about the relevancy of the music in the hope that each note is indispensable. Writing the *Stabat Mater* was slow and consuming work.

The five movement-sections of this choral-orchestra work are generated by an opening unifying idea: a Locrian motive introduced by a horn over a repeated-note pizzicato figure (see Example IX, 2). The modality fluctuates from the Locrian "lacrimosa" to a brighter series of tones in the "Paradisi gloria" at the end of the work.

EXAMPLE IX, 2

Chromatic elements of the basic theme are wound around the second movement's "O quam tristis" (see Example IX, 3), but

EXAMPLE IX, 3

polychordal shifting at the sound of the question "Quis?" uncovers a chorale-like "Quis non possit." The movement ends in tonal obscurity and "desolatum."

"Eia Máter" is probed by an insistent rhythmic figure (see Example IX, 4), while "Sancta Mater" returns melismatic at the tritone cries, "Cricifixi" (see Example IX, 5).

The "lowered Locrian" restlessness of the finale accumulates dissonances in the turbulent "Flammis" and polychordal "victoria" sections. An extended coda, marked by a timpani com-

EXAMPLE IX, 4

EXAMPLE IX, 5

plaint, snares "Quando corpus morietur" in a canonic mesh. Rich harmonic statements of "Paradisi gloria" precede the dark "amens" and the recollection of the initial Locrian horn line.

The *Te Deum* is as open and straightforward as the *Introit for Strings* is subdued and inward. One work requires heroic wind playing (I like the choral parts with young voices), and the other asks fine bow control and a subtly slow tempo. But both works pale as I hear a full-orchestra unison A, a short, strong A, with horns holding an octave A and the strings slowly and deliberately resisting an attacking B flat. There is friction and I believe ideas are forming for a new symphony—number "Eight."[1]

1 Vincent Persichetti's "Symphony No. 8" was completed in 1967.—R.S.H.

CHAPTER TEN: Gunther Schuller

GUNTHER SCHULLER (born in New York City on November 22, 1925), the son of a violinist with the New York Philharmonic Orchestra, did not become active in music until the age of twelve when he joined St. Thomas Choir School as a boy soprano. It was there that he became interested in instrumental performance and composition. Although his first instrument was the flute, he changed to the French horn at fourteen. His progress was so incredible that at sixteen he left high school and the Manhattan School of Music, where he had been studying horn, theory, and counterpoint, to play the horn professionally with the Ballet Theatre Orchestra. In 1943 at the age of seventeen, Schuller joined the Cincinnati Symphony as first horn. There he made his debut as composer and soloist in the *première* of his *Horn Concerto.* Schuller returned to New York in 1944 and played with the Metropolitan Opera Orchestra for the next fifteen years—nine as solo horn. An early work which brought wide acclaim for the young, self-taught composer was the *Symphony for Brass and Percussion* (1949) which Dimitri Mitropoulos performed with the New York Philharmonic and subsequently recorded. By 1959 Schuller had decided to resign his post at the Metropolitan Opera and devote his energies entirely to composing and other creative activities. There followed a continuous outpouring of significant pieces, chamber and large, in diverse vocal and instrumental forms. Freedom from a routine assignment also permitted him to gain recognition in other areas: as a conductor with the concert series known as "Twentieth Century Innovations," which he organized at the Carnegie Recital Hall, and as guest conductor with leading American and European orchestras; as an author with the manual *Horn Technique* and the book *Early Jazz,* both published by Oxford University Press; as a lecturer in a series of 150 radio broadcasts tracing

Contemporary Music in Evolution; and as a teacher of composition on the faculty of Yale University. From 1963–65 he was acting head of the composition department of the Berkshire Music Center, Tanglewood, and in 1965 he was appointed head of the department, succeeding Aaron Copland. In the fall of 1967 Schuller's career took a new turn when he began his tenure as president of the New England Conservatory of Music. In recognition of his musical composition, he was the recipient of the National Institute of Arts and Letters Award and the Brandeis University Creative Arts Award in 1960. During the years 1962–64 he held two Guggenheim Fellowships and was a special visitor to Yugoslavia, Poland, and West Germany for the U. S. State Department. The next year he received a grant from the Ford Foundation to take part in its Artists-in-Residence Program in Berlin. At the same time he received a commission from Rolf Liebermann of the Hamburg State Opera to write a jazz-oriented opera. The result of the commission was *The Visitation*, libretto by the composer, which has been hailed as one of the most significant operas in the second half of the twentieth century.

THERE IS MUCH DISCUSSION these days regarding the future of the symphony orchestra, the future—and indeed, the present—of orchestral music, and the place that both occupy in the view of today's composers. The most pessimistic prognoses predict the imminent demise of the symphony orchestra, or, at best, its maintenance as a mere museum custodian of eighteenth- and nineteenth-century European musical repertory. A corollary view claims that ever since the mid-1950's composers have been turning away from the orchestra for a host of practical and musical reasons. A few prominent conductors have even gone so far as to suggest that the young composers of today are no longer interested in writing for the orchestra and that the genre "symphonic music" has lost the attraction as a performance medium which it enjoyed earlier in the century.

Many of these dire prognostications are, of course, utter nonsense. To a large extent, they merely reflect in various ways the confusions and inner apprehensions of those who make such statements. While there are undeniably serious hazards and problems attendant to the performance of new music, which affect composers, performers, and orchestra managements alike—some of these problems are brilliantly dissected elsewhere in this book—it is simply an irresponsible generalization to say that composers are no longer interested in the orchestra as a medium.

There are, to be sure, a handful of composers who actually prefer to express themselves in terms of chamber music or who, as a result of some discouraging orchestral experiences, may momentarily claim a total disaffection for the orchestra. There may even be some composers who genuinely believe that the orchestra—along with opera, another favorite subject of the doom prognosticators—is dead. But surely the vast majority of composers would speedily accept an invitation or commission to write an orchestral work, not to mention the thousands of composers who, undaunted and unsolicited, have written orchestral works which for one reason or another languish on shelves or await the extraction of parts at the first sign of interest by a conductor.

This is not to deny that twentieth-century composition and its performance have changed in many fundamental ways. In recent years we have witnessed a serious widening of the gap between the composer's view of the orchestra and the actual performance capacities of most orchestral players and conductors. Ever since Schönberg's *Five Pieces for Orchestra* and certain passages in the late works of Mahler, composers have treated the orchestra more and more as a large "chamber music ensemble," thereby usurping the traditional structure and function of the symphony orchestra. This approach seems to have reached an ultimate stage in the works of composers like Penderecki and Xenakis, who frequently require even string players to perform completely individual and independent parts. It is a measure of the divergence between these two points of view that, although the use of the orchestra string section in this manner has been accepted for some ten to fifteen years by composers and conductors involved with new music, the vast majority of orchestral string players find this situation still completely novel, not to say suspect.

It is true that, given the problems in getting good performances of contemporary orchestral works, particularly complex or difficult ones, the young composer is apt to try his hand at chamber music on the simple premise that it is easier to gather together a woodwind quintet or even, let us say, a fourteen-piece chamber ensemble than an orchestra of eighty in order to organize a reading of his work. Lastly, it must be said that the orchestra, as a musical instrument—and probably as a social institution—will have to undergo some revitalization if it is to maintain itself artistically as well as economically.

It is inevitable that changes in the concept of the orchestra will originate largely with composers. Although it is sometimes difficult to see any order or pattern in some recent developments in contemporary music, it is clear that the extraordinary amount of experimentation already experienced in our century is beginning to wane and to coalesce into broader directions and schools of thought. Among these I see concepts of thinking and writing for the orchestra which, though new, have already demonstrated their viability and which are essentially within the reach of most enterprising orchestras and conductors.

The problem of artistic regeneration is not new, of course. It is certainly deplorable that many of our best orchestras are not capable of playing the works of Babbitt or Carter or Martino—not to mention late Webern—with anything approaching technical accuracy and stylistic conviction. But have we forgotten that Berg's *Wozzeck* took 137 orchestral rehearsals to prepare, and that a work like Stravinsky's *Le Sacre du Printemps* still presented enormous performance problems to an orchestra as fine as the New York Philharmonic nearly thirty years after the *Sacre* was first performed?

On the other hand, there is literally no orchestral work that I have yet seen—and I have seen many—that I would deem beyond the capacities of an ideal orchestra such as could easily be organized in the United States, given the appropriate financial support. This is tantamount to saying that there are no musical-technical problems in any score I have seen that inherently defy performance realization. That such an "ideal" orchestra does not exist is, of course, unfortunate, and is not in any way the fault of composers or their products. It is traceable, rather, to two primary causes: There is at present no conductor of any major orchestra who aspires to the formation of such an "ideal" orchestra, skilled in the performance of contemporary music; and the training and education of 90 per cent of those musicians presently populating our major orchestras was virtually devoid of any contact with the performance, conceptual, and stylistic problems of contemporary music. Only among the younger musicians of today—and even then still too infrequently—does one find an interest in and an awareness of these issues.

If we consider that the age of today's (1969) orchestral musicians averages out to about forty years, it follows that their education—again taken at an average—took place in the 1940's, a period when the works of Webern or Ives, for example, were still virtually unknown and unperformed. Schools and teachers were totally unaware of such "radical" new music and still taught their students in terms of nineteenth-century concepts of harmony, melody, and rhythm. Only the exceptional talent penetrated the mysteries of such "esoteric" composers as Schönberg, Bartók, or Messiaen. That generation of players grew up with all the erroneous preconceptions and deficiencies regarding new music which are almost inevitable when a language changes as dramatically as the language of music has in our time. These changes have manifested themselves in many ways: the move from tonality to atonality, from symmetrically patterned rhythms to assymmetrical, irregular rhythms, from closed, predetermined forms to open-ended, individualized forms, from the simple one-to-one relationships of nineteenth-century melody and its harmonic accompaniments to the multiple, complex internal relationships of today's music, and so on.

The younger players of today, on the other hand, are frequently free of these pre- and misconceptions. Their musical education took place at a time when in many ways—through recordings, live performances, analytical books or articles—an acquaintance with new music was at least theoretically possible. For many of them, the language of atonality, of "irregular" rhythms, of disjunct continuity is the natural language of their time, a language with which they have no basic aural or perceptual problems. Many others, of course, though young in age, have been subjected to older concepts of teaching and thereby indoctrinated with the notion that new music is meaningless and its performance a fruitless endeavor, or in any event not legitimized by "audience" support. These young players, of course, inherit the prejudices and limitations of their teachers. Music schools and publishers of teaching material—with some notable exceptions—have not yet recognized twentieth-century music as relevant to serious musical activity, a fact which greatly impedes the acquisition of those technical and perceptual skills required for the performance of new music.

Nevertheless many young musicians have broken through the various assorted educational-bureaucratic barriers and by one means or another have acquired some knowledge of contemporary music, or at least an open attitude towards it. That they are at the present time still outnumbered and often intimidated in their pursuit of new music by their older colleagues is as inevitable as it is deplorable. (It is worth noting in this connection that many superbly equipped young musicians today are not aspiring to play in symphony orchestras at all. They feel that they can better preserve their love for music, their artistic integrity, and their vital interest in new concepts of composition by playing chamber music and free-lancing on a selective basis, even at the risk of considerable financial insecurity.)

The dialogue between composers and orchestral players has always been a precarious and intermittent one. At times it seems to have broken down completely. It is quite pointless for composers to blame this or that orchestral player for his inability to cope with certain contemporary performance problems. The fault lies more with our conductors and our music-educational system. The latter clearly fails to provide sufficient training and opportunity to deal with these problems, while the majority of conductors avoid the confrontation with new music altogether or pay mere lip service to it.

There is, for example, no acceptable reason why our music schools should continue to turn out musicians who have never been taught how to play a quintuplet of eighth notes *evenly* against two quarter beats; or for that matter, against three quarters (5:6) or four eighth notes (5:4); or how to differentiate precisely between 𝄾♪., ⌐3¬𝄾♪𝄾 and ⌐5¬𝄾♩ or similar rhythmic differentiations. There is no reasonable excuse for our schools' failure to teach our instrumentalists and singers that the release of a note is just as important as its attack. There is no intelligent basis on which our schools and teachers can maintain the notion that "melody" must move conjunctly and within a reasonably close intervallic range—ignoring all the while the countless examples of two- or three-octave melodic leaps in Mozart's works, to cite only one example. There is no justifiable reason why our young students should not be taught the new function of dynamic indications in new music, that they are no longer merely decorative or expressive adjuncts of playing a note, but frequently define and delineate structural aspects of the work. There is no defensible rationale for the failure of many of our schools to teach ear-training which incorporates non-tonal intervallic hearing.

The list could be extended to alarming proportions. The fact is, however, that unless these issues can be effectively dealt with at the educational level, we can hardly expect to turn out professional musicians who will feel at ease in contemporary music. And inevitably the sheer accumulation of misconceptions spirals into a negative attitude on the part of musicians and conductors, which in turn transmits itself to the audience. The net result is that neither the audience nor the players establish sufficient rapport with the new music to acquire, in turn, the ability to discriminate between "good" and "bad" new music, between "significant innovation" and "faddish self-indulgence," between real talent and mere routine competence.

The conductor's role is just as critical as the "educator's," for he too must be, among other things, an educator—of the public and of the orchestra. An orchestra whose conductor cannot or will not consistently perform significant contemporary repertory can hardly become adept in it. An orchestra trained in a constant diet of Beethoven and Brahms gradually loses its mental, technical, and perceptual capacity to deal with anything but long-established musical ideas. Its intellectual and musical growth becomes stunted, and at the first encounter with a "new" rhythmic or stylistic problem, such musicians are apt to become defensive, automatically blaming the composer for their troubles and accusing *him* of unmusicality. The inevitable long-range by-product of this situation is the basic antagonism and mistrust between orchestral musicians and composers. This may not always become overt or harshly expressed, but the suspicion that all contemporary music is at worst the work of "fakes" and "frauds" and at best a nuisance or necessary evil lies just below the surface of most musicians' minds; and it doesn't take much to bring these feelings out into the open.

The conductor has it in his power to be the "mediator" between the composer and the musicians. He can bring to life for them—and for the audience as well—the lifeless blueprint which is a musical score. This he not only can do, but it ought to be his obligation. If he fails in this obligation, he not only thwarts the composer, who is after all the creative force keeping the art of music alive, but he deprives the musician of the opportunity to regenerate his intellectual and digital-technical capacities.

Human nature being as it is, it is inevitable that conductors—who are, I suppose, *human* beings—and musicians take the path of least resistance. Very few seem to identify with the sense of obligation, of responsibility, of dedication, and in turn of privilege that men like Mitropoulos, Hans Rosbaud, or Kleiber brought to this issue, or that such younger men as Boulez, Charles Rosen, Paul Zukofsky, Bethany Beardslee—to mention but a few—bring to it today. In this connection, it is well to recognize that the "specialists" in contemporary music, regardless of their ability, perform only a limited service to contemporary music. It is much too easy for the traditional establishment to ignore these specialists as peripheral outsiders and indeed to point to the many among them whose musicianship is somewhat suspect, as is evident when it is put to the test in the classical repertoire. The problem under discussion here will never be alleviated until someone like a Karajan or a Szell puts his reputation and abilities on the line, so to speak, on behalf of contemporary music—not just on behalf of a few selected, isolated, predominantly "conservative" composers, but contemporary music in all of its variegated and truly contemporary manifestations.

I have perhaps been more fortunate than some in my contacts with orchestras and conductors, and I could not complain about the numerous excellent performances which some of my orchestral works have enjoyed. However, having also experienced on a number of occasions under-rehearsed, ill-prepared, misunderstood renditions of my works, I know all too well the feeling of helplessness and bitterness which the composer experiences as he hears his work massacred and senses the hostility of the audience rising about him. If I have enjoyed a more favorable relationship in this quarter, it is probably due in part to the fact that I was privileged to grow up within earshot of one of the great orchestras of the world, the New York Philharmonic, and subsequently spent the better part of my adult life in a major orchestra as a professional instrumentalist. Viewing the orchestra, the conductor, the subtle psychological and artistic relationship that exists between an orchestra and conductor at close range and from the inside as it were, I am sure provided me with insights into this special world which in turn must have affected my writing for the orchestra. I must also qualify my small success in penetrating the repertory of many world-renowned orchestras by saying that I do not claim to be the most advanced radical innovator. Such evaluations are extremely relative and change from year to year, and though many conductors regard my work as *avant-garde* and are frightened into inactivity by it, an objective viewpoint would place me more towards the center, albeit on the left side of the stylistic spectrum. It must also be added that within my accumulated orchestral works, it is consistently those which avoid the more interesting and complex orchestral problems of texture, rhythmic structure, form, and continuity that are performed. As a result those works which I consider to be my most important orchestral works are rarely performed, largely because conductors are frightened off by the problems they present, and it is therefore easier to turn once again to the *Seven Studies on Themes of Paul Klee.*

Having thus cast myself in the role of the "conservative radical," or the "radical conservative," it might be useful to touch upon some of the performance problems in one of my major orchestral compositions, which—though the problems therein are elementary to *me*—seem to cause such concern among conductors and orchestral players. It is curious that musicians are not intimidated by even the most extreme demands upon their instrumental virtuosity, but they are turned off by the slightest demands on their intellectual capacities. It has always been a disturbing curiosity of the orchestral player's mentality that he is challenged by the former (technical virtuosity) and demoralized by the latter (intellectual, i.e., mental virtuosity). Moreover, even this technical virtuosity must be presented (and demanded) by the composer in more or less familiar formats (i.e., conjunct lines, regular rhythmic patterns, traditional continuity, etc.) or else he "loses" the player.

In my *Symphony* (1965), commissioned by the Fine Arts Department of the Dallas Public Library for the Dallas Symphony, I was preoccupied with developing in my own way contemporary analogues to certain eighteenth- and nineteenth-century concepts which have been considered obsolete and unusable in serial writing by many of the present-day style arbiters. Most particularly, I was interested in the symphonic form in the light of certain recently developed serial principles which permit the establishing of contemporary analogues for the basic precepts of diatonic tonality. The serial principles alluded to are those embodied in the concept of combinatoriality. I am assuming that this concept is familiar to the reader of this volume, or if not, he will turn to other sources for information on that subject. I will confine myself only to those external aspects of the work with which the conductor and musician must concern themselves if they are to perform the work adequately.

Most performers would define performing as consisting of an accurate rendition of all pitch, rhythmic, dynamic, and timbral events as notated by the composer. Most composers would wish to expand that definition to include an understanding of the basic internal relationships (intervallic, rhythmic, structural, formal, timbral) in a given player's part which may not be apparent immediately or after a single reading of the work. Since every responsible composer I know in one way or another occupies himself with the delineation and clarification—for the purpose of greater expression and communication—of such internal relationships, which, in composite, form the external sonic surface of the piece, it follows that the performers must work towards a fully realized performance *from the inside.* That is to say, a merely surface rendition, no matter how technically accurate or skillful, will not suffice if it ignores the inner preceptual demands of the work. This is equal to saying that every player in an orchestra should understand in regard to every note he plays—isolated, disjointed, or not—with which other note (or notes) the first one is to be structurally associated. Only then can he play that note with the right sonority, right dynamic, right duration, right attack and release, and right *feeling* so as to allow it to function properly in terms of the smaller and larger surrounding context, and finally, the grand design of the work. The ideal performance is one in which all the thousands of notes the composer has put down on paper after having carefully explored all the potential relationships radiating out from that note to all other notes in the work, are understood and performed in terms of those relationships. In some of today's more complex works, that is certainly a large order, but as I have stated before, far from inherently impossible.

Of course, the musician does not have a score in front of him; he has only a single part and his immediate sight-reading concern is whether a given passage is a solo and exposed, or whether it is an incidental part hidden in the total instrumental fabric. Perhaps one day a clever inventor will discover a means by which orchestra players can play from a full score, as all intelligent string quartets do nowadays. In any event it is the conductor's job to elucidate for the performer the role and function of individual passages or notes. And he must keep at it until all the performers involved understand and *feel* the relationships elucidated.

The roles and functions which a passage or a note may perform are of an infinite variety, and even a single work may involve the player in a variety of types of structures. My *Symphony*, for example, contains several types of timbre melodies (*Klangfarbenmelodien*). Some are embodied in "free" homophonic forms (as in the first movement) or in "strict" polyphonic forms (as in the six-part fugue and four-part double-canon-by-inversion in the second movement). The second movement is indebted conceptually to both Bach and Webern, perhaps the two greatest contrapuntal masters of their respective eras. The opening fugue is organized in the manner of Bach's so-called permutational fugues, in which the various contrapuntal lines are combined in strict patterns of order (chosen, of course, by the composer). Each individual line in my fugue, however, is orchestrationally fragmented in terms of Schönberg's *Klangfarbenmelodie* (literally, tone-color-melody, in which a single melody is played not by one instrument but by many, linked together into a sort of "chain" of colors and timbres). This instrumental fugue is interlocked with a recapitulation thereof, this time in the percussion instruments, the entire passage serving as an interlude to the next section: the aforementioned double canon, which again makes use of "tone-color-melody." This too is recapitulated by the percussion, leading this time to one of the two possible alternatives to polyphony: monody. In complete contrast then, the solo horn sings a long-line melody, accompanied sparsely only at cadential points.

The fugue, although harmless looking in each individual part, is quite demanding in its multiplicity of linear relationships between parts and from one instrumental timbre segment to another. Example X, 1, shows measures 1–15 of the fugue in its simplest reduced form. Example X, 2, shows measures 9–15 of the

Example X, 1

same music in full score, showing the orchestrational fragmentation applied. The linear relationship from one instrument to another is indicated either by connecting dotted lines or by parentheses in the preceding and succeeding instruments for each contrapuntal line. Thus each of the six lines is "handed around" from instrument to instrument, as if played on some gigantic multi-timbered organ on which, by merely pulling a stop, different timbres can be instantly chosen for individual notes or groups of notes.

As can be readily seen from Example X, 2, the trumpet in meas-

Example X, 2

Fl. 1 2
Picc.
Ob. 1
E. H.
Cl. 1
B. Cl.
Bn. 1
C. Bn.
Hn. 1 3
Tpt. 1
Trb. 1 3
Tuba
Hp.
Vln. 1
Vln. 2
Va.
Vc.
Cb.
Tutti con sord.
senza sord.
con sord.
poco dim.
poco cresc.
1 Solo
espr.
tutti
4 soli

ure 10 must know that he gets his note, as in a relay race, from the clarinet, and passes his line on to the oboe. The trumpet's *pp* F-sharp must match dynamically with the clarinet's three notes D, C-sharp, F-sharp. Likewise, the oboe in measure 11 must listen to the trumpet's crescendo in measure 10 and match its dynamic on the high C to the preceding F of the trumpet.

More difficult are the problems of attack and release. The trumpet's attack on the F-sharp in measure 10 must be such as to continue the contrapuntal line coming from the first violins and the clarinet, and so as not to interrupt the flow of the line by either too soft or too hard an attack. Similarly the release of the dotted-quarter F must be precise so as not to leave a gap before the incoming oboe, nor may it overlap past the oboe's entrance. In addition the exact release must be of such a nature as to musically pass the note on to the oboe. Beyond these points, of course, each line in its instrumental composites makes a single phrase unit, which in turn has to be balanced against the other contrapuntal lines. Even more problematic is the necessity to keep each line flowing, despite the fragmentation which permits each player to participate only in short segments of it. He must in other words feel the whole line, hear it along its entire course, insert his tiny segment, and pass it on to the next player, all the while feeling and hearing the over-all six-part progression of the fugue.

If one realizes that in the entire forty measures of this fugue there are nearly four hundred contact points which involve the precise matching of attacks, releases, and dynamics, one can gain an idea of the amount of rehearsal time required if, for instance, the orchestra is one that has never previously experienced this kind of orchestral writing. On the other hand, if the orchestra and each individual in it were aware of and experienced in this kind of orchestral technique by virtue of previous training and an occasional, though over a period of time consistent, encounter with such a problem, then the forty bars of this fugue could probably be sight-read nearly perfectly.

This, of course, brings us back to the point which I have already made in regard to education and training at the hands of our schools and teachers. If the musician encounters the particular technique under discussion here for the first time in, let us say, his third season as a professional in a major orchestra, when in fact this technique is already some sixty years old, then the education of that individual can only be considered inadequate. To further emphasize my point, I need only remind the reader that in this imaginary rehearsal of my *Symphony*, we have so far covered only 40 measures, whereas the entire work contains 401 measures, most of them with equally difficult problems to solve. Nevertheless, I maintain that with the afore-mentioned "dream" orchestra, the

Example X, 3

EXAMPLE X, 4

P4	C♯	D	F♯	B♭	A	F	C	A♭	G	B	E♭	E				
I11		A♭	G	E♭	B	C	E	A	C♯	D	B♭	F♯	F			
I5				D	C♯	F♯	A	B♭	F	E	B	C	E♭	A♭	G	
P10					G	A♭	E♭	C	B	E	F	B♭	A	F♯	C♯	D

Harp	C♯	C	A♭	E	F	A	D	F♯	G	E♭	B	B♭
Piano	F♯	G	B	E♭	D	B♭	F	C♯	C	E	A♭	A

entire work could be played to perfection and much of it virtually sight-read.

In the double canon of measures 65 through 106 there is, in addition to the timbre-melody fragmentation already encountered in the fugue, the problem of certain doublings in the harp and piano. The purpose of these doublings is to extrapolate from the double canon and to articulate in the harp and piano two forms of the twelve-tone set. As can be seen in Example X, 3, the harp and piano sets (encircled notes) are in the same inversional and combinatorial relationship to each other as the main sets of the canon itself (see Example X, 4).

In order for these doublings to function properly, they must be played with rhythmic accuracy. As measures 77 through 79 in Example X, 5, show (these three measures are presented in the pitch canon of Example X, 6, by the encircled notes), the piano and harp double various pitches in the strings and brass. Since one of the canonic lines is in 9/8, the other in 3/4, the piano and harp participate in the main canon with both triple and duple subdivisions of the beat, very often in close proximity. If all players play these rhythms accurately—and they surely cannot be deemed particularly difficult or novel—the doublings will automatically occur. Since there is only one correct way of playing 𝄾♫ or ³♫♪, one would think that there could not be any serious problems in achieving these doublings. But one would be amazed to see how

EXAMPLE X, 5

many inaccurate variants of these rhythms players are capable of finding. Painstaking and time-consuming rehearsing is then the only answer.

Example X, 6

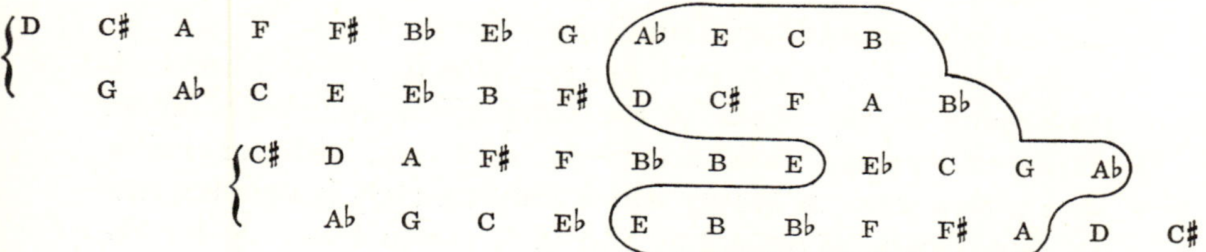

In this three-bar segment there is the added problem of the rapidly changing dynamics in piano and harp. As can be seen in Examples X, 3, and X, 5, these result from the fact that the two instruments are doubling isolated notes from various contrapuntal lines all with their own dynamic progression (not serialized). Incidentally, in measures 78 and 79 the brass takes over the canon from the strings, momentarily causing other doublings which must be rhythmically meshed and dynamically balanced.

I have discussed only two sections of the work in which a great deal of intricate detail must be worked out in order for the performers to realize what I have written and intended. Other sections call for other kinds of relationships to be worked out: the durational-proportional relationships of the Scherzo movement in which the ratios 4–2–2¼ are the primary determinants; the almost visual relationships in the first movement, in which an essentially vertical (chordal, non-melodic) music is gradually turned on its side, so to speak, to become an essentially horizontal (melodic, non-chordal) music. And finally there are the larger "key" relationships of the four movements of the *Symphony*, defined by the relationship of three different derived sets in the second, third, and fourth movements to the prime set of the first movement. I believe that the time will come when the twelve-tone language will be so familiar that sophisticated players and listeners will hear and "feel" derived sets, such as those used in this *Symphony*, much as sophisticated listeners and players hear and feel the key relationships in Mozart, Beethoven, and Brahms symphonies. To a sensitive musician, different keys have different weights, densities, consistencies, different moods. Analogously, combinatorially related and derived sets reveal differentiating properties upon repeated hearings and with familiarity.

In that ideal future a work like my *Symphony*—and hundreds of equally worthy works by the many gifted composers of our time—will be performed accurately, with ease, with conviction, and with a sense of beauty which unfortunately is now reserved by our symphony orchestras and their conductors only for the nineteenth- and late eighteenth-century classics.

CHAPTER ELEVEN: Michael Tippett

MICHAEL TIPPETT (born in London on January 2, 1905) began serious music study at the age of eighteen in the Royal College of Music, where he had composition under Sir Charles Wood and R. O. Morris, and conducting under Sir Adrian Boult and Sir Malcolm Sargent. In 1940 he was appointed musical director of Morley College, London, a position he held until 1952, when he resigned to devote full time to composition. During his tenure at Morley College, Tippett exerted a strong influence on all students and professionals who were associated with him. As a result of his intense interest in music from all periods, the Morley College Concerts Society programmed an unusually fine series of concerts of old and new music. Tippett has often appeared as a lecturer on BBC radio. A collection of these radio lectures, found in his book *Moving into Aquarius* (London, 1959), attests to his searching and comprehensive inquiries into many spheres of music as an art. Tippett's *Concerto for Double String Orchestra* is considered one of his most significant instrumental works, while *A Child of Our Time*, an impassioned plea against persecution and tyranny, is his best-known large choral composition. In opera, *A Midsummer Marriage* and *King Priam* are notable for their fresh approach to operatic form, and both works have had a profound influence on other compositions in all medias which followed. Tippett has been honored with several honorary doctorates, is a Commander of the Order of the British Empire and was knighted in 1966 by Queen Elizabeth II.

IN THE PRESENT PERIOD many older composers find the traditional titles for instrumental forms confusing. It is no wonder that the younger composers mostly eschew such titles altogether, because in an *avant-garde*-oriented time, all received remains must be excluded if possible. Also the received titles such as "symphony," "concerto," "sonata," and "suite" really are, at present, imprecise and confusing. I am not certain however that the confusion is absolute and that therefore the rejection of traditional titles must be absolute also. I think, on the contrary, that we should try to clarify the confusion by examining the historical titles more closely.

Symphony

I feel that much of the confusion that may arise when a contemporary instrumental work is called a "symphony" is due to the fact that we have habitually two differing uses of the word, implying two contrasting conceptions. Further, we are generally unaware of this division in use and pass from one use to the other, from one conception to the other, completely unawares. This practice must obviously result in confusion.

The two contrasting conceptions or ideas of what is meant by a symphony are: that we imply by the title a *historical archetype* (from which we depart and return), e.g., the middle symphonies of Beethoven; and that we imply a *notional archetype* (permitting endless variations to the end of time), e.g., the Mahler symphonies, as variations of a notional archetype, are as much symphonies as those of Beethoven (irrespective, of course, of pure value judgment). It is then surprising how easily we can say almost in the same breath that the Mahler symphonies are not true symphonies at all, because they do not conform to our historical archetype of the moment, and then say that Mahler gave the symphony a quite new and valid form, because we momentarily abandon the conception of a historical archetype for that of a notional archetype.

A nice public example of this was given in England by Leonard Bernstein, when he came to conduct the London Symphony Orchestra, in three programs for BBC Television, under the title "The Twilight of the Symphony." Mr. Bernstein introduced the programs himself in interview. Each program contained one work: Sibelius, *Symphony No. 5 in E♭, Op. 82*; Shostakovitch, *Sym-*

phony No. 5, Op. 47; and Stravinsky, *The Rite of Spring* (*La Sacre du Printemps*). Clearly the title of the series, "The Twilight of the Symphony," implies the historical archetype—that at sometime in the past, which Bernstein did not specify, the symphony had a noon. Unfortunately, the interviewer never pressed Bernstein on this point, and I suspect the interviewer himself had never properly cleared up this point in his own mind. But he did bring out the inherent confusion admirably—if, I guess, unconsciously—by pressing Bernstein to say whether then the three chosen modern works were symphonies at all in his opinion (especially *The Rite of Spring*) and whether the works as music exemplified a cultural twilight *in toto*. Bernstein said that all the works were symphonic in some sense and all were positive musically. This answer, of course, implies the notional archetype—that even an avowed ballet score like *The Rite of Spring* can rightly appear in a television program concerning the symphony, because it exemplifies, as Bernstein thinks, the kind of musical piece we may call "symphonic."

This is only Bernstein's view, of course. I might call *The Rite of Spring* "symphonic," but I doubt if I would want to call it a "symphony." Not because I have a true (for me) historical archetype to which I refer it and dismiss it, but because I dismiss it with reference to my notional archetype, which is probably not the same as Bernstein's. My notion is no more finally valid than his.

Concerto

With "concerto" for title, we have an added problem, in that the use of the word changed almost radically between the early eighteenth century and the late eighteenth century. Thus the concertos, the *Concerti Grossi*, to use their Italian title, of Vivaldi and Handel were suites of short instrumental movements some of which generally used the binary form which has been called "suite form" (in the sense that movements like the opening of Beethoven allegros have been called "sonata form"). This form is common in most of the innumerable single-movement harpsichord sonatas of Scarlatti. It is never found in the main music of

W. A. Mozart, Beethoven, and Schubert. But "concerto," as used exactly by the last-named composers, meant not a suite of movements but a three-movement display vehicle for solo instrumental virtuosity, accompanied by an orchestra. The movements used all the characteristic forms of this later period. On the whole we tend to think of "concerto" nowadays as referring to display pieces and use the word "*concertante*" when we need more precise reference to the older concertos of the Corelli-Vivaldi period.

Thus when Bartók invented the title *Concerto for Orchestra* he implied, once we had seen what the music was, two negatives and two positives. Negatively, since there was no solo instrument, it was not a standard display concerto, and since it was not a deliberate return to early eighteenth-century classicism, it was not a concerto in the older sense. Positively, through its succession of five movements, it suggested however that it had the suite in some sense in mind, and also that the orchestra itself might be the display instrument.

Orchestra

It is only dawning on us gradually that the term "orchestra" is in itself ambivalent. We can speak accurately enough about, say, Bach's orchestra, and in so far as we accept it as Bach did, then we are tending to use the "orchestra" as referring to a notional archetype—far too pretentious an expression, of course, because we only mean an ensemble of instruments beyond chamber music. But if we permit ourselves such statements as "Bach would have written for the *real* orchestra of today had he heard it," we are moving over to the idea of a historical archetype, viz., the Standard (whatever that might mean) Symphony Orchestra.

It is much clearer to us now than fifty years ago that this idea of some fixed or Standard Orchestra, with a capital O, has broken down. In their early days such revolutionary figures as Schönberg, Stravinsky, and Bartók all wrote exciting new-sounding pieces for this standard orchestra. But, of course, its very standard-ness came finally into question; its marvelous balance and smooth ensemble got in the way. There is a nice succinct account of how Stravinsky reacted to this feeling after the shattering experience of the 1914–18 war. It appears in Eric Walter White's recently published book on this composer:[1]

> A reaction against the full symphony orchestra set in;[2] and this manifested itself in different ways. In the first place, after *The Nightingale* he became convinced that the normal symphony orchestra could not provide him with the type of ensemble he needed for his next full-scale score for the Russian Ballet (*The Wedding*), and a nine-year search for the right combination of instruments ensued. Secondly, when he decided to adapt part of *The Nightingale* as a symphonic poem for orchestra, he not only chose a slightly smaller orchestra for the purpose (with double instead of triple woodwind, and other instruments scaled down in proportion) but also changed his attitude to the principle of orchestration. This change was typified by his growing interest in the *concertante* treatment of single instruments or small groups of instruments; and this in its turn, through the emphasis and prominence it gave certain instruments at certain moments, postulated their absence at many other moments. Instruments were no longer used as padding, or merely to fill in and inflate. The result was a purer palette of instrumental colors, lighter orchestral texture, a greater variety and contrast in the use of tones, and less insistence on the importance of "blend." The orchestra no longer sounded like a gigantic organ playing in an over-resonant cathedral. . . .
>
> In arriving at his orchestral specifications, he was always prepared to accept conditions dictated by outside circumstances (as in *The Soldier's Tale*) or a series of self-imposed restrictions. Early in the 1920's, for instance, he concentrated on writing for ensembles in which wind instruments predominated (the *Symphonies of Wind Instruments, Mavra,* the *Octet* and the *Piano Concerto*). Later on, he began to treat the orchestra on chamber-music lines; and this is particularly noticeable in the big serial works like *Canticum Sacrum,*

[1] *Stravinsky: The Composer and His Works* (Berkeley and Los Angeles, University of California Press, 1966), 515–16.—M.T.

[2] The term "full symphony orchestra" implies the historical archetype.—M.T.

> *Agon, Threni, Movements,* A *Sermon* etc., and *The Flood.* In fact, every time he wrote a full-scale composition, he deliberately rethought his orchestra.[3]

I think this is in fact where we have now arrived. But the social problems involved are acute. I mean, the standard symphony orchestra grew up during the nineteenth century, and concert halls were built to match the volume of the ensemble and to house the proportionate audience. If composers now change the volume of their orchestral ensemble for every piece, then clearly the fixed concert halls cannot always match up. The great standard orchestras, such as the Berlin Philharmonic or London Symphony Orchestra, naturally prefer to play as one body, and they are not enamored of the new demands upon them. The big public that still mostly lives by the idea of a "real" Orchestra, with a capital O, is slow to follow the changes. But these problems are not new, and they will be solved eventually.

In my own case I have been very slow to understand—and so to act upon—the general considerations outlined above. My best-known piece is a *Concerto for Double String Orchestra* of 1938–39. The title indicates my awareness of the problems, though it is not a revolutionary work in itself. It is clear that in calling the piece a "Concerto," I was harking back to the *Concerti Grossi* by Handel, which I knew and loved. In using a double string orchestra I was attaching myself to a specially English tradition, viz., the *Introduction and Allegro* for string quartet and string orchestra of Edward Elgar and the *Fantasia of a Theme of Tallis* of Ralph Vaughan Williams. It can almost be said that the string orchestra in this sense was an English invention. I know that I regarded the two orchestras as vehicles for *concertante* effects as are sometimes found between the *Concertino* and the *Concerto Grosso* of the Handel concertos. But the musical forms were Beethovenian: a succinct dramatic sonata allegro, a slow movement

[3] This sentence implies the complete going over to the notional archetype.—M.T.

which was almost modeled on a Beethoven quartet movement, and a sonata rondo with coda.

The *Symphony No. 1* of 1945 was for me the culmination of a long period of struggle with classical sonata forms (in the Beethoven sense) within the context of the musical life I lived at that time. That is to say, I still started with a dramatic sonata allegro laid out on a big scale. But I was already trying to add to the forms of the other movements. The slow movement was a set of mirror variations on a long ground bass. I could not have come to this conception without the prolonged preoccupation of that period of my life with the music of Henry Purcell. So once more it is clear that I was always reaching back behind the Beethoven period to older manners. In this sense I was perhaps acting out a delayed neoclassicism. (Many, many composers have worked in this field.) The third movement indeed, the scherzo, went back further still. I had observed how Pérotin wrote vocal trios all in triple time in which, after a few measures of plain-song in quarter notes, the voices took off in a flying hoquet on a chosen vowel in bumpy eighth notes. Yet the effect of these hoquets was always to have a very strong accent on each measure. This allied itself in my mind with the presto quarter notes of some Beethoven scherzos, which equally have an accent to each measure. Thus I saw what seemed to me a new material for a symphonic movement of a scherzo kind, and of course the bare, stark quality of the Pérotin allied itself easily to the starker sounds of my own music (starker, that is, than I had used before). This experience of agreement almost between late-medieval or very early renaissance sounds and contemporary sounds (outside serial music perhaps, which has to use so many minor seconds and minor ninths) is common to most composers who have been influenced in this way.

For the finale I called upon my natural gift for polyphony and counterpoint to the best of its powers and with a free use of the orchestra wrote a large-scale, unorthodox double fugue. But all along, despite the freedom with which I used the orchestra, the instrumental ensemble was that of a Standard Symphony Orchestra, just as I had studied it in the pages of Cecil Forsyth's manual of *Orchestration* (1914), with the addition of the instrumental balances enunciated by Rimsky-Korsakov, that in the forte, one trombone or one trumpet equals two horns or four wood winds or one line of the string body.

When I returned to the problem of orchestral music with the *Symphony No. 2* (1956–57), I had written a long opera, *The Midsummer Marriage,* in between. So I returned to the symphonic problems with a fresh mind, only to discover them to be as nearly intractable (in my sense) as ever. Yet the *Second Symphony* is the turning point. The work seems like a yet more concentrated example of neoclassicism, despite the use of broken tone clusters and a whole movement in additive rhythm (a method of composing entirely foreign to the Central European classicism). But of course, the fact that one of the movements *is* an additive structure is symptomatic of the change happening inside. I was at last ridding myself of the historic archetype of the symphony and going over decisively to the notional archetype.

Before I could put this change of emphasis to a further test, I needed to write another opera, *King Priam.* The dramatic processes demanded for this opera forced me to reconsider the standard orchestra radically. I began to realize that the sound of the standard orchestra has become so strong a historic archetype that contemporary music written for it gets inevitably drawn back in history by analogy to the period when the archetype was produced. To put it melodramatically and perhaps rudely, this may not matter to Shostakovich, but it matters to me. So I had to consider the matter systematically.

First, it was clear enough that Stravinsky had shattered the Rimsky-Korsakov balances, showing (as with much music from earlier periods) that any instrument can equal any instrument in the forte, *if played in the necessary way.* Also with a contemporary of mine like Olivier Messiaen, it is clear how exciting all kinds of unusual instruments can be within the non-standard orchestra. There is no dearth of examples from both sides of the Atlantic of this general process. But I had to take a rather more personal step. I had begun as a composer with an intense love of the string quartet, of which I have written three. I had written three pieces for string orchestra. With my natural feeling for this medium I realized that the use of the string body within the standard orchestra was for me the crux. For this body is historically the string quartet blown up, so that there is a terrific historic archetype embedded within it. I was at last ready to let go of this archetype and replace it with a body of string instruments whose number and layout would be entirely conditional on the piece to be composed. Essential to this understanding was the realization that there were to be no first or second violins, but just violins. (The idea of first and second violins is a very good touchstone indeed).

Once I had broken up the old string quartet conception of orchestral strings, it was no problem to reach the point described in the quotation from the book on Stravinsky, quoted previously: "in fact, every time he wrote a full-scale composition, he deliberately rethought his orchestra."

As I have already said, I reached this point first in the opera *King Priam*. When the opera was finished, I turned once again to pure instrumental music and began the *Concerto for Orchestra* (1962–63). Like the *Concerto for Double String Orchestra* of twenty-four years earlier, it is a three-movement work with obvious references to both concerti grossi and display concertos. But where the *Concerto for Double String Orchestra* used only Beethoven-type classical forms, the *Concerto for Orchestra* dispenses with a first-movement dramatic sonata allegro. Indeed, my advances, if that is the right word, in the problems of contemporary symphonic form and that of the nature of the contemporary orchestra were severely put to the test in this first movement.

The movement, and indeed the whole *Concerto for Orchestra*, is admirably described by Ian Kemp, the editor of the Faber and Faber *Symposium* on my music,[4] in his sleeve note to the recording. Kemp's description is clear and accurate and I cannot better it:

> Michael Tippett's *Concerto for Orchestra* was commissioned for the 1963 Edinburgh Festival and completed and first performed that

[4] *Michael Tippett: A Symposium on His 60th Birthday* (London, Faber and Faber, 1965).—M.T.

year by the same artists as on this recording. The work is dedicated "to Benjamin Britten with affection and admiration in the year of his fiftieth birthday." The *Concerto* of the title refers specifically to the grouping of the instruments into a number of small *concertini*, after the manner of a Baroque *concerti grossi*. The analogy should not be pressed too far, however, for there is no occasion for the contrast between the *concertino* and *ripieno*. This was not part of Tippett's intention. Rather he was concerned with the idea of basing a work on the combination and interaction of autonomous musical characters. This approach owes a good deal to the constructional methods of his second opera, *King Priam*, in which relations between personages are reflected in abrupt juxtapositioning of vivid musical motifs. It is also symptomatic of a growing impatience with the criteria and gestures of traditional forms. The result is unique—rather like a slice from a fascinating conversation piece. There is no sense of conclusion, no grand apotheosis, no "achievement" in a Beethovenian way. The listener is presented instead with a multiplicity of images locked together as in a painting. The effect is at its most radical in the first movement. Here Tippett uses nine *concertini*, grouped in threes, thus: flute and harp, tuba and piano, three horns; timpani and piano, oboe, cor anglais, bassoon and double bassoon, two trombones and percussion; xylophone and piano, clarinet and bass clarinet, two trumpets and side drum. This material is presented sequentially at first and then extended in combination by three "development" sections, using the three main periods of the first theme for flute and harp as binding elements. The climax is marked by a stroke on the gong, after which the music gradually returns to the calm of the opening, showing in the process that the apparently conflicting entities of the movement can be reconciled.[5]

I had, of course, rethought the orchestra specifically for this work. Thus the nine *concertini* of the first movement had to embody three musical functions. The first three (flute and harp, tuba and piano, three horns) were concerned with melodic line (see Examples XI, 1a, 1b, and 1c).

[5] *Concerto for Orchestra*, London Symphony Orchestra conducted by Colin Davis (Phillips).—M.T.

Example XI, 1a

Example XI, 1b

Example XI, 1c

The second three (timpani and piano; oboe, cor anglais, bassoon, and double bassoon; two trombones and percussion) were concerned with rhythm and dynamic punch (see Examples XI, 2a, 2b, and 2c).

The third three (xylophone and piano, clarinet and bass clarinet, two trumpets and side drum) were concerned with virtuosity of speed (see Examples XI, 3a, 3b, and 3c).

It takes at least a third of the movement to display all this section material. Then begin three of what Ian Kemp has called "developments," in quotation marks, simply because "development" is probably the only possible word, but not in the sense of the historic archetype of Beethoven. In reality it was chiefly a matter of effective juxtapositions and "jam sessions" (the *concertini* never changed their own ensembles throughout the movement). In his contribution to the book *Michael Tippett: A Symposium* mentioned earlier, Anthony Milner says this movement can be likened to "the so-called 'quilt'-canzonas of the early seventeenth century; these had between seven to ten short sections differentiated by tempo, time, and content, sometimes employing variation technique for a few consecutive sections."[6] I would accept this suggestion, though it is clear that I have widely extended the canzona form in all directions.

The slow movement of the *Concerto for Orchestra* brings strings into play for the first time. I stated its make-up in the

[6] "Style," 227.—M.T.

EXAMPLE XI, 2a

EXAMPLE XI, 2b

EXAMPLE XI, 2c

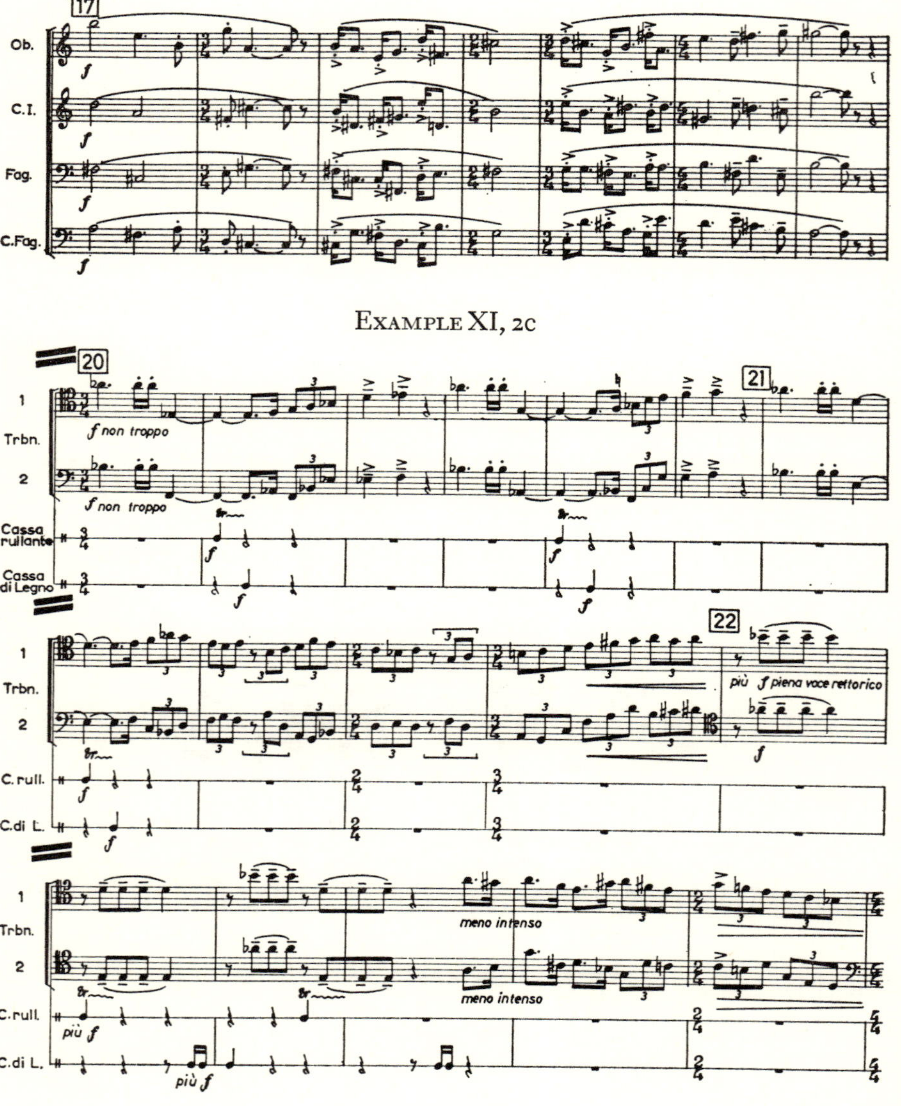

"Note to the Score" which appears in the Schott edition of the *Concerto*:

> The string body is a small one. It should not however be thought of as a scaled-down string section of a symphony orchestra with a conventional balance between Violins 1 and 2, Violas, Cellos and Basses, but a group of string instruments which divide up in various ways and produce, when they do in fact play together, a balance of their own. The overall number is left to the discretion of the conductor, but an optimum might well be six or eight Violins (i.e. three or four desks), four Violas, five Cellos (one generally playing solo) and four Basses. If this number is for any reason increased, the proportions should still conform.

The purpose of this particular proportion is to keep the light from the dark. The light violins are never asked to match in weight the dark violas, cellos, and basses. I specially wanted the sound of a small group of violins playing almost *concertante* and capable of great virtuosity.

In the finale I used mixed ensembles of strings and winds. Thus

Example XI, 3a

EXAMPLE XI, 3b

EXAMPLE XI, 3c

the six or eight violins play rapid triplets against a single trumpet in the forte. Then, at a repeat, the dark lower strings are added below in harmonically hard-sounding two-part chords. On another repeat the string two-part chords are replaced by the two trombones in other chords.

Finally it was clear that the composer needs to have some idea of the placing on the podium of his chosen orchestra to get the best ensemble. I made out, therefore, a possible plan, chiefly concerned by the need for the piano to be as close as possible to all the instruments it played with (see Example XI, 4).

EXAMPLE XI, 4

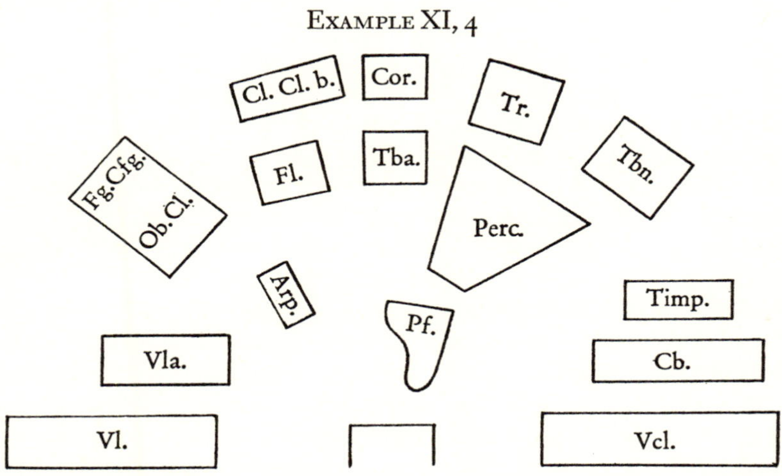

If we now look to the future, it seems to me that the present younger generation of composers in England, aged around thirty, whom I know and like, take the present position of a nonstandard orchestra in their stride. They are born free from the hangover of the old historic archetype. They accept the present condition that no fresh historic archetype of the Orchestra with a capital O is yet in formation. This is comparatively easy going. But the complementary freedom from any historic archetype of the Symphony, or symphonic music, is extremely difficult to manage and is as much an abiding problem to them as it is to me. It is never, of course, really evaded by the various literary or other titles which the younger generation feel compelled to use. The difficulties of how to write viable contemporary symphonic music are inescapable. Good luck to anyone capable of succeeding!

CHAPTER TWELVE: Wladimir Vogel

(Translated by Willis J. Wager)

Wladimir Vogel (born in Moscow on February 29, 1896, of a German father and a Russian mother) received private music instruction, and even during his early youth, there were efforts at composition. Later, Vogel was in contact with Alexander Scriabin, whose music influenced Vogel's youthful works up to "Sinfonischer Vorgang." From 1918 to 1933 Vogel resided in Berlin, where he studied with Heinz Tiessen and became acquainted with the early works of Arnold Schönberg and with Expressionist art. A synthesis of the Scriabin and the early Schönberg styles, in cyclic form, appeared in Vogel's *Komposition für 2 Klaviere* (1923). Between 1921 and 1924 he studied with Ferruccio Busoni at the Akademie der Künste in Berlin. It was during this period that Vogel taught composition and radio production at the Klindworth-Scharwenka Conservatory in the German capital. Vogel's first major international success came with his *4 Etüden für grosses Orchester* which were performed many times under Scherchen, Mitropoulos, Monteux, and others. In 1933 Vogel left Germany and, after a brief stay in France, settled in Switzerland where he is still living as a Swiss citizen. It was in 1936 that he turned to the twelve-tone technic of composition in the *Chormadrigalen* and the last two movements of the *Violinkonzert*. At the present time Vogel continues to write in the dodecaphonic idiom, but through the years it has evolved into a mode of expression which is unique and very much his own.

My large, purely symphonic works were almost all completed many years ago: "Sinfonischer Vorgang" (1922), lost as a result of the war, and *Sinfonia fugata* (*in memoriam Ferruccio*

Busoni) for full orchestra (1925). This was my last purely symphonic work. Between 1930 and 1934, I wrote the following orchestral pieces: *4 Etüden für grosses Orchester* (1930–32); *Tripartita* for large orchestra (1934); and *Violinkonzert* (1937).

After a rather long interruption during which I concerned myself with the twelve-tone technique, there followed: *Sieben Aspekte einer Zwölftonreihe* for normal orchestra (1950); *Spiegelungen* for orchestra (1952); *Preludio, Interludio lirico, Postludio* (1954); and a *Konzert für Violoncello* (1954). All other and succeeding compositions are either vocal works with orchestra or chamber ensemble. So far as both musical material and intellectual and aesthetic assumptions are concerned, a return to the large symphonic form seems inappropriate to me today. An analysis of the orchestral works just mentioned appears to me rather superfluous—not because these pieces are without interest (they all present personal solutions to problems of content and form), but because they scarcely may be taken to represent my method of composing today.

The large symphonic form demands, along with other things, themes and thematic complexes which permit themselves to be elaborated and worked together in closed movements and in various ways: contrasting sectional conceptions, dynamic crescendos and climaxes, and differing activities in typified and discrete movements. This was still possible in a strictly or freely tonal musical idiom. Procedure and technique were either polyphonic-contrapuntal or melodic-homophonic, or polymelodic; "rhythmics" served as the ultimate basis of a movement; harmonic complexes set the stage, as it were, in terms of sonority.

With the adoption of the twelve-tone manner of composing, most of these assumptions necessary for large symphonic works fell away. Still the largest purely orchestral form is provided by "variations," which serve to contrast and unify.

The trend toward athematic thinking in composition, characteristic of most present-day twelve-tone or serial music, demands another conception and technique, as also another aesthetic, which must confine itself to concentrated, rather short forms. Particularly the development of serial music, as it has emerged in recent years in younger composers' works, led to a state of quiescence and undergirded all dynamic mobility in favor of small, as it were, self-multiplicative constellations of sound, sonorous procedures, and micro-temporal structures. All these and many other factors led to the turning away from symphonic form, whether of Classical or Romantic persuasion.

The expansion and introduction of new or previously little-used instruments, particularly of percussive and other distinctive timbres, considerably enlarged the number of instruments in the orchestra, so that one cannot speak unqualifiedly of a turning away from the "full" orchestra. On the other hand, these tendencies make such unusual technical and musical demands on the performers that they must have the abilities of soloists. The mixing of electronically generated tones and noises with those produced by normal orchestral instruments does not alter the fact that today one could largely or entirely dispense with the conventionally instrumented orchestra. As to what the future will bring forth, no one today can foresee.

As for me, I have sought to find the way to the great forms of music and of composition in areas where they are linked with words,[1] partly to break away from the purely formal and the merely material, but also (and this is perhaps still more important) partly to fulfill a need to approach human beings with works that could be done and re-experienced, with contents that might speak to them—even though I might run a risk of "swimming against the stream." In orchestral instrumentation, I had already renounced excessive effects of tone-color in favor of "limited" classical instrumental sonority. Linear and vertical elements are characterized by re-emphasis on actual and not "estranged" tone and return to intervals which determine the course and framework of musical structure. The range of the instruments prevents continual exaggeration in the direction of height and depth and holds itself in general within normal limitation and economy, to

[1] See my choral work *Wagadus Untergang durch die Eitelkeit* (*Wagadu Destroyed*).—W.V.

be replaced in characteristic passages all the more effectively. Every mannerism is avoided, but the traits of the dodecaphonic style are retained.

The axioms of composition proposed by me and tried out in several vocal works are in many respects "new," and in fact stand boldly over against tradition. Yet, without sacrifice of principle, they are perhaps suited to making the New Music more available and accessible to experience.

My aim has been to convert and integrate textual content and emotional elements of the sung and spoken word into a formal language arising from absolute music, presented on various levels—as, for example, I have done in my drama-oratorio *Flucht*. The late great director Hermann Scherchen, shortly before he died, was able to look at and read the score, and characterized it as a composition that opened up "new dimensions."

Today I can see that, from 1930 on, there was gradual development in one area of my creative activity: in my larger vocal works a new type of oratorio was constantly and consistently taking shape, the germ of which is discernible as early as my first choral work, *Wagadus Untergang durch die Eitelkeit*, and the form of which comes out more and more crystal clear in the succeeding major works.

As early as 1922 I wrote a series of *Sprechlieder* for low voice and piano on texts by the German poet who had died in World War I, August Stramm, one of the most typical of the Expressionists. These *Sprechlieder* I consider even today to have some validity as an especially characteristic expression of that time and of my own creative work. In them I distribute the words and word-formations into spoken and sung portions (in a manner different from that of, for example, Schönberg's *Pierrot Lunaire*, where the *sprechstimme*, though speaking at prescribed pitches, does not pass on over into actual song).

In 1930 I completed my first large choral work, *Wagadus Untergang durch die Eitelkeit*, after a Kabyle Riff legend recorded by the well-known Africanist Professor Leo Frobenius, set to music by me for three soloists, mixed chorus, and five saxophones.

In this work, the text, both solo and chorus, was sung and also spoken.

In 1938 I composed, as my next big vocal work, the first part of the epic oratorio *Thyl Claes,* after Charles de Coster's legend *Thyl Ulenspiegel et Lamme Goedzak,* for two solo-*sprechstimmen,* soprano, choral-speaking group, and orchestra. In this the spoken word was assigned a predominating role. What determined my doing this was, primarily, the text itself—the persecution of the Reformers by the Spanish Inquisition under Charles V in Flanders, presented through the fate of individuals—and, secondarily, the source of the commission: the Renaudins' choral-speaking group in Brussels, which had already performed works with speaking chorus by Darius Milhaud and Plisnier.

The relative proportion of text and music in this part of the work—as compared with traditional oratorios—has been consciously reversed: more spoken text, less music. The spoken text transmits in a more direct way the content of what is reported than the music would if it had tried to convey the report and in so doing had weakened its direct effort. On the other hand, the less frequent passages of song and wordless music, which interrupt the spoken text, are felt either as oases of relaxation or as dramatic climaxes.

During and influenced by World War II, I wrote the second part of the work, for the same combination as the first. In this second part, it is no longer a matter of the fate of individual persons but that of the whole people. The over-all character of this part thereby becomes more epic than dramatic. The relationship between the spoken text and the music is somewhat equalized, though the spoken word remains of decisive significance and effect.

In clearer and clearer relief, the mutual relationship between the word as spoken and the word as sung began to stand out in my mind—leading to a type of composition in which the dramatic and the epic-oratorical elements fuse.

The next work was the oratorio *Yet Jonah Went to Ninevah* (*Jona ging doch nach Ninive*), after the biblical translation by

Martin Buber, for baritone, speaker, speaking chorus, mixed singing chorus, and orchestra. In this work, special functions with regard to the text are assigned to the collaborating groups and tie the whole together. In the portions where God speaks, moreover, a new element appears in the splitting up of the words into syllables and their assignment to various voice-groups.

The little *Pergolesi Cantata,* composed at the request of the Pergolesi Festival Committee in Zurich, for tenor and strings, can be considered under the category of further development in that it, perhaps for the first time in the history of music, had as its content a biography: thus it represented an extension of the subject-matter for vocal works.

The ensuing large cantata, *Meditation on Amedeo Modigliani* (*Meditazione su Amedeo Modigliani*), had as its subject-matter a portrait of this painter and originated from a text by Felice Filippini, being composed for a solo-*sprechstimme,* singing quartet, mixed chorus, and orchestra, and having been commissioned for the dedication of the new radio studio at Lugano. This work combines epic-oratorical, dramatic, and operatic elements into a whole (see Examples XII, 1 and 2).

A later member in the development which has led to the precise form of the "drama-oratorio" and has united all the preceding and the new is again a portrait, this time that of the Swiss poet Robert Walser, under the title *Flight* (*Flucht*). It is written for four solo-*sprechstimmen,* singing quartet, speaking chorus, and orchestra, on poetry by Robert Walser and biographical data compiled by Paul Mueller in Herisau, where the unfortunate poet died in 1956.

Also in this work, which constitutes a full evening's program, I combine elements from the regular theater, the oratorio, and the opera.

There are, finally, two further compositions still to be noted: *Arpiade,* for soprano, speaking chorus, and instrumental quintet, on texts by Hans Arp, and the Schiller Anniversary composition

EXAMPLE XII, 1

EXAMPLE XII, 2

for Radio Zurich "Song of the Bell" ("Lied von der Glocke"), for *a cappella* speaking chorus—in both of which, it seems to me, some fortunate formulations have been found.

The works cited have been performed often and successfully, both in Switzerland and abroad, and have left strong impressions behind, each in its own way. These compositions have also won critical recognition. Yet so far no one has attempted to establish the connections among these works or to get down to the unity of development and conception, recognizing here the advent of the means and the bases for a new type of oratorio.

When one considers precisely the through-composed texts of late Romantic, Modern, and some Contemporary vocal works—particularly of many operas and oratorios—one observes that by no means all texts, words, sentences, and expressions necessarily need music in order to be perceived and understood. On the contrary, song often hides the verbal content, and makes it inaudible and unintelligible. Song, on the other hand, is hindered and distorted in its free unfolding by texts that are overloaded in content and language. Thus music is not called for by every word, in terms of its phonetic aspects (e.g., short words with many consonants, long compound nouns) or of its meaning; nor does every sentence, according to the statement it makes, cry out for music, need it, or even bear it. This is so if the words and sentences, in terms of their content, harbor within themselves little or nothing of the Muses and cannot without much ado be linked up with or related to music: texts, words, and assertions whose sense and effect are completely expended in and through themselves and require no projection onto the musical plane.

The manner of "through-composing" the entire text and thus unifying everything sung has not existed from all eternity. Quite the contrary. At the time when the number-opera had achieved its classical form and status, the text-distribution functions were —as is well known—more highly differentiated. I am using the term "classical" here in the sense in which Busoni used it; it has nothing to do with the concept of the Classical, Neoclassical, or Pseudoclassical, but rather with the dictionary definition of the "classical" as the "exemplary," thus being not confined to any one epoch or to any one particular style, but attainable in every epoch and in every style.

At that time, accordingly, we find in the opera *secco* and melodic recitatives, the texts of which were important in preserving the continuity of the events or in characterizing personage and situation. Linked with them were arias, in which song was given freer development, the actual statements being limited but effective; then, too, the ensemble movements and the orchestra performed a multiple role. In the course of music history, this important differentiation was lost, and texts were "through-composed."

The same thing is true of the oratorio: at one time there was the chronicler, the narrator; there were recitatives of the same sort, leading on to arias, which in turn carried the events—on the basis of often-repeated words and sentences—into the level of contemplation, of expression; furthermore, the chorus had substantial pieces, the propositional aspects of which were restricted to a limited amount of text but were heightened in effect. Finally, the orchestra, sometimes independent, sometimes accompanying. Thus far matters had already gone by Bach's time.

In the oratorio, too, this wise and valuable discipline of the functional distribution of text was lost. As a result, choral texts, for example, were laden with statements, and hearers could follow them only through books of words—consulted, moreover, usually for the first time after the performance.

Since in the opera visible action on stage is superadded to strictly auditory perception, one can guess at the purport of texts that are often unintelligible. But in a non-scenic presentation, the word itself remains mainly—if not exclusively—the vehicle and bearer of the content and the action. The more important it is, the more decisive its significance becomes for the listeners' receptivity and understanding.

As one can extract the individual tone from its surrounding tonal relationships and consider it autonomously or relate it, for example, only to its immediate neighbors (as in the dodecaphonic method), I extract the word as an autonomous element from the logical context of a sentence and examine it according to its idea, its phonetics, its tone-color, its hidden associations of content of phonetic sonority, and any rhymes or assonances it may yield by itself or in the possible succession of neighboring words (as, for example, in the *Arpiade*, the *Mondträume*, the *Worte*, and so forth). On the other hand, I also proceed from the actual conceptual meaning of the word. I proceed to transform and project the word onto another plane so far as either the poet himself has done so or I have undertaken to do so myself. But I avoid any deformation of the words for the sake of mere phonetic and acoustical play or for comic effect, the outcome of which soon proves cheapening and deadening.

Since the world and the ideas, thoughts, and feelings of men seem to me all of like importance, I take—in principle—every kind of textual content as artistically realizable and make of it a direct or indirect connection with the sum total of our life. Within our ken, accordingly, emerge many subjects, themes, problems, and questions which perhaps heretofore have found no entry into a work of musical art. A basic consideration in the choice of texts for works of rather large proportions is provided by the possibility of introducing new content into the area of expression in musically related art, thereby involving all levels of the human—with the important presupposition, of course, that they are feasible and susceptible of being re-experienced.

I purposely use texts that are already texts (i.e., no fabricated librettos), and I use everything that seems to me valuable in them: assertions, descriptions of nature, psychological processes, conversations, scenes, the real and the unreal, the commonplace, the dramatic, and the lyric. Since however, as I indicated, not every text, not every word in the sentence is suitable to be sung, a division into spoken and sung portions ensues.

The apportionment of text to the various groupings within the whole ensemble lies at the very heart of the artistic undertaking; it demands delicacy of feeling, a sense of the outward acoustical and phonetic effects of language and the inward intellectual and emotional connections. Through the division of the functions among the participants, heterogeneous elements and contents are assigned to different acoustical and sonorous levels and thus are unified in their diversity. Such a procedure would have previously been scarcely conceivable. Only modern world-knowledge and philosophy, modern art, and the modern theater have opened up and made possible the phenomenon that I should like to call "unity in diversity."

This principle characterizes the position which I take with regard to the present day and represents, as it seems to me, an example of the modern conception of a vocal work. The fact that this upsets various theories previously considered unshakable goes without saying. The listener who is accustomed to look on an oratorio as a primarily musical matter assigns only an intermediate and transitory function to the texts spoken or half-sung on pitches in recitative. For him, what is sung or played on instruments is the main thing.

In the "drama-oratorio" as I conceive it, a significance of equal rank is intended for both the freely spoken and the rhythmically spoken word, as well as for what is sung and what is played on instruments. The listener who is traditionally oriented must accordingly accustom himself in his auditory receptivity and imagination to both levels, the one presented as speech and the other as music, to unite them into one single event.

The elements of my material and its utilization, in so far as they now permit themselves to be given currently final form in the Walser composition, had come into existence and use earlier in my works: freely speaking solo voices (actors), rhythmized solo-*sprechstimmen,* singing soloists, singing chorus, rhythmized speaking chorus, and orchestra.

Their entries occur according to the following principles:

To the *sprechstimmen* various functions are assigned. A freely speaking voice is, for example, the chronicler, the narrator (not to be confused with the announcer), whose duty it is to convey data and course of the action, with or without participating in it—i.e., either taking part in the action or standing off from it. This voice usually appears at the beginning or end of the piece. The actors speak naturally, though with volume suited to the space.

If *sprech*-soloists speak in pieces with music, they do so principally on held notes or chords and thus during moments when the ear of the listener can be entirely directed to receiving the spoken text.

Sprechstimmen carry first-person speeches as well as direct discourse and assertions needed for understanding the abstract or—if these voices speak in place of an acting personage—for giving life to forms.

For this reason conversations, dialogues, scenes, byplay, and discussion are spoken—not sung, as in opera.

Along with these *sprechstimmen,* solo voices also come forth from the speaking chorus: these—like the whole speaking chorus—are rhythmized and speak either *a cappella* or to an orchestral passage, which, dry and transparent, fits itself in with the volume of tone being used by the speaking voices. The speaking voices are supplanted by the singing voices when the utterances have a higher sense, are to be raised to another level; the singing voice can be suddenly blended in at the point where the meaning of the statement is raised, and thereby the prose style can be effectively interspersed with poetic elements.

To be sung, moreover, is indirect discourse, if it is to convey epic or lyric utterance, poetic turns, sententious remarks, poems, and matters of nonrealistic content.

Duets and trios in the sense of reciprocal dramatic give-and-take—of "welcoming each other in song," as occurs in opera—are not sung, but are spoken in dialogue. Duets, trios, and quartets, however, do appear in impersonal or madrigalesque sections, as is characteristic of the oratorio. In the process, lyric and even highly dramatic climaxes of one or more voices may even occur, as in opera where they are usually to be encountered in solo arias. Thus all possibilities of expression lie open to the solo singers, and the invitation to avail themselves of them is just as great as in the opera or oratorio.

In song, in the twelve-tone technique as I use it, one will be struck by the fact that words and syllables are often divided among the four vocal soloists. Usually the twelve-tone technique of composition employs wide tonal leaps into very high and low vocal registers, often demanding sheer vocal acrobatics of the singers. Since every voice has a typical timbre and level, and its own special charm, range, and so forth, the "uniformed voice," at home at all levels, must become a characterless voice. This manner of singing required by the twelve-tone technique is harder on men's voices than on women's. For this reason, as one can observe, most twelve-tone vocal works are written for the female solo voice.

I have, accordingly, in many instances adopted a simple solution: I let the low voices sing the low tones and the high voices the high. Also, after one voice begins a text, the second carries it further, and the third and fourth bring it up to the high point, without the individual voice being forced to go against nature or to attempt impossible leaps. Of course, ability as a composer figures in here, if this is to be given artistically meaningful form. On the other hand, use of this method is thinkable only where people have freed themselves from the traditional idea of song, which in accordance with the naturalistic-realistic conception, as the occasion arises, entrusts the part to a single figure, a single person, and identifies itself with him.

This principle of mine is thus opposed to that of opera, which is tied up with the figure of the performer.

Thus there arises also a new style of vocal quartet, which receives a new meaning, a new form. The development begins from within the musical material and style, from its inner laws, and thus from a nonmaterial conception with immanent aesthetic. The four singing voices are thus often conceived of as almost a single voice. Accordingly, the phrases that belong together in content are not held together by one and the same singing voice, but often by an underlying organ-point, which forms the bridge, the ground, on which the splitting of the phrase takes place and can be held together by the hearer precisely by means of the underlaid common notes (often two appogiaturas). Over this, however, the singing voice and the instruments follow and fulfill the technical function in the series. In the relation of the spoken to the sung parts, and vice versa, doublings occur. Thus, for example, a youthful, clear male speaking voice can be doubled by the tenor singer, and a clear female speaking voice by the soprano. In this way, the material can be divided without a break in the style and without abandonment of meaningful statement, whereas with only singing there is a loss in intelligibility, and with only speaking a loss in effect on the subconscious. This makes possible also an uninterrupted transition from one level to another. Two or more dimensions are thus united; in fact, there is no break in what happens musically (in contrast to—and, at the same time, in line with—such earlier devices as the *secco*-recitative). As a result, by the very nature of things, there is elimination of numbered pieces.

Thus, as has already been explained, the intelligible will be spoken by a clear male voice, and the emotional will be sung at the same time by a tenor voice. Everything is brought together: reality and imagination, "unity in diversity."

The singing choruses undertake to present no important statements or bits of information (and nothing at all in the first person), but they are brought in for dramatic mass-effects or symbolic high-points that have been projected beyond the usual dimensions. They also form the background for a realistic or unrealistic actuality. The singing chorus also takes over functions that are purely musical and—by means of vocalises—even orchestral.

On the other hand, I have introduced the speaking chorus for group statements, reactions, massed replies, and so forth. Held to a polyphonic method of composition, it takes over everything descriptive and illustrative, whether belonging to the external world or to the world of the inner emotions. With the speaking chorus I also associate the naturalistic, the agogic, and everything that can be interpreted as extramusical (e.g., descriptions of nature, dramatic discussions, rejoinders to the purely musical matter of the singers and the orchestra). Renunciations of such elements and contents would cut down the thematic complexes, rule out much that is lively and spontaneous, and thereby cause impoverishment.

Upon the speaking chorus there often devolves the task of creating shock effects or of carrying on further and expanding impressions that have been produced in the audience. For this reason, the emotionally dramatic and the background elements are reproduced by the speaking chorus, as it is its legitimate role to narrate, to represent. The speaking chorus stands in the closest relationship to the listener: it directly transmits to the public its reactions, identifies itself also often with the hearer, embodies him, as it were, on the platform, and speaks directly to the listener. Hence, too, its powerful effect.

The orchestra—particularly as it appears in the Walser composition—has a purely musical function. It does not participate in "illustrative effects" (as in Impressionism), nor—or rarely—does it participate in dramatic excesses (as in Verism). Holding itself in the background, it accompanies singers or sung or spoken interludes; it provides transitions; or it blossoms out in rather large, independent orchestral pieces. The task of the orchestra is to exhaust the possibilities of the musical material, while using, in my case, the dodecaphonic structure as its basic element.

With the music itself, I proceed from the same starting point as I do with the word, the text, and its treatment. As I evaluate the individual word in its meaning, I also evaluate the individual tone, to make it clearly perceivable and intelligible. Estrangement of tones I call for only in quite particular places that absolutely require it. The device of blurring the tone-color of the individual instruments I employ, likewise, in only very special situations.

A conception such as that which I have followed requires also a simplification of the complex musical structure, but also increases its effect, thereby preserving the stylistic unity of the dodecaphonic principles intact without demanding of the musical procedures functions or effects foreign to the discipline; thus genre-music is ruled out, all local-color pieces being assigned, for example, to the speaking chorus, which is open to their world.

A consequent renunciation of the Wagnerian music drama, of the Verdian dramatism, of Verism, of mere Impressionism, or exaggerated Expressionism, in favor of true expression, and a return to reality and its transformation (being led over onto other levels without the substance being deformed)—these are the basic elements of what I call "concrete reality."

Thus, possibly, my attempted integration of all life into the realm of musico-vocal works may assure their living on, and following the means I have proposed may perhaps close the regrettable gap between the composer's work and the larger public, and bring the latter to the new music.

This conception, which has been presented in rough outline, dispenses with much that has heretofore been respected. Right from the selection of the text to the final fashioning of the work, it contradicts many of the still-cherished traditions in the field of opera and oratorio. It creates, however, the basis for a new type which I call the "drama-oratorio" and which stands on ground other than does opera—"that anachronism," as Theodor Adorno calls it. Over against opera, which is a somewhat realistic unreality, played figuratively and represented on a spatially localized stage, I place the "drama-oratorio," which conveys a nonfigurative reality, at once imagined and concrete, on a nonlocalized stage, the podium.

I am aware that my ideas will encounter opposition and may even upset certain circles and be rejected by them. I realize too that these ideas, oversimplified, can be easily vulgarized. On the other hand, some composers have taken over my ideas with success. This is in the very nature of things.

Yet the fact that the principles here set forth have been arrived at not through armchair theorizing, to be later applied, but from already existing and proved works, and that their basic formulation has been only now arrived at, vouches—so far as I am concerned—for their correctness, quite over and above the effectiveness of the works.

Catalogues of Composers' Works

Following is a list of abbreviations used for the publishers in these Catalogues of Composers' Works:

AMP	Associated Music Publishers, Inc., New York
Ars Viva	Ars-Viva-Verlag, Mainz
B&B	Bote & Bock KG, Berlin, Wiesbaden
Broude	Broude Bros., New York
BV	Bärenreiter-Verlag, Kassel, Basel, London, Paris
CF	Carl Fischer, Inc., New York
Ditson	Oliver Ditson Co., Boston
EV	Elkan-Vogel Co., Inc., Philadelphia
GS	G. Schirmer, Inc., New York
H-C	Hansen-Chester, Copenhagen, London
Henmar	Hemar Press Inc., New York
HMV	Hermann Moeck Verlag, Celle
Malcolm	Malcolm Music Ltd., Delaware Water Gap, Pa.
Marks	Edward B. Marks Music Corp., New York
Mentor	Mentor Music, Inc., New York
Merion	Merion Music, Inc., Bryn Mawr, Pa.
MJQ	MJQ Music, Inc., New York
MS	Not published—in manuscript form only
Oxford	Oxford University Press, London, New York
Pegasus	Pegasus-Verlag, Wilhelmshaven, Locarno-Monti
Peters	C. F. Peters Corp., New York
PWM	Polskie Wydawnictwo Muzyczne (Polish Music Publishers), Warsaw, Cracow; representative: SESAC, Inc., New York

Ricordi	Edizioni G. Ricordi & C., Milan, New York
Schott	Schott and Co., Ltd., Mainz, London, New York
Selbsverlag	Composer's publication
S-Z	Edizioni Suvini Zerboni, Milan
UE	Universal Edition, Vienna, Bryn Mawr, Pa., London
Valley	Valley Music Press, Northampton, Mass.

WILLIAM SCHUMAN

Orchestral Music

American Festival Overture, GS, 1939.
Newsreel, suite, GS, 1941.
Symphony No. 3, GS, 1941.
Symphony No. 4, GS, 1942.
Prayer in Time of War, GS, 1943.
Concerto for Piano and Small Orchestra, GS, 1943.
Symphony No. 5 (Symphony for Strings), GS, 1943.
"Steel Town," music for a film, MS, 1944.
Circus Overture, GS, 1944.
Undertow, choreographic episodes, GS, 1945.
Night Journey, ballet, Merion, 1947.
Concerto for Violin and Orchestra, Merion, 1947 (revised 1950 and 1954).
Symphony No. 6, GS, 1949.
Judith, choreographic poem, GS, 1950.
Credendum, Merion, 1955.
New England Triptych, Merion, 1956.
"The Earth Is Born," music for a film, MS, 1957.
Symphony No. 7, Merion, 1960.
A Song of Orpheus, fantasy for cello and orchestra, Merion, 1962.
Symphony No. 8, Merion, 1962.
Variations on "America," an orchestration of the Charles Ives organ work, Merion, 1963.
Orchestra Song, Merion, 1964.
The Witch of Endor, ballet, Merion, 1965.
Symphony No. 9, Merion, 1968.
To Thee Old Cause, Merion, 1968.

MILTON BABBITT

Orchestral Music

Relata I, AMP, 1965.
Correspondences for string orchestra and synthesized tape, AMP, 1966–67.
Relata II for large orchestra, AMP, 1967–68.

ELLIOTT CARTER

Orchestral Music

"Tarantella," four-part men's chorus and orchestra, MS (score and parts property of Harvard Glee Club), 1936.
Pocahontas, ballet suite, AMP (score published, parts rental), 1939.
Symphony No. 1, AMP (score published, parts rental), 1942.
Holiday Overture, AMP (score published, parts rental), 1944 (new version, 1961).
The Minotaur, ballet suite, AMP (score published, parts rental), 1947.
Variations for Orchestra, AMP (score published, parts rental), 1955.
Double Concerto for Harpsichord and Piano with Two Chamber Orchestras, AMP (score published, parts rental), 1961.
Piano Concerto, AMP (score published, parts rental), 1965.

ROSS LEE FINNEY

Orchestral Music

Concerto in E minor for Violin and Full Orchestra, Peters (rental), 1933 (revised 1947).
Bleheris for tenor and contralto soloists and orchestra (MacLeish), Peters (rental), 1937.
Slow Piece for string orchestra, Valley, 1940.
Symphony No. 1 (Communiqué, 1943), Peters (score published, parts rental), 1942.
Hymn, Fuguing, and Holiday, CF (score published, parts rental), 1943 (revised 1950).
Concerto in E major for Piano and Orchestra, Peters (rental), 1948.
Variations, Peters (score published, parts rental), 1957.
Symphony No. 2, Peters (score published, parts rental), 1959.

Symphony No. 3, Peters (score published, parts rental), 1960.
Three Pieces for Strings, Winds, Percussion, and Tape, Peters (rental), 1962.
Three Studies in Fours for percussion orchestra, Peters (rental), 1965.
Concerto for Percussion and Orchestra, Peters (score published, parts rental), 1965.
Symphony Concertante, Peters (rental), 1967.
Second Concerto for Piano and Orchestra, Peters (rental), 1968.

PETER RACINE FRICKER

Orchestral Music

Rondo Scherzoso, Schott (score and parts rental), 1948.
Opus 9. *First Symphony*, Schott (score published, parts rental), 1948–49.
Opus 10. *Prelude, Elegy and Finale for String Orchestra*, Schott (score published, parts rental), 1949.
Opus 11. *First Violin Concerto*, Schott (piano reduction published, parts rental), 1949–50.
Opus 13. *Concertante for English Horn and String Orchestra*, Schott (score and piano reduction published, parts rental), 1950.
Opus 14. *Second Symphony*, Schott (score published, parts rental), 1950–51.
Opus 15. *Concertante for Three Pianos, Strings, and Timpani*, Schott (score and parts rental), 1951.
Opus 18. *Concerto for Viola and Orchestra*, Schott (piano reduction published, score and parts rental), 1951–53.
Opus 19. *Concerto for Piano and Orchestra*, Schott (piano reduction published, score and parts rental), 1952–54.
Opus 21. *Rapsodia Concertante (Concerto No. 2) for Violin and Orchestra*, Schott (piano reduction published, score and parts rental), 1953–54.
Opus 22. *Dance Scene*, Schott (score published, parts rental), 1954.
Opus 26. *Litany for Double String Orchestra*, Schott (score published, parts rental), 1955.
Fantasie on a theme of Mozart, Schott/Universal (rental), 1956.

"Waltz for Restricted Orchestra." For mouthpieces, reeds, strings *col legno* for the Hoffnung Interplanetary Festival. MS, 1958.

Opus 32. *Comedy Overture,* Schott (rental), 1958.

Opus 33. *Toccata for Piano and Orchestra,* Schott (piano reduction published, score and parts rental), 1958–59.

Opus 36. *Third Symphony,* Schott (score published, parts rental), 1960.

Opus 39. *O long desirs* (Louise Labé), song cycle for soprano and orchestra, Schott (piano reduction published, score and parts rental), 1963.

"Introduction and Postlude to Othello," MS, 1964.

Opus 42a. "Four Songs" for high voice and orchestra, MS, 1965.

Opus 43. *Fourth Symphony, in memoriam Mátyás Seiber,* Schott (rental), 1966.

Opus 45. *Three Scenes for Orchestra,* MS, 1966.

Opus 47. "Seven Counterpoints for Orchestra," MS, 1967.

HANS WERNER HENZE

Orchestral Music

"Chamber Concerto," MS, 1946.

"Concertino for Piano and Wind Orchestra with Percussion," MS, 1947.

Concerto for Violin and Orchestra, Schott (score published, parts rental), 1947.

"Symphony No. 1," MS, 1947 (new version, 1963).

"Ballet-Variations" for full orchestra, MS, 1949.

"Jack Pudding," ballet suite, MS, 1949.

Symphony No. 2, Schott (score published, parts rental), 1949.

Symphony No. 3, Schott (score published, parts rental), 1949–50.

Concerto for Piano and Orchestra, Schott (piano reduction published, score and parts rental), 1950.

"Rosa Silber," ballet scenes for orchestra, MS, 1950.

"Symphonic Variations" for chamber orchestra, MS, 1950.

"Boulevard Solitude," symphonic interludes from the opera, MS, 1951.

"Labyrinth," choreographic fantasy on the Theseus-motif, MS, 1951.

"Tancredi e Cantilena," suite from the ballet, MS, 1952.

Ode to the Westwind, music for cello and orchestra on the poem by Percy Bysshe Shelley, Schott (score and piano reduction published, parts rental), 1953.

"Quattro Poemi" for full orchestra, MS, 1955.

Symphony No. 4, Schott (score published, parts rental), 1955.

"Three Symphonic Studies for Orchestra," MS, 1955 (revised 1964).

"Jeux des Tritons," divertissement from the ballet Ondine for piano and orchestra, MS, 1956–57.

"Maratona," ballet suite for two jazz bands and orchestra, MS, 1956.

"Hochzeitmusik" ("Wedding Music"), from the ballet *Ondine* for symphonic wind orchestra, MS, 1957.

Sonata per Archi for chamber orchestra, Schott (score published, parts rental), 1957–58.

Ondine, Trois pas des Tritons, from the ballet, 1958.

"Ondine, First Suite," from the ballet, MS, 1958.

"Ondine, Second Suite," from the ballet, MS, 1958.

Three Dithyrambs for chamber orchestra, Schott (score published, parts rental), 1958.

L'Usignolo dell'Imperatore (The Emperor's Nightingale), pantomime, Schott (score published, parts rental), 1959.

Antifone, Schott (score published, parts rental), 1960.

Symphony No. 5, Schott (score published, parts rental), 1962.

"Los Caprichos, Fantasia per orchestra," MS, 1963.

"Der junge Lord (The Young Lord)," symphonic interludes from the opera, MS, 1964.

"In Memoriam: The White Rose" for chamber orchestra, MS, 1965.

"The Bassarids: Maenad Scene," MS (rental), 1966.

Muses of Sicily, concerto for two pianos, chorus, and wind instruments, Schott (score published, parts rental), 1966.

Double concerto for Oboe, Harp, and Strings, Schott (score published, parts rental), 1966.

Concerto for Double-bass and Orchestra, Schott (score published, parts rental), 1966.

Telemanniana, Schott, 1967.

Concerto No. 2 for Piano and Orchestra, Schott, 1967.

ERNST KRENEK

Orchestral Music[1]

Opus 7. *First Symphony*, UE, 1921.
Opus 11. *Symphonic Music* for nine instruments, UE, 1922.
Opus 12. *Second Symphony*, UE, 1922.
Opus 16. *Third Symphony*, UE, 1922.
Opus 18. *Piano Concerto No. 1 in F-sharp major*, UE, 1923.
Opus 25. *Concerto Grosso No. 2*, UE, 1924.
Opus 27. *Concertino*, UE, 1924.
Opus 29. *Violin Concerto No. 1*, UE, 1924.
Opus 31. *Seven Orchestra Pieces*, UE, 1924.
Opus 34. *Symphony* for wind instruments and percussion, UE, 1924.
Opus 44. *Three Jolly Marches*, UE, 1926.
Opus 54. *Potpourri*, UE, 1927.
Opus 58. *Little Symphony*, UE, 1928.
Opus 69. *Theme and Thirteen Variations*, UE, 1931.
Opus 80. *Campo Marzio, Overture*, UE, 1937.
Opus 81. *Piano Concerto No. 2*, UE, 1937.
Opus 86. *Symphonic Piece* for string orchestra, Schott-UE, 1939.
Opus 88. "Little Concerto" for organ, harpsichord, and chamber orchestra, MS, 1940.
Opus 94. "I Wonder as I Wander," symphonic movement in the form of variations on a folk song from North Carolina, MS, 1942.
(105.)[2] *Symphonic Elegy* for string orchestra, EV, 1946.
(107.) *Piano Concerto No. 3*, Schott-UE, 1946.
(113.) "Fourth Symphony," MS, 1947.
(116.) "Five Pieces for String Orchestra," MS, 1948.
(119.) "Fifth Symphony," MS, 1949.
(123.) *Piano Concerto No. 4*, BV, 1950.
(124.) *Double Concerto for Violin and Piano*, Marks, 1950.

[1] A few minor works, such as those written for special occasions, are not included in this list.—E.K.

[2] For private reasons the composer has omitted opus numbers after 96. For filing and research purposes order numbers (given in parentheses) were assigned later to the works not numbered.—R.S.H.

(126.) *Concerto for Harp*, UE, 1951.
(127.) *Concerto for Two Pianos*, BV, 1951.
(131.) *Sinfonietta* "A Brasileira," UE, 1952.
(133.) *Concerto for Cello*, BV, 1952.
(137.) *Symphony Pallas Athene*, excerpts from the opera *Pallas Athene Weeps*, Schott-UE, 1954.
(140.) *Violin Concerto No. 2*, Schott-UE, 1954.
(142.) *Eleven Transparencies*, Schott-UE, 1954.
(145.) *Cappriccio for Cello*, Schott-UE, 1955.
(146.) *Seven Easy Pieces* for strings, Schott, 1955.
(147.) *Suite for Flute and Strings*, Broude, 1954.
(148.) *Suite for Clarinet and Strings*, Broude, 1955.
(160.) *Circle, Chain, and Mirror*, BV, 1957.
(162.) *Marginal Sounds*, Broude, 1957.
(167.) *Hexahedron*, BV, 1958.
(170.) *Quaestio temporis (A Question of Time)*, BV, 1959.
(177.) *From Three Make Seven*, BV, 1961.
(196.) *Horizon Circled*, BV, 1967.
(199.) *Perspectives*, BV, 1968.
(200.) *Exercises of a Late Hour*, chamber orchestra and electronic tape, BV, 1968.
(203.) "Six Profiles for Orchestra," MS, 1969.
(205.) *Fivefold Enfoldment*, BV, 1969.

WITOLD LUTOSLAWSKI

Orchestral Music

Symphonic Variations, PWM (score published, parts rental), 1938.
Symphony No. 1, PWM (score published, parts rental), 1947.
Overture for string orchestra, PWM (score published, parts rental), 1949.
"Little Suite" for chamber orchestra, MS, 1950.
Little Suite for full orchestra, PWM (score published, parts rental), 1951.
"Five Folk Melodies" for string orchestra, MS, 1952.
Concerto for Orchestra, PWM (score published, parts rental), 1954.
Postludium, PWM (score published, parts rental), 1958.

"Two Postludiums," MS, 1960.
Jeux Vénitiens, HMV (score published, parts rental), 1961.
Symphony No. 2, H-C and PWM (score published, parts rental), 1967.
Livre pour Orchestra, H-C and PWM (score published, parts rental), 1968.

FRANK MARTIN

Orchestral Music

Rythmes, 3 mouvements symphoniques, UE, 1926.
Concerto for Piano and Orchestra, UE, 1934.
"Symphonie," MS, 1937.
Ballade for alto saxophone, string orchestra, piano, and percussion, UE, 1938.
Sonata da chiesa for viole d'amour and string orchestra or flute and string orchestra, UE, 1938.
Ballade for flute, string orchestra, and piano, UE, 1939.
Ballade for piano and orchestra, UE, 1940.
Ballade for trombone and orchestra, UE, 1940.
Passacaille for organ with string orchestra or large orchestra, UE, 1944.
Petite Symphonie Concertante for harp, clavecin, piano, and two string orchestras, UE, 1945.
Ouverture from "Musique de Scène et choeurs pour L'Athalie de Racine," UE, 1946.
Concerto pour 7 Instruments à vent, UE, 1949.
Ballade for cello and small orchestra, UE, 1949.
Concerto for Violin, UE, 1951.
Concerto for Clavecin and Small Orchestra, UE, 1952.
Études for string orchestra, UE, 1956.
Ouverture en Hommage à Mozart, UE, 1956.
Ouverture en Rondeau, UE, 1958.
Inter Arma Caritas, UE, 1963.
Les Quatre Éléments, UE, 1964.
Concerto for Cello and Orchestra, UE, 1966.
Maria Tripticon (Ave Maria, Magnificat, Stabat Mater) for soprano, violin solo and orchestra, UE, 1968.
Erasmi Monumentum for orchestra and organ, UE, 1969.
Concerto for Piano and Orchestra, UE, 1969.

VINCENT PERSICHETTI

Orchestral Music

Opus 16. *Concertino for Piano and Orchestra,* EV (rental), 1941. (Two-piano version also published.)
Opus 18. "First Symphony," MS, 1942.
Opus 19. "Second Symphony," MS, 1942.
Opus 20. *Dance Overture,* EV (score published, parts rental), 1942.
Opus 23. *Fables for Narrator and Orchestra,* CF (rental), 1942.
Opus 25. *The Hollow Men, for Trumpet and String Orchestra,* EV, 1944.
Opus 30. *Third Symphony,* EV, 1946.
Opus 43. *Serenade No. 5,* EV (score published, parts rental), 1950.
Opus 48. *Fairy Tale,* CF (rental), 1950.
Opus 51. *Fourth Symphony,* EV (score published, parts rental), 1951.
Opus 61. *Symphony for Strings (Symphony No. 5),* EV, 1953.
Opus 80. *Seventh Symphony (Liturgical),* EV (score published, parts rental), 1958.
Opus 90. *Concerto for Piano and Orchestra,* EV, 1962.
Opus 92. *Stabat Mater* for chorus and orchestra, EV, 1963.
Opus 93. *Te Deum* for chorus and orchestra, EV, 1963.
Opus 96. *Introit for Strings,* EV, 1964.
Opus 106. "Symphony No. 8," MS, 1967.
Opus 107. *Pleiades for Chorus, Trumpet, and String Orchestra,* EV, 1968.

Band Music

Opus 42. *Divertimento,* Ditson, 1950.
Opus 53. *Psalm,* EV, 1952.
Opus 59. *Pageant,* CF, 1953.
Opus 69. *Symphony for Band (Symphony No. 6),* EV, 1956.
Opus 85. *Serenade for Band,* EV, 1960.
Opus 87. *Bagatelles for Band,* EV, 1961.
Opus 91. *Chorale Prelude: So Pure the Star,* EV, 1962.
Opus 102. *Masquerade for Band,* EV, 1965.
Opus 105. *Chorale Prelude: Turn Not Thy Face,* EV, 1966.

GUNTHER SCHULLER

Orchestral Music

"Concerto for Horn and Orchestra," MS, 1944.
"Concerto for Cello and Orchestra," MS, 1945.
"Vertige d'Eros," MS, 1945.
Symphonic Study, AMP, 1947.
"Suite for Chamber Orchestra," MS, 1949.
Symphony for Brass and Percussion, Malcolm, 1949–50.
Dramatic Overture, Schott, 1951.
Recitative and Rondo for Violin and Orchestra, AMP, 1954.
"Symphonic Tribute to Duke Ellington," MS, 1955.
Contours, Schott, 1955–58.
Little Fantasy, Malcolm, 1957.
Spectra, AMP-Schott, 1958.
Concertino for Jazz Quartet and Orchestra, MJQ, 1959.
Seven Studies on Themes of Paul Klee, UE, 1959.
Capriccio for Tuba and Orchestra, Mentor, 1960.
Variants, MJQ, 1960.
Contrasts, AMP-Schott, 1961.
Composition in Three Parts, AMP-Schott, 1962.
Concerto for Piano and Orchestra, AMP-Schott, 1962.
Five Bagatelles, AMP, 1962.
Journey into Jazz, AMP, 1962.
Movement for Flute and Strings, AMP-Schott, 1962.
Music for "Journey to the Stars," AMP, 1962.
Threnos for solo oboe and orchestra, AMP-Schott, 1963.
Five Shakespearean Songs for baritone and orchestra, AMP, 1964.
American Triptych, AMP, 1965.
Symphony, AMP, 1965.
Concerto for Orchestra, AMP, 1966.
Five Etudes for Orchestra, AMP, 1966.
The Visitation, AMP-Schott, 1966.
The Five Senses, ballet, AMP, 1967.
Triplum, AMP, 1967.
Colloquy for Two Pianists and Orchestra, AMP, 1968.
Concerto for Double Bass and Orchestra, AMP, 1968.
Shapes and Designs, AMP, 1969.

MICHAEL TIPPETT

Orchestral Music

"Concerto in D," for two flutes, two oboes, four horns, and strings, MS, 1928–30.

"Incidental Music to Fletcher's 'Don Juan,' " MS, 1930.

"Symphony in B-flat," MS, 1933–34 (revised 1935).

Concerto for Double String Orchestra, Schott (score published, parts rental), 1938–39.

Fantasia on a Theme of Handel for piano and orchestra, Schott (reduction for two pianos), 1939–41.

Symphony No. 1, Schott (score published, parts rental), 1944–45.

Little Music for string orchestra, Schott (score published, parts rental), 1946.

Suite in D, Schott (score published, parts rental), 1948.

Ritual Dances from "The Midsummer Marriage" for orchestra with optional chorus, Schott (score published, parts rental), 1953.

Fantasia Concertante on a Theme of Corelli for string orchestra, Schott (score published, parts rental), 1953.

Divertimento on "Sellinger's Round" for chamber orchestra, Schott (score published, parts rental), 1953–54.

Concerto for Piano and Orchestra, Schott, 1953–55. (Reduction for two pianos also available.)

Symphony No. 2, Schott (score published, parts rental), 1956–57.

Praeludium for Brass, Bells, and Percussion, Schott (score published, parts rental), 1962.

Concerto for Orchestra, Schott (score published, parts rental), 1963.

WLADIMIR VOGEL

Orchestral Music

"Sinfonischer Vorgang," MS lost, 1922.

Sinfonia fugata (in memorium Ferruccio Busoni), B&B, 1925.

4 Etüden für grosses Orchester, B&B, 1930–32.

Tripartita, B&B, 1934.

"Rally," MS, 1936.

Violinkonzert, B&B, 1937.

3 Suiten (aus Thyl Claes I. Teil), Ricordi, 1945.

Cortège de Noces (aus Thyl Claes II. Teil), Ricordi, 1945.
Passacaglia, Ricordi, 1946.
Sieben Aspekte einer Zwölftonreihe, B&B, 1950.
Spiegelungen, UE, 1952.
Interludio lirico, Ricordi, 1954.
Preludio, Interludio lirico, Postludio, Ricordi, 1954.
Kozert für Violoncello und Orchester, S-Z, 1954.
Orchestersuite (aus Thyl Claes II. Teil), Ricordi, n.d.

Speaking Chorus a Cappella

"Das Lied von der Glocke" (Schiller), soli speakers and double speaking chorus, MS, 1959.
Mondträume / Mondsand (Arp), speaking chorus, Selbstverlag, 1965.

Vocal and Choral Music with Accompaniment (Abridged)

"3 Sprechlieder" (Stramm), low male voice and piano, MS, 1922.
Wagadus Untergang durch die Eitelkeit (Frobenius), soprano, alto, and bass-baritone soloists, mixed chorus, and five saxophones, Ricordi, 1930.
Thyl Claes der Kohlenträger, I. Teil (de Coster), soprano, two solo-*sprechstimmen*, speaking chorus, and orchestra, Ricordi, 1938.
6 *Fragmente aus I. Teil: Thyl Claes der Kohlenträger* (de Coster), soprano, two solo-*sprechstimmen*, and orchestra, Ricordi, n.d.
Thyl Claes der Kohlenträger, II. Teil (de Coster), soprano, two solo-*sprechstimmen*, speaking chorus, and orchestra, Ricordi, 1943–45.
5 *Fragmente aus II. Teil: Thyl Claes der Kohlenträger* (de Coster), soprano, two solo-*sprechstimmen*, and orchestra, Ricordi, n.d.
Arpiade (Arp), soprano, speaking chorus, flute, clarinet, viola, cello, and piano, Ars Viva, 1954.
"Antigone" (Sophocles/Hölderlin), male speaking chorus and percussion, MS, 1955.
Jona ging doch nach Ninive (Buber), baritone, speaker, speaking chorus, mixed chorus, and orchestra, B&B, 1958.
Rezitativ und Epitaph "Alla memoria di Giovanni Battista Pergolesi" (Brezzo), tenor and string orchestra, Ricordi, 1958–59.
Meditazione su Amedeo Modigliani (Filippini), solo quartet, speaker, mixed chorus, and orchestra, Ricordi, 1960.

An die akademische Jugend (Vadian), mixed chorus and nine winds, Selbstverlag, 1962.
Worte (Arp), two female speaking voices and small string orchestra, Pegasus, 1962.
Flucht (Robert Walser), solo-quartet, mixed chorus, speaking chorus, and orchestra, BV, 1964.
"Hörformen 1–6," MS, 1967–68.

Index

The composers who have contributed to this book are listed in the index only when mention of them appears outside their own essays.—R.S.H.